THE AMERICAN SPIRIT
IN EUROPE

Publications of

THE AMERICAN INSTITUTE

University of Oslo

In coöperation with the

DEPARTMENT OF AMERICAN CIVILIZATION

Graduate School of Arts and Sciences

University of Pennsylvania

The
AMERICAN SPIRIT
in EUROPE

A SURVEY OF TRANSATLANTIC INFLUENCES

By

HALVDAN KOHT

UNIVERSITY OF PENNSYLVANIA PRESS

Philadelphia

1949

THE MAPLE PRESS COMPANY, YORK, PA.

PREFACE

AMERICA in this book means the United States of America. The subject of the book, however, is not America. It is rather Europe. The plan of the book is to present a comprehensive view of the effect of American activities, struggles, and efforts upon European life and progress.

The United States of America was born as a loosely knit union of thirteen small States comprising a population of no more than three millions. It has grown to be one of the greatest powers of the earth.

Since the very beginning of its existence, however, it has been a real power in the life of nations and has greatly affected the growth of the rest of the world. Its influence has made itself strongly felt in many different fields—in international relations, in political thought, in economic development and policies, in the shaping of daily life, in literature and journalism. Indeed, it is scarcely possible to point to a single aspect of modern civilization in which America has not exerted a certain degree of influence; in many important matters it has been a determining influence. Once upon a time many people spoke apprehensively of the complete "Americanization" of the world. In many ways the United States of today seems to be the very center of Western civilization.

The American nation was in its origin an offshoot of European growth and enterprise, and many scholars have examined and demonstrated all kinds of European influences in the history of the United States. Only a few efforts have been made to define the impact of American life and activities upon world affairs or upon the conditions and development of the European nations. I do not dare to hope that, at the present stage of research, I may be able to offer a complete picture of this aspect of history. But even a preliminary survey may be useful and may provoke further, more profound studies.

v

The influences of one nation upon others are very difficult to trace with any degree of exactitude. They are always so intimately mingled with domestic elements as to make it well-nigh impossible to discern the definite limits between foreign and native. Material importations can be described on the basis of objective evidence. Mental influences, however, are often so subtle as to evade observation. Sometimes they may come with such a shock that they cannot be mistaken. In other cases, they may conceal themselves under national slogans; even illusions may play their part.

In the search for American influences upon Europe, an American will easily find that much of what he may deem most valuable in the achievements of his nation or essential in its domestic history has remained purely American and passed unnoticed abroad. Influences are determined not only by the strength and vitality of the one party but equally by the receptivity of the other. Therefore, in this study the European point of view must be just as important as the American.

In the course of previous studies of both American and European history I have had the opportunity to make many observations regarding American occurrences that left their mark on European development. For the present book I have, of course, made an extensive use of facts and connections brought to light by other students. At the end of the book I have added a short bibliography of works on which I have drawn for whole chapters or for more extended episodes. It would have been impracticable to indicate the authorities for every single statement. In some cases I have mentioned in the text the authors to whom I am specially indebted for some interesting information or observation. As far as possible, I have gone to the primary sources, and I have tried to verify dates wherever possible.

H.K.

ACKNOWLEDGMENT

In presenting this first volume of publications of the American Institute of the University of Oslo, the University of Pennsylvania Press takes pleasure in acknowledging its indebtedness to Sigmund Skard, Professor of Literature, especially American, University of Oslo, and Robert E. Spiller, Professor of English, University of Pennsylvania, through whose good offices the series was initiated.

Thanks are also due to Frederick B. Tolles, Assistant Professor of History, Swarthmore College, who prepared the manuscript for the press.

CONTENTS

Chapter   *Page*

     PREFACE   v

   I INTRODUCTION: THE COLONIAL PERIOD   1

  II THE AMERICAN REVOLUTION AS A EUROPEAN
       REVOLUTION   7

 III CHALLENGE TO THE EUROPEAN POWERS   26

  IV REFORMS AND MOVEMENTS FOR REFORM   34

   V THE LAND OF OPPORTUNITIES   60

  VI PROGRESS THROUGH INVENTION   79

 VII AMERICA ENTERS WORLD LITERATURE   99

VIII INTERNATIONAL POLITICS AND CIVIL WAR   124

  IX ECONOMIC POWER   152

   X THE AMERICAN TECHNIQUE   163

  XI THE ALMIGHTY DOLLAR VERSUS AMERICAN
       IDEALISM   179

 XII WORLD CO-OPERATION IN TECHNOLOGY AND
       SCIENCE   205

XIII ONE WORLD OF IDEAS   218

XIV AMERICA AS A WORLD POWER   244

 XV OUTLOOK   274

     SELECTED BIBLIOGRAPHY   279

     INDEX   281

I

INTRODUCTION: THE COLONIAL PERIOD

As long as America was nothing but colonies it could mean to Europe little more than an object of exploitation. Colonial politics was one feature of the mercantilistic system, and thus it was highly fitting that the discovery and conquest of America should have started from Spain, the country where the principles of mercantilism were first elaborated and put into practice.

As a territory for exploitation America offered to Europe new sources of wealth, and the conquest of the New World disturbed the balance of economic as well as political power in Europe. It became the foundation of the first world empire created by any European nation since the Romans.

The Spaniards came in search of silver and gold, and some new articles of production were found in the new lands. It is, however, a remarkable fact that the largest parts of the New World could not be profitably exploited until staple products of the Old World were transplanted there and manpower from the conquering nations was imported. America offered Indian corn, tobacco, and potatoes. But wheat and most of the other grains were brought over from Europe. So were all the most important domestic animals, including cattle and horses. So too were even such characteristic "colonial" articles as sugar, coffee, and rice, and the chief varieties of cotton. European colonists had to come to perform the very labor of production.

This holds particularly true for the British colonies in North America which were finally to become the United States. The only native article to be found there that could constitute a profitable article of commerce was tobacco, and that was, in the beginning, condemned by governments and by cultivated opinion as a corruptive and indecent element of social life. Actually, tobacco was the first American product to effect a lasting transformation in European customs and tastes, and it became an

1

important element in European economy. Its importance for Europe was matched and surpassed only by the much later reception of the South American potato.

In the Spanish dominions the colonists remained a superior class, employing colored labor. In the British settlements the colonists themselves constituted most of the laboring classes, except on the tobacco and cotton plantations, where colored slaves did the work. In all the colonies intellectual and social life mainly followed European patterns; in the British provinces, however, there was the significant exception of the absence of an organized class of noblemen. This fact was to be an important element in shaping social thought in the United States throughout its whole history. It made bourgeois and business ideas much more predominant than in Europe and, what first of all struck the European imagination, it made British America appear much more democratic than any country of the Old World. Europeans came to look at the British colonies as a land of liberty as compared with their home countries, and freedom-loving people in Europe early began to look to this part of America as a haven for the oppressed. Immigrants turned their steps thither not only from Great Britain but also from Germany and France.

This notion of America as the home of liberty sometimes intermingled curiously with the romantic idea of freedom as existing most perfectly in primitive society. Such a conception of the happy "state of nature" was apparently confirmed by many of the descriptions sent back to Europe, in particular from French Jesuit missionaries, and published and republished through the whole eighteenth century. It was a natural consequence that some of the dreamers of a new and perfect society placed their utopias in faraway America; thus the French philosopher Morelly (1753) and the Swedish clergyman Bergeström (1770). The other idea, however, of British colonial society as one of true freedom had much more reality in it and therefore could determine practical action on the part of large groups of European people.

By reason of the great distance severing them from the mother countries, the colonies in the American hemisphere were early compelled to build up their own institutions of intellectual life.

But the activities fostered by such institutions remained essentially parts of the life of the home nations. They could not represent independent contributions to universal civilization. Even the British colonies, which were organized on a basis of much stronger and more active self-government than the others, were mentally dependent on British models for all their achievements. Their civilization was English, not American. Even when, during the latter half of the eighteenth century, French ideas came to influence American thought, they were, in fact, the same ideas that entered England, and they arrived in America partly by way of England. Although the colonies produced both men and actions which advanced human civilization in different fields of activity, they were calmly and naturally accepted and appropriated by the mother country as belonging to its proper development. And the Americans conformed spontaneously to this way of thinking. Both distance and peculiar conditions gradually shaped a specifically American type of men, and deep in their souls independence was slowly preparing. But the colonial character of American life was preserved throughout and was not to be completely uprooted even by the Revolution.

The situation is strikingly illustrated by the early history of American art. In the eighteenth century America gave to the world three prominent painters—Benjamin West, John Singleton Copley, and Gilbert Stuart. West left America as a young man in 1759, settled down in England in 1763 and remained there until his death in 1820. He was even president of the Royal Academy for almost thirty years, so completely was he absorbed by English society. His contribution to the preparation of an American school of art consisted chiefly in his having been the teacher of a number of young American painters. Copley left America just before the Revolution, in 1774, and he too stayed in England for the remainder of his life, until 1815. Only the youngest of the three, Gilbert Stuart, returned to America—in 1792, after a stay of seventeen years in England. But truly he appears in his production still more Anglicized, presenting if possible still less of an American character, than the two elder artists; he belongs completely to the English school of painters of that period.

Corresponding was the situation in science. The brilliant physicist Benjamin Thompson of New Hampshire, the man who first established the fact that heat is a form of energy due to vibration of the particles of matter, fought for the British in the American Revolution and afterwards left for Europe, where he made all his experiments and discoveries. This might be called an extreme case, but even nationalists like the physician Benjamin Rush of Philadelphia sought their scientific education in Great Britain, studying medicine preferably at the great University of Edinburgh. There was no American institution able to offer an education of equal character. The American Philosophical Society, founded by Franklin in 1743, did not attain a broad scientific standing until well into the nineteenth century.

As a matter of fact, in many respects American civilization remained colonial after the Revolution. Most people in the United States still looked to England as the mother country. Men of literature as well as men of art continued to go there to learn and were absorbed by the master nation. Though Noah Webster proclaimed the linguistic independence of America, another American grammarian, Lindley Murray, who had kept aloof from the Revolution, went to England as soon as peace was reëstablished, and composed the English Grammar and English Reader which for half a century dominated English schools.

The very Declaration of Independence was intrinsically, and in some parts literally, based on English political doctrine, specifically that expressed by John Locke in his defense of the English Revolution. It was an Englishman, Thomas Paine, who wrote the first, most vigorous, and most effective pamphlet for independence. Of the two men most influential in the development of Thomas Jefferson's thought, one, according to his own admission, was the Scotchman William Small, Professor of Philosophy at the College of William and Mary. The other was the American jurist George Wythe, a student and interpreter of English common law, and himself a signer of the Declaration of Independence. American independence may well be defined as a true product of the British spirit.

Before the Revolution America produced only one man who

represented an independent expression of truly American civilization and who thus offered a sign of a new age. That man was Benjamin Franklin. He was the first American to win world fame, and his character was so complete a prototype of what was later conceived as distinctively American as to impress Europe with something genuinely new and peculiar. He not only became famous, but he exerted a strong and lasting influence on European thought, and for the first time made America an active power in European life.

Franklin won his fame first by his invention of the lightning conductor in 1752. That was a feat of truly American character. Six years before, he had begun experiments on electricity. With extremely small means, but with an eminently practical grasp, he succeeded in establishing a whole series of fundamental facts regarding electrical phenomena. His observations effectively advanced the understanding of the character of electricity and, when published in England, aroused the attention of the whole scientific world. His description of his experiments was immediately translated into French, and he received doctor's degrees from the University of St. Andrews in Scotland and the University of Oxford in England. He himself, however, was most interested in the practical effect of his discoveries; he not only proved the identity of lightning with electricity, but gave to the world an instrument to avert the dangers of lightning. This invention made his name universally known through Europe. The picture of Franklin and the boy with their kite drawing the lightning down from the clouds became immensely popular, and for more than a hundred years appeared in innumerable textbooks for elementary schools in all countries. It caught the imagination of adults and children alike, of poets as well as practical people, and Franklin was celebrated as the man who had mastered the forces of heaven.

The practical genius of America impressed itself on Europe by still another invention of Franklin's—the Pennsylvania Fireplace, later called the Franklin Stove, constructed so as to utilize the hot air that otherwise went uselessly up the chimney .

Such achievements were, however, only one aspect of his

fame. Another, and still more far-reaching, was the popularity of his writings. His philosophical and didactical tracts, his *Autobiography*, his *Way to Wealth*, were translated into all European languages and republished year after year. In particular, the sayings of Poor Richard were quoted over and over again in newspapers and in books. Although not always original creations of his own (some of them were borrowed from Solomon's Book of Wisdom, others were traditional proverbs), all of them were stamped with the shrewd humor of the writer and appealed to the practical sense of the common reader. Through them Franklin became an educator of the masses; he taught them a bourgeois philosophy that helped prepare them for the social transformation that was on the way.

Franklin's prominent activities in Europe for the cause of the American colonies made him a conspicuous man among his contemporaries. In particular, his examination before the House of Commons in 1766 was a widely publicized event; his cool presence of mind in the face of harassing questions, his lucid answers, always to the point and often with a sly irony, exasperated the ruling classes in England, but won universal admiration outside the circle of his opponents. It was like a parcel of schoolboys interrogating the master, said Edmund Burke.

Franklin resided in England for sixteen years, and in France for nine years. He knew these countries better than most men, and he maintained a large correspondence all over Europe. He might well be called a "good European." But he had a balance of mind that did not allow him to be conquered by the superiority of European civilization, though he enjoyed all the amenities of it. His thoroughly practical orientation, his business realism, and his humorous complacency made him a perfect American, and it was in that quality that he impressed the European public so profoundly.

More than anybody else he prepared Europe for the American Revolution.

II

THE AMERICAN REVOLUTION AS A
EUROPEAN REVOLUTION

DIRECTLY and indirectly, by its immediate as by its subsequent effects, the American Revolution involved such changes in the conditions of Europe as virtually to amount to another revolution.

The very external events were far-reaching in their consequences. The war of independence of the English colonies became a European war. In the course of the eighteenth century England had grown up to be the largest sea power of the world, and it used its supremacy in such a way as to rouse the anger and hostility of all other seafaring nations. The rebellion of the colonies meant a breaking away of that part of the British Empire which possessed a considerable part of its marine, and all of Europe seized upon the opportunity of weakening the British superiority. Some powers—France, Spain, Holland—joined the war against Great Britain. Well-nigh all the other powers of Europe united into the Armed Neutrality in order to safeguard the freedom of the seas. Confronted with such formidable opposition, Great Britain chose to lay down her arms and recognize the independence of the colonies. On that occasion Edmund Burke said:

A great revolution has happened—a revolution made, not by chopping and changing of power in any of the existing states, but by the appearance of a new state, of a new species, in a new part of the globe. It has made as great a change in all the relations, and balances, and gravitations of power, as the appearance of a new planet would in the system of the solar world.

England still remained the largest sea power, and in another war, some few years later, was able to assert its supremacy more completely than at any time before. But it had been compelled to acknowledge the existence and the freedom of a new rival on the seas, the United States of America.

There are no accurate statistics as to the size of the merchant

7

marines of the world at the outbreak of the American Revolution. It may, however, be estimated that while England had a fleet of approximately 1,000,000 tons, the American colonies had no more than 200,000, ranking behind both Holland and Denmark-Norway. Nevertheless the historian of British shipping, William L. Lindsay, declared in 1874 that the separation of the colonies from their motherland "produced a complete revolution in the relative position of the great maritime nations." The marines of both countries suffered severe losses during the War; American tonnage decreased to less than 125,000. But the years of peace that followed witnessed amazing progress on both sides of the Atlantic, relatively greater, however, on the American side. Ten years after the peace was concluded, the American merchant fleet had jumped to more than 500,000 tons and was already equal to a third of the English fleet which, at that time, was approaching 1,500,000 tons. At that moment the United States not only had reached the point at which it was carrying almost all of its commerce in its own ships, but had started on a successful competition with other nations in foreign waters—in the Baltic and the Mediterranean as well as in the trade with China. Everywhere it broke through the barriers of former monopolies. Thus the young American nation early entered upon a career as an independent economic power in international commerce, and during the world wars which were to pit England and France against each other in rivalry for world power, the United States became the leading champion of the freedom of the seas.

*   *   *   *   *

The rebellion of the colonies was directed against the commercial and political rule—branded as "tyranny"—of England, but it had larger consequences for England than merely to rob it of one element of power. The rebels founded their claims on good English principles, and they were supported by at least a minority of English public opinion. To the eternal honor of England be it said that there have at all times been people able to look beyond bare national interests and bold enough to stand up for justice to other nations. So it was on this occasion. Many Englishmen grasped the intimate connection between their fight for freedom at home and the fight of the Americans. From England came, as late as 1774, the fearless revolutionary Thomas Paine, who first ventured to raise the cry for unconditional American independence. The very title page of his *Common Sense* carried the statement "Written by an Englishman." In the British Parliament a small party of courageous speakers never tired of defending the cause of America. They were a minority, but their number was increasing, and they asserted that out in the country the majority was on their side.

At the very beginning of the crisis, in 1766, the national hero William Pitt (shortly to become Lord Chatham) hurled against the royal cabinet the famous and often quoted words: "I rejoice that America has resisted. Three millions of people, so dead to all the feelings of liberty as voluntarily to submit to be slaves, would have been fit instruments to make slaves of the rest. . . . America, if it falls, would fall like the strong man with his arms around the pillars of the Constitution." When his son, the younger William Pitt, entered Parliament in 1781, at a moment when the American Revolution was drawing near to final victory, he took the first opportunity to reassert the opinions of his father, declaring unequivocally that the war to suppress the revolution was "a most accursed, wicked, barbarous, cruel, unnatural, unjust, and diabolical war." The vehement oppositionist John Wilkes declared in 1780 that if an arbitrary administration had succeeded in its plan of "dragooning the colonists into unconditional submission," the liberties of England would not long have survived those of America. Every friend of the constitution, he went on, regarded support of the American cause as a vindication of the rights of Englishmen. Similar declarations came from statesmen like Charles James Fox and Edmund Burke.

The American question became a matter of internal British politics and considerably influenced their development. The feeling of frustration in regard to America created a better understanding of the Irish claims. The very war led to a measure of religious toleration: for the benefit of the volunteers the government assented to a bill releasing Irish dissenters from the sacramental test. Then in 1780 the system of restriction on Ireland's trade was abandoned; her trade with the colonies was thrown open, and the acts restraining the exportation of her woolens and glass were repealed. In 1782 Irish legislative independence was conceded. Later, no doubt, the experiences of this war largely determined the liberal policies pursued towards Canada.

The struggle over the war even involved an important constitutional question. Just as the colonies presented their rebellion as directed primarily against royal tyranny, so in England the war was generally called "the King's War." The opposition understood very well that on the issue of the war depended the question whether the king would be able to maintain his system of personal government. They reckoned on failure in America and hoped that (to quote a recent history of England) "by exposing the errors and corrupt practice of the government, they would so rouse public feeling that, when the war ended in national humiliation, the king would be forced to accept a minister imposed on him by his people." Their expectation proved right. The king was defeated in America, and that meant the deathblow to his system in England. He had to accept a prime minister who enjoyed the confidence of the nation. Thus was initiated the long rule of the younger William Pitt.

Undeniably, the defeat of England in the American war was at least partly attributable to the political corruption which, in the course of the eighteenth century, had infected the whole administration and was gnawing at the strength of the nation. Naturally, therefore, the opposition directed their attacks against this pernicious system, which had demonstrated its dangers by the lax conduct of the war. Burke moved and spoke for economic reform; Pitt took up the matter of parliamentary reform. Their proposals did not succeed at once, but the question was put on the order of the day and could not be removed until it was resolved. The sanitation of English political life began.

*   *   *   *   *

The effect on England of the American Revolution was only a part of its effect on the whole of Europe. Perhaps nobody foresaw the universal consequences of the rising of the colonies as clearly as the French statesman Turgot. In an official memorandum of April 6, 1776 (three months before the Declaration of Independence) regarding the attitude of France toward the colonial conflict, he stated that whatever might be the wish of the government, nothing could avert the final and absolute independence of the English colonies in America; and the inevitable consequence of this event, he said, would be a total revolution in the relations of Europe with America. Even though the Anglo-Americans, "enthusiasts of freedom," were overwhelmed by arms, their will could not be crushed. He understood that the opposition in England would ally themselves with the rebels in order to shake off the yoke of the king, but he added that the emancipation of the colonies would also mark the epoch of the greatest commercial and political revolution not only in England but in all of Europe.

Economist as he was, even in the narrower sense of a physiocrat, he fixed his attention particularly on the commercial aspect of the revolution to come. He pointed out that the Americans would have no need to make conquests in order to extend their commerce; for them it would suffice to open their ports to all nations, who would then hasten to bring them all that they needed in exchange for their own goods. Therefore they would not maintain the mercantilistic system against which they were rebelling. Already they had broken through it by their extensive smuggling, and if necessary they would fight to assert the freedom of commerce. Sooner or later, voluntarily or forcibly, all the European nations would have to concede this liberty to the colonies, nay, to all colonies.

"I firmly believe," Turgot concluded, "that all the metropolitan countries will be compelled to abandon all command of their colonies, to allow them a complete freedom of commerce with all nations, to be content to share this freedom with the others and to preserve with their colonies only the bonds of friendship and fraternity." He called that nation wise and happy which would be first to arrange its policies according to the new circumstances and to conceive its colonies as allies, not as subjects. He expected that "when the total separation of America shall have forced the whole world to acknowledge this truth and have cured the European nations of the jealousy of commerce, there will exist among men one great cause of war the less," and he added, "it is very difficult not to desire an event which is to accomplish this good for the human race."

Like all prophets Turgot saw the achievement of his wishes nearer than it was to be in reality. But he was right in the conception that a breach had been made in the mercantilistic system. It has often and justly been pointed out that the American Declaration of Independence was simultaneous with the appearance of Adam Smith's epoch-making work *The Wealth of Nations.* But it must not be forgotten that the physiocratic school, the "economists," had been proclaiming the principle of laissez-faire for twenty years, and that it had won the adherence of leading men in many countries. It was not a conscious tenet of the American revolutionaries, but by necessity they opposed the policies of mercantilism and thus led the way to a freer commerce.

For a long time the treaties of commerce concluded by the United States with European nations achieved only small steps in this direction. The first two to be signed after the end of the war with Great Britain—that with Sweden in 1783 and that with Prussia in 1785—marked a distinct breach with the principle of the navigation acts, which had restricted mutual commerce to vessels belonging to the parties to the treaty. They stipulated explicitly that each party should have the right to carry its own produce, manufactures, and merchandise in its own or any other vessels to any parts of the dominions of the other. But the long wars that filled the world during the period down to 1815 prevented negotiations for treaties of commerce on a larger basis of freedom. Nevertheless, the first tariff act adopted by the United States in 1789 broke away from mercantilism insofar as it was essentially a tariff for revenue. Though protectionism followed, the prohibitions and monopolies inherent in the mercantilistic system did not find a place in the American trade regulations. Then, when peace was reëstablished in the world, the American example and American insistence worked for commercial freedom everywhere.

It was an important gain when Great Britain in 1815 accepted the American proposal of complete reciprocity in the adjustment of duties. In a special treaty the two parties agreed that they should not impose higher duties in their ports on vessels of the other country than those payable by their own vessels. In the negotiations that were entered into immediately afterwards with Sweden, the American minister demanded the same equality for commerce with that country. Repeatedly he urged upon the Swedish government the "liberal policy" or the "superior liberality" of the United States, and he succeeded in having the principle of equal port duties included in the treaty signed the next year and made valid for Norway as well as for Sweden. By the same treaty both parties agreed to abstain completely from all prohibitions regarding either importation or exportation.

Still more remarkable was the victory won for free trade a few years later in the intercourse with Norway, and in this case the American example was clearly working. The first American consul in Norway, the wealthy shipowner Peter Isaachsen in Christiansand, by his own initiative in 1816 presented to the Norwegian government a petition for allowing American ships access to the ports of the country without any discriminating conditions, and finally in January 1821, a royal decree provided that American ships might bring products of any and all parts of the world into Norwegian ports without any restriction or qualification. The same principle was included in the treaty with Denmark in 1826, and in the new one with Sweden in 1827. This was the definitive breach with mercantilism in that part of the world.

Now the United States did not wait any longer to extend the principle of free navigation to intercourse with all countries. By an act of 1828 it opened all its ports to the vessels of all nations on the same terms as for its own vessels without discrimination as to the origin of the cargoes. Thus the prediction of Turgot in this regard finally came true.

    ✿ ✿ ✿ ✿ ✿

The political effects of the American Revolution materialized much more quickly and obviously than the economic ones. The American rebels had partisans not merely in Great Britain but

still more in other countries of Europe where there were no national interests opposed to sympathy with the revolution. On May
1, 1777, after four months in France, Benjamin Franklin wrote
home:

> All Europe is on our Side of the Question, as far as Applause and good
> Wish can carry them. Those who live under arbitrary Power do nevertheless
> approve of Liberty, and wish for it; they almost despair of recovering it
> in Europe; they read the Translations of our separate Colony Constitutions
> with Rapture. . . . Hence 'tis a Common Observation here, that our Cause
> is *the Cause of all Mankind,* and that we are fighting for their Liberty in
> defending our own.

Certainly "all Europe" was an exaggeration. But articulate public
opinion was so strongly in favor of America as to give the impression of true unanimity. Mirabeau used the same expression in
1782: "All Europe has applauded the sublime manifesto of the
United States of America." Such leaders of the Enlightenment as
Voltaire and Lessing hailed the rising of the Americans.

The general enthusiasm manifested itself in the number of
volunteers who crossed the Atlantic to fight at the side of the
American patriots. From France came Lafayette; it was the perusal of the Declaration of Independence that determined him to
go—"his heart," he said, "was enlisted." From Poland came Kosciusko and Pulaski, from Prussia von Steuben. And besides such
celebrated heroes many unknown people offered their lives to
the liberty of America.

The King of England, in his own way, tried to enlist Europe
against the revolution. As early as February 1776, he decided to
hire mercenaries from the small German principalities to fight the
rebels, and he contracted for troops from Brunswick and Hesse.
No action on his part roused such anger as this—a sentiment quite
incomprehensible from his point of view as he was merely following earlier instances of the same policy. (In the past, however,
foreign troops had been employed only in foreign wars, not
against subjects of the crown.) The act gave the final impulse to
the adoption of American independence. It was bitterly criticized
in the British Parliament, Burke observing that the mercenaries
snuffed the cadaverous taint of lucrative war; and the disgust of

public opinion abroad was not less outspoken. The German princes who, it was said, "sold the blood of their people" to fight against the cause of liberty, won the contempt and odium of "all Europe." From a temporary refuge in Holland Mirabeau hurled against the German soldiers his denunciation of the shameful traffic and exhorted them to imitate the example of the Americans by breaking their chains and fighting for freedom. One of the princes, whose recruits mutinied and refused to march, was obliged to disarm and fetter them and drive them to the ports of embarkation with the help of his guards. On his return, we are told, he was publicly hooted by mobs in every town through which he passed in Holland, with all sorts of reproachful epithets. All liberal Europe laughed and applauded when they heard that the King of Prussia, Frederick II, demanded the same toll per head for the men driven through his dominions as was paid for cattle.

The vital matter was that this revolutionary sympathy naturally transformed itself into a dynamic force within European society. The ideas that had been discussed and elaborated by philosophers, the liberty that had been praised in works on political theory, the republic that had been presented to a reading public as the basis of civic virtue—all this suddenly appeared as an actual reality. It was no longer a chimera: it existed in the New World and, by irresistible logic, it must be attainable and capable of realization in the Old. Men who had fought for the freedom of America returned to Europe to continue the fight in their home countries. Kosciusko came back to Poland to fight for Polish independence. Lafayette came back to France to fight for revolution there. Danish and Swedish officers who fought with the French forces in America, even if they did not carry home revolutionary ideas, nevertheless acquired a liberalism and an independent attitude that did not conform well with absolutism.

In 1787 an experienced observer of international politics, the German Emperor Joseph II, remarked in a letter that the assistance which the French had afforded to the Americans gave birth to ideas of freedom in their own country. Certainly in France, the home of the new radical philosophy, the effect of the American

Revolution was explosive. Thomas Paine's call to arms, the pamphlet *Common Sense,* was immediately translated into French, the first edition appearing in Rotterdam and later ones in France itself. One of the foremost historians of the French Revolution, A. Aulard, has stated that "its bold phrases resounded through France." The Virginia Declaration of Rights and, a few weeks later, the Declaration of Independence were hailed with an outburst of enthusiasm.

When, at the end of 1776, Franklin arrived as the envoy of the new republic, he was received with general rejoicing as the apostle of liberty. He became the favorite of the leading intellectual circles of Paris and almost a legendary figure in popular conception. He piqued the curiosity and won the admiration of the French because, in the words of a French historian, he "proved the possibility of associating friendship for France with fidelity to American virtues." He was portrayed as the man who "conquered the lightning and triumphed over the tyrants." The Queen dubbed him "our dear republican," and republicanism became the fashion of the day. People fixed upon a phrase of his, used in the days of military reverses: "*Ça ira, ça ira,*" and it was later made the motif of a revolutionary battle song. Then he was joined by John Paul Jones, who made his famous raid of the North Sea in a French cruiser, named for Franklin *Bonhomme Richard.* He became the popular naval hero of the young republic, admired by men and loved by women. Monarchical France identified itself with rebellious America.

All this was much more than a passing infatuation; it meant a lasting orientation of the French mind. It led directly to the French Revolution. The American war for liberty inspired the French to produce a large number of narratives, histories, books of travel, and prints concerning America. Translations of the various American state constitutions were published in many editions, partly through Franklin's efforts. The adoption of the Federal Constitution in 1788 confirmed the stability of the new republic, and the stream of books and articles about America steadily continued. Several of them were written by the most prominent French philosophers and statesmen, men like Turgot,

Condorcet, Mirabeau. American freedom was praised, and the authors generally stressed the high morals and the profound religious character of the American nation. All such writings were propaganda for revolution.

Franklin, who knew how to combine grave dignity with jocular wit, made the republic attractive and respected. Thomas Jefferson, who followed him as American minister, was less in the public eye but was nevertheless able to maintain the prestige of his country. He was overshadowed by Franklin's immense reputation and also by Lafayette, who was regarded as the French symbol of American ideas and ideals, the unofficial protector of American interests. Yet behind the scenes Jefferson was more directly active for revolution than Franklin ever had been. He took full advantage of Lafayette's invaluable coöperation, associated with him on terms of intimacy and affection, and helped keep his republican interests warm. For Lafayette's use Jefferson made suggestions as to the desirable course of procedure for the assembly of Notables, and immediately upon the meeting of the Estates General, submitted to Lafayette a draft of a constitution for France.

After his return to France from the American war Lafayette was often heard to say: "When shall I see myself the Washington of France?" Both in speaking and writing he affected the phrase "We other republicans." In his house in Paris he installed a large copy of the American Declaration of Independence, with a vacant space beside it awaiting the declaration of the rights of France. In military reviews he wore the American uniform, decorated with an emblem representing the tree of liberty above a crown and a broken sceptre. On all occasions he defended the "American principles": religious toleration, abolition of slavery, freedom of the press, parliamentary rule. Around him gathered what was called the "American party," chiefly consisting of liberal young noblemen.

Another American party, of bourgeois members, formed itself around Brissot, who had been a friend of Franklin's. Following the American example, they called themselves Patriots. Brissot organized them in 1787 into a Gallo-American Society. He published a pamphlet in defense of the United States against English calumnies, and even went on a visit to America.

When in 1787 the King found himself compelled to call the meeting of the Notables and, in the next year, the Estates General, Lafayette was one of the leaders in attacking the abuses of absolutism and in uniting a party of revolutionaries. He was one of the first to demand the summoning of the Estates General, and he was active in preparing the petitions for reform from his home province. After the nobility, of which he was a member, had joined the third estate in the National Assembly of France, he was elected vice-president of the Assembly and, on the same day, July 11, 1789, he made the proposal to vote a declaration of the rights of man.

It has been denied that in this action he was motivated by the example of the American states, and in his speech on this occasion he did not explicitly refer to the American model. But there is no reason to doubt the statement in his memoirs that he really wanted France to imitate America by such a declaration. He was not alone in this desire. During the preceding months, pamphlets had appeared calling for a declaration of rights according to the American pattern. When the committee charged with the task of elaborating the declaration laid its report before the assembly, it did not hesitate to state the original source of the proposal:

This noble idea, conceived in another hemisphere, should, by preference, be transplanted among us at once. We have coöperated in the events which have established liberty in North America; she shows us on what principles we should base the conservation of our own; and the New World, into which hitherto we have borne only a sword, teaches us today to guard ourselves from the dangers of carrying it to our own hurt.

There can be no disagreement about the fact that the French declaration of rights shows a decided superiority in clarity of style and thought to the various American declarations. But it appears indisputable that the idea of such a proclamation of the fundamental principles of the French Revolution was borrowed from America. Nor was this an isolated instance of imitation. Part of the very vocabulary of the French Revolution was American; the French did not forget that America had had National Conventions, Committees of Public Safety, and Committees of General Security. When Lafayette was made chief of the Civil Guard of Paris, he hoped that by virtue of this authority he might become the French Washington, leading a national army, and on his suggestion the Guard was renamed the National Guard.

One of the members of the Constituent Assembly reported that in its meetings he observed a distinct "American inoculation." Another member wrote that he found there a party which "regarded the federative republics of America as the best model" for the constitution of France and had a committee which carried on secret correspondence. During the first discussions of the new constitution, in the summer and fall of 1789, the party of the Patriots met in the house of Jefferson; they considered with him the various forms of a parliamentary system, e.g., the questions of the royal veto and of organization into one or two houses, and arranged with his assistance the necessary compromises. Roland and other revolutionists publicly referred to the American example and inspiration.

During the first two years of the French Revolution, the United States and its institutions were much discussed in pamphlets and newspapers. Brissot published a book about his visit to America. Franklin's death in 1790 occasioned great demonstrations. The National Assembly voted public mourning, and accepted Houdon's busts of Franklin and Washington; Mirabeau proclaimed that the world owed liberty to America; and the opportunity was taken for republican propaganda.

In its further progress the French Revolution followed its own ways; very soon the representatives of the French nation became satisfied that the conditions of France demanded another system than the American one. But that does not diminish the importance of the American example or, more particularly, of the American impulse to revolutionary action.

In the beginnings of the French Revolution, many people expected and hoped that it might lead to a universal European revolution, and Americans were active to this end. Just at the time Jefferson left France, toward the close of 1789, another American revolutionist arrived—no less a person than Thomas

Paine. For a couple of years he alternated between Paris and London, as has been said, "as a self-appointed missionary of the world revolution." When Edmund Burke, once the defender of the American Revolution, vehemently condemned the French, Paine answered him with his *Rights of Man,* which was not only an eloquent defense of the French Revolution but at the same time a passionate appeal to the English people to rise against their tyrants and set up a democratic republic. For this call to revolution Paine was outlawed in England, but he was made a citizen of France, and was immediately elected by four departments as a representative to the National Convention. The revolutionary development, however, soon passed by him, and in the next year, 1793, he was deprived of his French citizenship and put into prison, where he wrote *The Age of Reason,* another plea for universal revolution, this time in the domain of religion. He was presently released, but in the period of reaction that followed he found no place for his ideas. His life of action was finished, and he died a solitary man.

One of the poets of the American Revolution, Joel Barlow, was simultaneously working for the same purposes. He went to France in 1788 as agent for a company of speculators in Ohio lands. The speculation proved a failure, but he stayed on in France as an agent of revolution, traveling about the country lecturing and organizing societies in favor of the revolutionary party. He too looked beyond the frontiers of France. Close on the heels of Paine's *Rights of Man,* he published both in Paris and in London a work in two volumes on "the necessity and propriety of a general revolution," in the form of *Advice to the Privileged Orders in the Several States of Europe.* Later he addressed a letter to the Italian people "on the advantages of the French Revolution." He even put his talent for versification to the service of revolutionary propaganda in a poem on *The Conspiracy of Kings,* also printed in London as well as in Paris. He remained faithful to the French Revolution through all its periods. His activities, however, could not prevent the reaction; still less could they bring about a general revolution.

Nevertheless, though suppressed by force of arms, the ideas of the Revolution lived on and in the course of time were to rise again.

*   *   *   *   *

In terms of future developments the effects of the French Revolution by far overshadowed those of the American. Even in the countries outside France, however, the American Revolution prepared the ground for revolutionary action. It is a significant fact that the great prophet of the Italian *risorgimento*, the poet Vittorio Alfieri, in 1784 published a cycle of odes on *America liberata* and, in the next year, dedicated his revolutionary drama *Bruto* to George Washington. At the other end of Europe, in Sweden, the constitution of the United States was immediately published in translation; members of the nobility, infected by the American ideas, began whispering about a *coup* against the absolute monarch, and when finally, in 1809, the revolution was achieved, some of them wanted to establish a congress after the American pattern. Class interests, however, proved superior, and the old Riksdag of four estates was reconstituted.

In the neighboring country, Norway, the people of Bergen at an early date demonstrated their sympathy for the American rebels as against British supremacy on the sea. In 1779 some American prizes, captured from the English by John Paul Jones's squadron, came into Bergen and were detained there by the authorities. The Danish King regarded it as his duty according to the rules of neutrality to deliver up these prizes to the English government, but the citizens of Bergen were highly dissatisfied with this act.

An event of a similar character is reported thirty years later. At that time Denmark-Norway, much against the wishes of the Norwegians, were at war with Great Britain, and American vessels suspected of trading for the English were often captured in the North Sea and brought into Norwegian ports, particularly to Christiansand. Reports from American captains in 1809 tell of the friendship and assistance they met with both there and in Bergen, and John Quincy Adams, just passing through Christiansand on his way to St. Petersburg, tells the same story. It was then that the foremost shipowner of the city, Peter Isaachsen, was made the first American consul for Norway, and on his petition the temporary War Governing Board of Norway agreed to release the American ships detained in Christiansand for condemnation as prizes. Again, however, the King in Copenhagen was of another opinion and quashed the friendly act of the Norwegians.

Norwegian discontent with the union with Denmark was to a large extent motivated by opposition to the mercantilist system practised by the Copenhagen government. Although the business people of Norway felt strongly attached to England by intellectual as well as economic bonds, the idea of liberty was the fundamental element of their thought, and they felt inspired by the rising of the Americans.

One of the leaders of the Norwegian revolution of 1814, Judge C. M. Falsen, who is justly remembered as the Father of the Norwegian Constitution, named his son, who was born that year, George Benjamin for Washington and Franklin.

When the King had been forced to cede Norway to the King of Sweden, and Great Britain, on the insistence of Sweden, declared a blockade against rebellious Norway, the Norwegians could feel it a source of strength that the United States still kept up the fight against such policies of oppression. On the initiative of Consul Isaachsen the Prince Regent of Norway addressed himself to President Madison beseeching the friendship of the United States.

The example of America directly influenced the shaping of the new constitution of Norway. One of the delegates to the constituent assembly that met at Eidsvoll in April 1814 brought along a copy of the French translation of the American state constitutions published under Franklin's auspices in 1783 (this very copy is still preserved at the Independence Hall at Eidsvoll). The federal constitution of 1787 too was studied. Many models were used for the instrument that was finally signed on May 17 and is still valid for Norway. Most important were the first revolutionary constitution of France and the constitutional practice of England. The influence of the American models, however, is clearly visible in several articles of the Norwegian document, as in the definition of the legislative power of the Storthing, in the provisions for compensation to members and for their security from arrest, and in the rules for impeachment of members of the royal cabinet.

By a curious coincidence, the same months (April and May 1814) which saw the elaboration of the Norwegian constitution also witnessed the constitution of another country, France, being formed on the American model. But what a difference! The first draft of the new French constitution was initiated by Talleyrand, who himself had lived for a while in America as a political refugee; it was founded, like the Norwegian constitution, on the principle of popular sovereignty, although without applying it to the building up of a true democracy. The final proclamation, however, by King Louis XVIII on June 4 transformed the sovereignty of the people into that of the absolute monarch; the constitution was made, in name as in reality, a charter—a grant by the King according to his sovereign will to the nation. He created a legislature for the adoption of laws and of a budget; but the royal power was supreme, and nothing but the external forms of the American constitution were retained. The Senate became a Chamber of Peers. One important freedom, which had been the primary demand of the Norwegians and in fact was a vital condition of democracy, could not be omitted from the charter. That was the liberty of the press. That would make the winning of all other liberties possible.

The next time a European nation set out to give herself a free and truly democratic constitution, the United States was again used as an important model. This occurred when the Belgian nation rose for independence in 1830. It is a strange fact that the leaders of the Belgian revolution were not aware of the democratic constitution of Norway, although in many respects their problems and their goals were remarkably similar to those of the Norwegians. They imagined that their new democratic constitution was the first of its kind in Europe and therefore the most democratic in existence.

Many years later, at the close of the American Civil War, the priest Désiré de Haerne, who had been active in shaping the

Belgian constitution of 1830 and for almost half a century thereafter remained a member of the national parliament, spoke in the House of Representatives:

We are the only nation [he said] that has remained faithful in spirit to traditional rights and has followed America from the foundation of her political establishment and her liberal institutions. Yes, we looked upon England, on the one hand, as worthy of imitation in the march of progress in the path of true and practical liberty; but, at the same time, we were conscious that there were certain customs in the institutions of that country we could not adopt, and we cast our eyes beyond the Atlantic, where we found a great people worthy of entire imitation, and it is the institutions of that people we have chiefly inscribed upon our organic charter. We have followed their example in all that regards public liberty, the distribution of power, the election of representatives and decentralization of rule.

In this speech, de Haerne did not specifically mention the most striking feature in which Belgium in 1830 had followed the American example. He only faintly suggested it by referring to "all that regards public liberty." Presumably he did not want to touch the matter just then because it was a source of the bitterest party conflict at the moment. Already before the revolution of 1830 the division of party lines in Belgium had been drawn between Catholics and liberals. The revolution was possible because the two parties agreed to coöperate for independence, and de Haerne was one of the Catholic leaders who contributed most effectively to the temporary solution of the religious question by the adoption of the American principle of the complete separation of church and state. That was in Europe a radical innovation, and Belgium was the first country to adopt it. De Haerne was a follower of the great French Catholic rebel Lamennais who, immediately upon the Belgian revolution, started the newspaper *L'Avenir*, in which he advocated the freedom of the church by making it absolutely independent of the state. De Haerne was the champion of this idea in the Belgian national congress, and he pointed to America to show how well it worked. One of the leading liberals, Nothomb, did so too. To both of them, the separation of church and state seemed a consequence of the general principle laid down for the constitution: liberty in all for all.

In other respects, the constitutional ideas borrowed from America had no such revolutionary character. De Haerne had wanted, in order to secure the church against all interference from the state, to have Belgium established as a republic; he was afraid of the ambitions of a monarchy. In this he was defeated. When, in the speech quoted, he stated that the Belgian constitution, like the American, was founded on the division of power, he was not absolutely accurate. To be sure, the independence of the judiciary was guaranteed. But the executive was made largely dependent on the legislative by the parliamentary system. The parliament, however, was not made as democratic as that of Norway. It was built up on the two-chamber system. For the adoption of that system, America was referred to as the convincing proof. The advice of Lafayette was taken on this question; he too urged the American example. There was a party that proposed to create a kind of House of Lords, like that of England, by having the King appoint members of the Senate for life. That was defeated, and the American system of indirect elections was adopted.

Thus half a century after the American Revolution, its acts and its work were a power in the struggle for freedom in Europe. The American example was to become even more influential in time to come.

III

CHALLENGE TO THE EUROPEAN POWERS

THE Monroe message of 1823 was in itself a challenge to the Great Powers of Europe, a protest hurled against the plans of the Holy Alliance to interfere in American affairs. By that declaration the United States for the first time announced itself as a world power. The world importance of the doctrine thus proclaimed was not diminished, was rather confirmed, by the fact that it came to support one of the European Powers, Great Britain.

Until then, the governments of Europe had not taken the United States much into consideration in their fight for power. In the great revolutionary and Napoleonic wars the New World nation appeared almost a nonentity. Its incessant pleas for the rights of neutral trade fell on deaf ears. Its protests against injuries and violations were treated with neglect and contempt even by small powers like Denmark-Norway and Sweden, still more so by the great powers. Its "quasi-war" with France (1798–1801) and its open war with Great Britain (1812–14) led to no lasting gain. In European works on this period of crises and conflicts the interference of the United States is often passed over in complete silence. When at last in 1815 peace was reestablished in Europe, the Great Powers considered themselves the appointed guardians of universal peace and founded their Holy Alliance for the purpose of keeping down all disturbing elements. They wanted to dictate peace to the whole world.

In this regard, however, they were not very successful. Their agreement was more manifest in the suppression of revolutions than in maintaining general peace. At the Congress of Vienna in 1815 the Powers endeavored to concert measures to put an end to the piracy of Algiers and the other Barbary states of North Africa and to the system of tributes paid to the sovereigns of the corsairs since the seventeenth century. But it was the United States that really acted decisively. Sending a naval force to the Mediterranean, she compelled the Barbary rulers not only to desist from piracy against American ships but actually to pay indemnities. That was in the year 1815; by this vigorous action America set the pace for Europe. The American example induced first Great Britain and then other European countries to use their forces for getting rid of the rule of the corsairs.

In the matter of suppressing revolutions, however, the United States took a position completely opposite to that of the European Powers and helped to break their agreement on this point.

When peace was made in Europe there was a part of the world, indeed almost a world by itself, which stood in open rebellion against European dominion. That was Spanish America. The problem for the Powers was: Should they interfere to quell the rebellion and restore the colonies to Spain? The question brought them squarely up against the United States, and it split the alliance of the Powers.

The rebellion of the Spanish colonies could not but excite the sympathy of the United States. The rising was in no small measure inspired by the example of the North American colonies, and its victory would mean another defeat for the mercantilistic system of monopoly so hateful to the rebels of the North. Both continents of the western hemisphere were truly fighting for a common cause. Officially the government at Washington maintained neutrality, although it had been lending both moral and material support to the rebel colonies since 1810.

When, in the summer of 1818, rumors were heard of an intended European intervention, the United States gave notice to Great Britain that the basis of every international arrangement ought to be the autonomy of the Spanish colonies. At the beginning of 1819 President Monroe informed the British government that he planned, at the first opportunity, to recognize the independence of Buenos Aires. As a matter of fact, Great Britain had just as much, or indeed even more, interest in the abolition of the Spanish monopoly in South America. Although reluctant to see the spirit of revolution victorious, the conservative government of Castlereagh aimed at commercial liberation, and for that reason was unwilling to share in or to connive at intervention by force.

At the congress of the allied Powers at Aix-la-Chapelle in 1818, Czar Alexander of Russia had proposed a common guarantee of the territorial status quo and of all legitimate sovereignty. Castlereagh refused to join in any common action. The revolutions that broke out in southern Europe in 1820 stimulated the Czar's anxiety to crush all such movements, and despite the opposition and ultimate abstention of Great Britain, the continental Powers started a policy of active intervention. This policy roused in Europe a growing public opinion in favor of the liberal and democratic revolutionists, which found its outlet in a movement for support to free Greece. The first public act for the cause of freedom, however, came from the United States.

In Congress, Henry Clay, who had tried as early as the spring of 1818 to carry a resolution for the recognition of the first South American republic, succeeded in the fall of 1820 in having the House of Representatives adopt a resolution assuring the President of its support whenever he might deem it expedient to recognize the sovereignty and independence of the Spanish provinces. A year later, President Monroe, in his annual message to Congress, pointed to the success of the revolutions in South America and stated publicly that it would be the object of the government of the United States to promote the independence of the new republics. In fact, as he subsequently informed Congress, he had already "duly apprized" several of the European governments of his plan to recognize the revolted colonies. He was well acquainted with the disagreements of the Great Powers, and he cherished, as he said, "a sincere desire" to act in concert with at least some of them in the proposed recognition. He had, however, received no assurance regarding their attitude when, in March 1822, he laid his plan before Congress in a special message. He thought the moment had come for independent action on the part of the United States.

"When we regard," he wrote to Congress, "the great length of time which this war has been prosecuted, the complete success which has attended it in favor of the provinces, the present condition of the parties, and the utter inability of Spain to produce any change in it, we are compelled to conclude that its fate is settled, and that the provinces which have declared their independence, and are in the enjoyment of it, ought to be recognized." He felt himself authorized to predict that other governments would soon follow the American example, and he concluded: "The measure is proposed, under a thorough conviction that it is in strict accord with the laws of nations; that it is just and right as to the parties; and that the United States owe to their station and character in the world, as well as to their essential interests, to adopt it."

The last words demand particular attention. The consciousness of having won a "station in the world" that entitled it to act independently in important international matters was a new fact in American politics and led to a change in the world position of the United States.

The House of Representatives (with but one dissenting vote) immediately adopted a resolution concurring in the opinion expressed by the President, and before the end of the next month Congress voted the necessary appropriations for missions to be sent to the new independent states. Thus the President had the support of the nation for his policy. Very soon afterwards, he received in solemn audience the first diplomatic representative of the republic of Colombia. Further action was postponed until the beginning of the following year. Presumably Monroe was waiting to see the reaction in Europe to the decision taken in America.

In Europe a new conference of the Great Powers was called for the autumn of 1822 at Verona, and one of the subjects to be treated there was the question of intervention against revolutionary Spain and the Spanish colonies. In fact it became the only one. And it shattered the Holy Alliance. Canning, who had succeeded Castlereagh as the shaper of British foreign policy, took a still more decided attitude against intervention than his predecessor. Great Britain had already recognized the *de facto* existence of the Spanish American republics by maintaining commerce with them, and Canning said frankly that "the course of events, the interests of commerce, and the state of navigation in the American seas" might soon oblige the cabinet to come to an understanding with the revolutionary governments, even finally to recognize them *de jure*. When the other Powers agreed to authorize France to intervene in Spain in order to restore the monarchy there, Canning publicly warned the French government that if it should later help Spain subdue the colonies, he would promptly acknowledge their independence. According to his famous phrase, if France should have Spain it should be "Spain without the Indies."

After Verona the defection of Great Britain from the Alliance was manifest to the whole world, and in January 1823 President Monroe took the decisive step in the recognition of the Spanish American republics by appointing ministers to four of them (Colombia, Buenos Aires, Mexico, and Chile). The French army that crossed the Pyrenees in the spring of 1823 triumphed easily over the revolutionary Spaniards; immediately afterwards, the King of Spain with the support of France asked the Powers for assistance in subduing the rebel colonies. Thereupon Canning proposed common action by Great Britain and the United States.

President Monroe was in favor of it. But he let himself be persuaded by his Secretary of State, John Quincy Adams, to take parallel action rather than to act in direct coöperation with the British statesman. The result was the famous message of December 2, 1823, which proclaimed the Monroe Doctrine.

One part of the message directly pointed to the ambitions of the Russian Czar on the west coast of the American continent. In relation to them the President laid down the principle that the American continents were no more to be considered as subject for future colonization by any European power. At that moment the Czar had virtually abandoned the claims he had previously put forth to exclusive trading privileges far south along the American coast, and there was no real conflict between the two governments. An important principle, however, had been proclaimed for future policies. It was a word spoken on behalf of all America.

Still more does this hold true for the other part of the message in which the President declared that the United States must regard it as an unfriendly act, dangerous to its own peace and safety, if any European power should attempt to extend its own political system, that of the Holy Alliance, to any portion of the western hemisphere or try to oppress the governments recently recognized as independent by the United States. In this case, too, the words were a defiance to the Russian Czar, the moving spirit of the Holy Alliance, the man who had been most anxious to see an action against the Spanish-American republics. But of course the declaration directed itself against all policies of the same character, and it raised the prospect of united American resistance against the tyrannical powers of Europe.

The American minister in London, Richard Rush, tells us in his memoirs:

> When the message arrived in London, the whole document excited great attention. It was upon all tongues; the press was full of it; the Spanish-American Deputies were overjoyed; Spanish-American securities rose in the stock market, and the safety of the new States from all European coercion was considered as no longer doubtful.

Some critics have tried to minimize the actual effect of the Monroe message by asserting that at that moment no real danger existed of European intervention in South America, and it may truly be said that the menace of such intervention was effectively averted by the fierce protestations of Great Britain. It is, however, evident that the British government found itself powerfully strengthened in its opposition to the Allied powers by the unambiguous attitude of the United States. Canning did not like the proclamation of principles that might be turned against British policies also. Still less did he like the fact that the United States had gone ahead of Great Britain by its independent action. But he took all the advantage of it that he possibly could. When, the next year, on the insistence of the King of Spain, invitations were issued for another congress of the Great Powers to discuss the Spanish-American question, Canning exulted that the message of Monroe had given this congress the *coup de grâce*. He refused to attend.

The other Powers were irritated by the interference of the United States in what they regarded as their proper affairs. They persisted in regarding the American republic as an inferior power, not entitled to any voice in large international matters. When Canning suggested that the government at Washington ought to be invited to the projected congress on Spanish-American affairs, the French government which in 1818 had desired the coöperation of the United States because it hoped to see it combine with France against revolution, now found it a senseless idea to offer a seat to America in European councils. Chateaubriand, the Foreign Minister of France, thought it better to have no congress at all than to admit a country "whose political principles are directly at variance with those of every other Power." He declared that it should rather be an "article of public law of Europe" that the United States should be kept out of all European gatherings.

But the very irritation manifested offers a witness of the profound impression exerted by the American proclamation. In January 1824, the Austrian chancellor Metternich wrote to his Russian colleague Nesselrode:

These United States of America which we have seen arise and grow, and which during their too short youth already meditated projects which they dared not then avow, have suddenly left a sphere too narrow for their ambition, and have astonished Europe by a new act of revolt, more unprovoked, fully as audacious, and no less dangerous than the former. They have distinctly and clearly announced their intention to set not only power against power, but, to express it more exactly, altar against altar. In their indecent declarations they have cast blame and scorn on the institutions of Europe most worthy of respect, on the principles of its greatest sovereigns, on the whole of those measures which a sacred duty no less than an evident necessity has forced our governments to adopt to frustrate plans most criminal. In permitting themselves these unprovoked attacks, in fostering revolutions wherever they show themselves, in regretting those which have failed, in extending a helping hand to those which seem to prosper, they lend new strength to the apostles of sedition, and reanimate the courage of every conspirator. If this flood of evil doctrines and pernicious examples should extend over the whole of America, what would become of our religious and political institutions, of the moral force of our governments, and of that conservative system which has saved Europe from complete dissolution?

When the Russian minister to the United States proposed to the Czar to issue a solemn answer to the American document he was informed that "the document in question enunciates views and pretensions so exaggerated, it establishes principles so contrary to the rights of the European powers, that it merits only the most profound contempt."

The masters of oppressed Europe felt themselves attacked in the very heart of their principles by the action of the United States. But the friends of liberty exulted. Lafayette, still the close friend of America and Americans, declared the message of Monroe "the best little bit of paper that God had ever permitted any man to give to the world."

At the end of 1824, Canning saw to it that Great Britain recognized the independence of three of the Spanish-American republics, and after concluding a treaty of commerce with them on January 1, 1825, he boasted to the Parliament: "I called the new world into existence to redress the balance of the old."

The Russian Czar and the Emperor of Austria as well as the Kings of France and Spain solemnly protested against this act of recognition, and the supporters of the Holy Alliance were anxious to make it appear as though the whole of continental Europe stood united on the same side. But one of the American diplomatic representatives in Europe, the chargé d'affaires at Stockholm, felt authorized to report that those who said so either were deceived or wished to deceive others. "Our and the English doctrine," he wrote, "as to national rights and what constitutes national independence, has many staunch Friends and Supporters among the *Governments* as well as among the *people* of this Continent." He was correct, at any rate, regarding the King and government of Sweden and Norway, still more so as to the peoples.

The establishment of a series of republics in the New World was a distinct blow to the belief in the divine right of monarchy, and in the period of reaction that gloomed so darkly over Europe, it came like a ray of light carrying hope for new freedom.

The United States had first of all had the courage to proclaim the right of revolution, and the message of Monroe meant that it would firmly stand up for this right in the entire hemisphere where it had its own home. It was not yet accepted as an equal of the Great Powers. But it had dared to defy them. It rose once more as the champion of freedom in the world.

IV

REFORMS AND MOVEMENTS FOR REFORM

THE European system born of the convulsions that followed the French Revolution was one of general reaction and oppression. The idea of freedom was anathema to the monarchs and the ruling classes. Democracy was identified with mob rule and lawlessness.

In the face of this wave of reaction, the example of American democracy was a continuing stimulus to movements for popular self-government. The United States, as the aged James Madison said in 1835 to an English visitor, had been "useful in proving things before held impossible." One such thing he himself had been eminently instrumental in achieving—the establishment of a lasting Constitution founded upon general experience and philosophy. Another thing was the capacity of mankind for self-government. Both facts exerted far-reaching influence upon Europe.

The more the peoples of Europe began to shake the shackles laid upon them by their monarchical tyrants, the more wistfully they looked upon the freedom prevailing across the ocean. Before and after 1830 America was a powerful element of discussion and propaganda in European political struggles. Anti-democrats held it up as a warning, champions of freedom as an object of admiration and imitation. This is not the place to review in detail the voluminous literature produced by foreign visitors to the United States in the second quarter of the nineteenth century. It is important to observe, however, that essentially it was a literature of propaganda rather than of objective study and that it provided an arsenal of weapons for the battle of ideologies which was taking place on the continent of Europe.

Thus hostile and condescending critics like Captain Basil Hall, Mrs. Frances Trollope, Thomas Hamilton, and Captain Marryat looked upon the American experiment in democracy and were horrified; committing their reactions to print, they proclaimed that democracy was almost universally pernicious in its influence upon manners, morals, political behavior, and the social order. On the other hand, friendly observers like Harriet Martineau, Alexis de Tocqueville, and Fredrika Bremer found in American life much that was hopeful and worthy of imitation by the Old World.

The books of these travelers, widely circulated and read in Europe, provided arguments for both sides in the political controversies which racked the continent in the years which saw the revolutions of 1830 and 1848 and their aftermath. Despite their greater celebrity and the sensationalism which marked their reports, the spokesmen of reaction (and the disappointed liberals like Charles Dickens) did not succeed in making American politics and society such a bogey of corruption and vulgarity as to overawe the spontaneous sympathy of the broad masses that were struggling towards freedom.

Particularly, the work of Tocqueville made the example of America felt in all quarters of the European world. While the first two volumes, published in 1835, chiefly offered factual information about the functioning of democratic government in the United States, the two later volumes, appearing in 1840, contained a broad study of the influences of democracy on intellectual and social life, and this part of the work, though critical in some respects, was essentially an eloquent vindication of democratic government. By 1850, the work had passed through thirteen French editions, and it was translated into all the principal languages—English, German, Italian, Spanish, Danish, Russian, Serbian, etc. Everywhere it was hailed as one of the great contributions to the cause of democracy, everywhere it was discussed, impugned, or applauded. Few books have ever made such a profound and universal impression. In France it was said: "To speak of democracy is to speak of Tocqueville's book"; and the same holds true of many other countries. The work was an event in European history. Through its pages America spoke to Europe more forcefully than it had spoken since the Revolution.

❋   ❋   ❋   ❋   ❋

One feature of American life that struck—and for once agreeably struck—all foreign visitors to the country was the spirit of philanthropy expressed in the many charitable institutions, private and public, which they found, particularly in New England and in Pennsylvania.

Humanity and philanthropy were inseparable links in the great movement of enlightenment of the eighteenth century. They were proofs that this movement was not merely one of intellectualism, that it was intimately connected with sentiments of human love embracing all mankind. Pity and mercy, which nowadays seem so absolutely bound up with the Christian religion, came in fact to maturity very late within the Christian nations. The strengthening of these qualities in modern times may perhaps be regarded as the one real change that has been produced in the human mind in the course of historical development; other changes seem rather to have affected external conditions, and in that way to have determined the ideas and acts of the individual. Even pity and mercy, however, being profound elements of personal character, demand expression in social action. This they found most early and most generally in the British colonies in America. There deep-rooted religious sentiments combined strongly with the influx of the Enlightenment, as witnessed, among other things, by the peaceable transition from Puritanism to Unitarianism in New England. Moreover, Tocqueville was indubitably right when he derived the new humane spirit to a great extent from the conception of equality prevailing in an essentially democratic society. Thus philanthropic institutions in America could well offer examples and inspiration to European philanthropists.

At first sight it may appear strange that the very first American institution after the Constitution of the United States to be consciously imitated in Europe was the system of prisons. But it is less surprising when penal laws are seen as evidence of the degree of humanity to be found in a country. It was a writer on crimes and penalties (the Italian Beccaria in 1764) who formulated the political program of the age as the demand for "the greatest happiness for the greatest number." And democratic

America was the first country to abandon the old conception of punishment as retribution. There the individual states began to experiment with systems of another character in which the principle was the reformation of the criminal. On the basis of that principle two different systems were developed, both of which, however, were founded on the idea that the convicts should be kept out of touch with each other in order to prevent mutual contamination. The one system, that of New York, placed the prisoners in isolated cells during the night but let them work together during the day, though in complete silence. The other system, that of Pennsylvania, kept them in solitary confinement day and night. When Basil Hall saw the latter in operation in Philadelphia in 1828, he found it exceedingly cruel and not at all conducive to the end intended, because it kept the convicts completely unoccupied except by their solitary thoughts. But in that very year an important reform of the system was accomplished by prescribing regular work of an educational character for the prisoners.

These American experiments attracted a good deal of attention in Europe, and it is significant of European development that, immediately upon the advance of democracy in the revolutions of 1830, students were sent out to investigate penal reform in America. From France in 1831 came Tocqueville and other experts, from England in the next year came William Crawford. The result of the French inquiries was published in 1833, that of the English in 1834. Both works concluded with the recommendation of the Pennsylvania system. That seemed to them to lead to the promised goal: solitary confinement, with the addition of moral and religious instruction, in the words of Crawford, "might be made permanently efficient not only in deterring but in reforming the offenders." In accordance with this recommendation the system was adopted in both France and England, and new prisons were built in which it could be put into practice.

The Pennsylvania or Philadelphia system, as it was popularly called, won a great renown all over Europe. It impressed the older school of philanthropists as something very fine and humane, as it really was in comparison with the methods of former times. The great Swedish historian E. G. Geijer published in 1839 a series of articles concerning the treatment of the poor, and in these articles he included a recommendation of the Pennsylvania penitentiary system according to the French and English reports. The Crown Prince of Sweden and Norway, later King Oscar I, a man of liberal inclinations, published a whole book about the new system in 1840; it was translated into Norwegian by the great poet and spiritual leader of young Norway, Henrik Wergeland. Prince Oscar recommended the system for prison terms of less than six years. It was adopted in that form by the Swedish Riksdag in 1841, by the Norwegian Storthing in 1842. Later it spread to Denmark, to Belgium, to Prussia, to Italy, and to some Swiss cantons.

When Charles Dickens visited the solitary prison of Philadelphia in 1842, he was deeply impressed with the horrors of long years of solitude, and he felt sure that such a punishment dulled the senses and by degrees impaired the faculties of the prisoners. Modern criminologists may have other objections to the system. It must be noted, however, that most European countries adopted it in a modified form. What was of lasting value was the stimulus to penitentiary reform which came from America.

Other features of the American penal laws were also made objects of study in Europe. In particular their humane character, pointed out by Tocqueville, made a lasting impression. By a peculiar coincidence this influence was to a great extent exerted by a code of laws that was not adopted—the criminal code for Louisiana elaborated by Edward Livingston. As early as 1795, as a young member of Congress from New York, he had moved to revise the penal code of the United States, which he considered far too sanguinary—but nothing was done. He continued his studies of crime and punishment, and in the works of Jeremy Bentham he found the systematic expression of his ideas. When in 1821, as a member of the legislature of Louisiana, he was commissioned to revise the penal laws of the state, he made what was actually the first attempt to construct a criminal code on the basis of these ideas. In 1825 he presented to the legislature a complete system of laws; in every article it consistently aimed at the prevention rather than the avenging of crime. It proved too radical to be adopted, but the publication of the proposal made the author famous throughout the civilized world. The great English authority on laws, Sir Henry Maine, called Livingston "the first legal genius of modern times," and he was chosen foreign associate of the Institute of France. More important, his work encouraged reform in many European countries. Among other things, it furthered the movement toward limiting and even abolishing the use of capital punishment. Several of the European countries gradually advanced further on the way to reform than America did. The field for experimentation, however, has generally remained more open in America than in Europe.

As democracy won ground in Europe, the English and American system of trial by jury in criminal cases became part of the democratic program, and students came to America to see it in practice; for instance, an expert was sent by the government of Norway in 1846. It was an encouragement to European democrats to observe how deep-rooted the jury system was in American life and thought. But one characteristic element of the English-American system, the grand jury, did not take hold on the European continent. In this simplified form the jury system was triumphant in most European countries in the course of the nineteenth century. Even if it only reflected American influence to a limited degree, it led at any rate to an increasing assimilation between America and Europe.

* * * * *

When Tocqueville discussed the influence of democracy in mellowing manners and character, as for instance in the more humane treatment of criminals, he also pointed to the increasing love for peace in a democratic nation. At the same time he stressed the eminently religious character of American thought. Both elements united in forming a movement for international peace which intermittently became an animating force in European life.

The Anglo-Saxon nations have perpetuated to an extraordinary degree the tendency so dominant in the Middle Ages to transform all social and political questions into moral or religious ones. This tendency, strengthened by the English Revolution of the seventeenth century which made the Puritans political rebels, was inherited by the Americans. Both in England and in America the first peace movement had an outspoken religious character.

In both countries it was born in protest against the long-drawn-out Napoleonic wars. It started in America and was carried thence to England. In 1815 no less than three independent peace societies were formed in the United States—the first in New York by a Presbyterian who had announced his program by a pamphlet entitled *War Inconsistent with the Religion of Jesus Christ,* the second by Quakers in Ohio, the third by Congregational ministers in Massachusetts. The next year, Quakers in London founded a peace society after the pattern of the Massachusetts society. The English as well as the American societies displayed great activity in issuing tracts, mostly of a religious character, designed to convert people to their cause. Hundreds of thousands of such tracts translated into different languages were spread all over the world. A member of the Massachusetts society organized the first French peace society in Paris in 1821, and it carried on correspondence with the sister societies in America and England, besides holding communication with individuals in Switzerland and Germany. A peace society was founded in Geneva in 1830 by a woman who happened to read a copy of the organ of the London society.

An organization on a broader basis was begun in America by the founding of a national peace society in 1828. At that date there were already in the United States as many as fifty independent peace societies, besides a dozen branches of the Massachusetts society. The founder of the American Peace Society, William Ladd, explained his enterprise by saying: "I felt it a duty which I owe to God and my fellow-creatures to do something to hasten the glorious era when men shall learn war no more." In the first circular of the new organization he stated its program in these words: "We believe the custom of war to be contrary to the principles of the Christian religion, subversive of the liberty of mankind and destructive to their happiness."

Already the time seemed ripe for an international movement. From 1835 on, American representatives frequently came to the meetings of the Peace Society of London, and acting upon an American suggestion, this society called an international convention of delegates of peace societies to meet in London in 1843. Most of those who attended (more than a hundred persons) were English; but in addition there were fourteen from the United States and six from France. Letters were read from people who were unable to attend from Holland, Switzerland, Sweden, and Canada. It is significant for the moral background of this convention that it was organized in connection with the anti-slavery convention of the same year, and it was called on the principle that "war is inconsistent with the spirit of Christianity and the true interest of mankind."

The convention of 1843, however, did not result in more concerted action of all the peace societies or in the formulation of a more practical program. The initiative for such a reshaping of the peace movement came from America. On the one hand, political developments had led the American peace societies to bombard Congress with petitions for the promotion of their principles. They had practical proposals for the solution of the problems involved: they demanded the organization of a general congress to codify international law, the establishment of a court of nations, and the conclusion of treaties of arbitration with foreign nations. On the other hand, the magnetic personality of Elihu Burritt, "the learned blacksmith" of Connecticut, proved a powerful force. He too first approached the peace problem from the religious point of view; he began in 1844 the publication of a weekly called *The Christian Citizen,* devoted to all kinds of moral reforms—abolition of slavery, peace, temperance, and so on. As to war, his attitude was of a terrific consistency; he clung passionately to the Bible's precept of never taking up arms. But he was at the same time a shrewd Yankee, and he seized upon the economic causes of international conflicts, explaining that free trade would be the surest way of establishing a lasting peace.

Shortly after he had joined the peace movement by becoming a member of the executive committee of the American Peace Society, the United States surprised the world by annexing Texas in 1845, thus risking war with Mexico, and by following up the action with a claim to all of the Oregon territory, thereby defying Great Britain. Governments and people in Europe stood aghast at this sudden outburst of the lust for conquest; they could not conceive of a hardihood that made it seem a matter of indifference to the American nation whether the Great Powers might like or dislike their action. In European eyes the United States at this stage could not but appear an extremely bellicose nation. When war with Mexico actually ensued, this impression was confirmed.

These very events stimulated the peace movement in America to vigorous advance, and Elihu Burritt became the chief exponent of the will to preserve peace. During the Oregon crisis in the first months of 1846, he inaugurated an intimate coöperation with English friends of peace, and he brought about an exchange of "Friendly Addresses" between British and American cities, merchants, ministers, and laborers, which, with a keen sense of publicity, he managed to have published in some eight hundred newspapers.

The outbreak of the Mexican War in the summer of the same year led to a rupture in the American Peace Society. The majority thought it their duty to support their national government. In consequence, Burritt and other members who were uncompromising in their opposition to war withdrew from the society. Immediately afterward, he went to Europe, ostensibly to attend the general temperance convention to be held in London. He made use of the convention to launch his plan to establish a world organization for peace, the League of Universal Brotherhood, which was finally organized in 1847. It became the chief instrument of his world-embracing activities during the next years.

Immediately on the outbreak of the February Revolution of 1848, he decided that the moment had come to summon all the peace friends of the world to united action. He therefore called a universal peace congress in September of the same year in Brussels. One hundred and fifty Englishmen went over to this meeting, while only one other American accompanied Burritt. Other attenders were from Belgium, France, Holland, Spain, and Italy. Before this assembly Burritt propounded the program which from now on he made his special project and which came to be generally known as the American Plan. It was presented in a paper on "The Propriety of Convoking a Congress of Nations, the object of which shall be to form an International Code, in order, as far as possible, to settle on a Satisfactory Basis, Moot Questions, and generally to secure Peace." The congress adopted resolutions for this purpose as well as for international arbitration and universal disarmament.

A series of annual congresses followed, all of them organized by Burritt in coöperation with the new secretary of the English Peace Society, Reverend Henry Richard. The most resounding of them was that at Paris in 1849. For that congress Burritt succeeded in enlisting the assistance of prominent Frenchmen like Victor Hugo, Lamartine, and the liberal economist Bastiat. Tocqueville, who momentarily was the French minister for foreign affairs, accorded all kinds of facilities and honors to the congress. This time almost seven hundred Englishmen came to attend, and there were a hundred French delegates, twenty Americans, and fifty from other countries.

Victor Hugo presided. Throwing out the slogan of the United States of Europe, which would join the United States of America to create a fellowship across the ocean, he prophesied:

A day will come when the only battlefield will be the market opened to commerce, and the mind opening to new ideas. A day will come when bullets and bombshells will be replaced by votes, by the universal suffrage of nations, by the venerable arbitration of a great sovereign senate. A day will come when a cannon will be exhibited in public museums, just as an instrument of torture is now, and people will be astonished that such a thing could have been.

People will nowadays recall with a bitter smile that even instruments of torture have been put into use again in our own times, and that cannon have been perfected as a means of destruction more terrible than ever. But the peace congress of Paris, and the other congresses held for the same purpose, first posed the idea of organized international peace as an actual problem for the nations. Most leading newspapers had nothing but ridicule for the champions of this idea, but as each year passed they felt compelled to take it more seriously.

In Paris Burritt made an impassioned appeal for the calling of a congress of nations to codify international law and for the establishment of a general court of arbitral justice; and resolutions to this effect were adopted. The next year, 1850, the peace congress met in the free city of Frankfort where, the previous year, a parliament had been engaged in abortive efforts to create a liberal constitution for Germany. This time Burritt had gone in advance to the United States and had toured the country in order to secure a larger number of American delegates; thirty-six Americans answered his call. One of the results of this congress was the formation of the first peace society in Germany, appropriately located in Königsberg, the city of Immanuel Kant who, half a century before, had propounded the first realistic plan for a peaceful society of nations. This peace society was immediately suppressed by the Prussian police—a striking evidence that the idea of peace had become an actuality, a danger to the dominating military coterie of Prussia.

The largest congress in this series was that of London in 1851, attended by no less than twelve hundred delegates, most of them, of course, from Great Britain. In addition there were sixty from the United States, almost forty from Germany, many from France, and further delegates from Austria, Belgium, Italy, Netherlands, Norway, Spain, Sweden, and Guatemala. But after this meeting the general reaction in Europe affected this movement as it did others. New congresses were held in Manchester (1852) and Edinburgh (1853). Increasingly, however, they lost their international character, and after the outbreak of the Crimean War peace congresses were not called again for a full generation.

Meanwhile Elihu Burritt had undertaken other kinds of work for propagating the cause of peace. In 1852, under the sponsorship of the League of Universal Brotherhood, he managed the exchange of "Friendly Addresses" between British and French cities, and he went personally to France to deliver the messages of friendship to the municipal authorities there. Still more important was the inauguration in 1850 of the "Olive Leaf" mission. This was a journalistic enterprise of unprecedented dimensions, the first international syndicated newspaper column. Burritt obtained the agreement of forty influential continental papers to accept from him, or from the League of Universal Brotherhood, monthly articles, called "Olive Leaves for the People," containing peace propaganda. They were printed by popular newspapers from Stockholm, Oslo, and Copenhagen to Vienna and Madrid, and were reprinted in many liberal papers which had not contracted for them. In 1856 Burritt estimated that they had reached one million European readers each month, and that was, in my judgment, a rather low estimate.

After the meetings of the universal peace congresses were terminated, Burritt went back to the United States. During the eight years of his activities in Europe he had influenced public opinion more than any American before him. It may truly be said that he was the man who first created a public opinion in favor of peace in Europe. At the same time he lifted the program of peace out of the purely religious context of the older Anglo-American movement. He gave it practical aims, and connected the cause of peace integrally with the liberalism of the age, in particular with the demand for free trade. Henceforth the European peace movement could advance independently under its own leaders. But it was owing to him that it had reached so far.

*   *   *   *   *

All foreign visitors to America, at least before liberalism had won the field in Europe, observed with pleasure or distaste the personal freedom that prevailed in this democracy. Tocqueville had some misgivings on account of the pressure of public opinion that weighed upon and curbed the individual, but even he had to state that American freedom of action and thought far exceeded what he had experienced in Europe. This freedom even extended to women. America thus became the starting point of the feminist movement. From there it was carried to Europe.

Feminism has often been explained as a result of the Industrial Revolution. That does not, however, mean that the women who were taken out of their homes and put to work in factories were those who started the battle for women's rights in social and political life. Had that been the case, one would expect feminism to have begun in England, the first country to be thoroughly industrialized. As a matter of fact, the movement was started by women of the bourgeois class who, by the invention of spinning and weaving machines and later the sewing machine (an American invention), were largely set free from their old duties of housework—free to acquire a higher education and to take up social tasks of different kinds. The movement appeared earliest in America because there both laws and social customs presented fewer obstacles and a freer spirit reigned.

At the close of the 1820's the conservative-minded Captain Basil Hall noticed that the young girls of America displayed more independence of conduct than he could approve. But he was happy to add that after they had married they were content to give themselves completely up to their duties as wives and mothers. Tocqueville, who came to the country only a couple of years later, had another interpretation of this latter fact. He explained it as an actual consequence of their freedom before marriage. He observed what to a Frenchman perhaps was more striking than to anybody else, that American girls were not given away in marriage against their own will; therefore they would naturally be more faithful to their husbands. On the other hand, he remarked in another connection that even married women often went to public meetings and listened to political speeches, in that way "relaxing from the tediums of housekeeping." The fundamental fact, however, was that he found American girls better educated than European, and this was the fruit of conscious efforts which were just at that time beginning to reach out from America to Europe.

The pioneer of higher education for women was Emma Willard who, by her *Plan for Improving Female Education* (1819), persuaded the legislature of New York to grant state support to a seminary for girls. She was a pedagogical genius whose elementary textbooks in geography, history, and other disciplines were translated and adopted even in Europe. She herself went to Europe and, by a series of addresses on the advancement of female education, helped establish a female seminary in Athens. Partly as a consequence of the movement she started, women were admitted to Oberlin College in Ohio in 1833, and in 1836 the first chartered women's college in the world was established at Macon, Georgia, by the Methodist Church. That was only the first step, and inevitably, as the field of higher education was opened to more and more women, new interests and new claims were evoked.

Both in Europe and in America individual women had been able to accomplish remarkable feats in different domains, and isolated voices for equal rights had lifted themselves in both hemispheres. But in America, for the first time, women began to organize themselves for entrance upon public life. A Female Peace Society was formed as early as 1820, but it was the women's work in another moral movement that was more determinative for the general development of feminism.

Within some of the Christian denominations, particularly among the Quakers (or Friends) and the Methodists, women's rights as religious preachers were acknowledged as a matter of course, and in a social movement of an eminently religious character where the Quakers were largely leaders, women quickly advanced to the forefront. This was the fight for the abolition of slavery. And with this movement American women carried the fight for their own freedom over to Europe.

When the American Anti-Slavery Society was founded in 1833, the women thought it natural that they should not join the organization of their husbands and male friends. They could not, however, stay out of the movement and consequently they immediately formed their own organization, the Female Anti-Slavery Society. Its president was Lucretia Mott of Philadelphia, already at that time a famous Quaker preacher. This society held annual national conventions during the years 1837–39, this being another novelty in women's history. It began to seem unnatural and impracticable, however, that men and women should work separately in the same cause, and in 1839 women were admitted to equal membership with men in the American Anti-Slavery Society. This change was not carried without resistance. In fact, it was adopted by a very small majority, and it rent the society in twain; the opponents withdrew and formed an organization for themselves. The victory, none the less, was won by the women.

In Europe, the forces of resistance were stronger. It happened that in the same year the British and Foreign Anti-Slavery Society in London called friends of their cause in all countries to a general conference to commence on June 12, 1840. The two chief branches of the American Anti-Slavery Society, the one in Pennsylvania, the other in Massachusetts, resolved to send delegates, and both of them elected female as well as male representatives. All together eight women were sent to London; one of them was Mrs. Mott, who went along with her husband, James Mott.

The British Society was informed before the convention that women delegates were coming, and the news created much excitement. When the Americans arrived in London, one of the English delegates came to them and remonstrated against such unprecedented action. "We endeavored," says Mrs. Mott in her diary, "to show him the inconsistency of excluding women delegates, but we soon found he had prejudged . . . therefore all reasoning was lost upon him and our appeals made in vain." She understood what the outcome would be, and she called a meeting of women who adopted a protest against the expected exclusion.

The battle was fought on the first day of the conference. After the solemnities of opening, the leader of the Massachusetts delegation, Wendell Phillips, immediately moved that a committee on credentials should be instructed to accept all members, including women, delegated from any anti-slavery body. He pointed out that the invitation was extended to all "friends of the slave," and, he said, "we stand here in consequence of your invitation." He tried to appeal to the sentiments of the assembly by urging that it would not appear just or equitable to refuse a place in the deliberations to people who had come three thousand miles in order to attend.

One of the English Quakers supported the motion. Recalling that his society had always given to its women members a great, honorable, and religious prominence, he declared: "I look upon this delegation from America as one of the most interesting, the most encouraging, and the most delightful symptoms of the times." But he stood almost alone. Another English minister stated that the British society had not intended to invite women, and he made "a most touching appeal" to the American ladies to "conform to English prejudice and custom" by withdrawing their credentials. He declared that it would be better to see the whole convention dissolved right away than to have the motion of admission adopted. A Scotch minister said that to him it was a matter of conscience not to allow females to sit and deliberate in such an assembly as this. Even an American minister affirmed that the reception of women would be not only a violation of the customs of England but of the ordinance of Almighty God. Finally an English minister warned that the discussion might be hurtful to "the delicacy, the honor, the respectability of those excellent females who have come from the Western World," and he begged the Americans to spare the ladies "such exposure."

In vain did Wendell Phillips urge that he and his colleagues could not go back to America and ask the assistance of women in the anti-slavery cause if they deserted their rights here. By a large majority the women were excluded. Sadly Lucretia Mott had to note: "The Friends present were nearly all opposed to women's admission." They were allowed only to sit and listen behind the bar that separated the assembly from spectators.

The convention lasted almost two weeks, and it was concluded by a large public meeting at which even royalty were present. But there too the American women were excluded. At a final afternoon tea, Mrs. Mott was called upon to speak. One representative tried to protest, but was drowned by cries of "No! no! Mrs. Mott!" She made a brief speech which was, she relates, "patiently heard."

One day during the convention an English lady came and said to the American ladies: "You are held in high estimation, and have raised yourself by coming." No doubt the occurrence made a profound impression on English women who were witnesses to it. But it did not arouse very wide attention. The London *Times* reported from the opening meeting that the motion of Wendell Phillips "gave rise to a very long and irregular discussion" and then proceeded to summarize the arguments against the motion in a very few lines. That was all. The *Annual Register* for 1840 did not contain the slightest allusion to the convention, although it devoted four full pages to a meeting of the Society for the Extinction of the Slave-Trade; that meeting, to be sure, was presided over by the Prince Consort.

The fact remained, nevertheless, that the rights of women had become an object of struggle in Europe. Further impetus from America created a real women's movement. Bitter memories of London lay smoldering in women's minds on both sides of the Atlantic. During the Anti-Slavery Convention Mrs. Mott had made the acquaintance of young Elizabeth Cady Stanton, a pupil of Emma Willard, who had accompanied her husband as a bride to the meeting; and before departing, the two ladies promised each other to organize American women for a general program of social and political equality. They did not carry their plan into effect until 1848. In that memorable year they called a meeting to discuss women's claims at Seneca Falls, New York; there a platform was adopted of which the chief plank was the demand for suffrage at all public elections. In the next few years similar meetings were held at different places. In 1850 a national Women's Rights Convention was held at Worcester, Massachusetts, to be followed by more such conventions in 1852 and later. In this way a women's movement was firmly established.

The rumors of this new rising reverberated in Europe. The Worcester Convention was reported (anonymously) in the liberal *Westminster Review* in July 1851 by Mrs. John Stuart Mill in a long article, entitled *Enfranchisement of Women*, which presented to the British public the arguments later to become so well known, for women's emancipation. Mrs. Mill did not write simply as the mouthpiece of her famous husband; on the contrary, it was rather she who made him embrace the cause of women with conviction and consistency. She stated clearly that it was an American movement which she now wanted to transplant to Europe. She opened her article with these words:

Most of our readers will probably learn from these pages, for the first time, that there has arisen in the United States, and in the most civilized and enlightened portion of them, an organized agitation on a new question, —new, not to thinkers nor to anyone by whom the principles of free and popular government are felt as well as acknowledged, but new, and even unheard of, as a subject for public meetings and practical political agitation. This question is the enfranchisement of women; their admission, in law and in fact, to equality in all rights, political, civil, and social, with the male citizens of the community. It will add to the surprise with which many will receive this intelligence, that the agitation which has commenced is not a pleading by male writers and orators *for* women; those who are professedly to be benefited remaining either indifferent or ostensibly hostile. It is a political movement, practical in its objects, carried on in a form which denotes an intention to persevere. And it is a movement not merely *for* women, but *by* them.

And she continued:

Not only to the democracy of America, the claim of women to civil and political equality makes an irresistible appeal, but also to those Radicals and Chartists in the British islands, and democrats on the Continent, who claim what is called universal suffrage as an inherent right, unjustly and oppressively withheld from them.

With these words the women's movement was linked with the great democratic movement which had started in 1848, and in the years to come it became even more indissolubly bound up with the general advance of democracy. In England it was already on the way. Mrs. Mill was able to refer to the fact that on February 13, 1851, a petition of women adopted by a public meeting in the industrial city of Sheffield, claiming the elective franchise, had been presented to the House of Lords. This was the first step to follow the American example. And it is worth noting that when the World's Educational Convention met in

London in 1854, Emma Willard with other women were accepted as members without objection.

American impulses were active in other ways also. While Fredrika Bremer, the Swedish novelist, was traveling in the United States (1849–51) she met several of the "emancipated ladies" and observed the increasing appreciation of women's value in the life of the nation. She found educational institutions for women much superior to those of Europe, and she was surprised to find even a woman physician. This was Elizabeth Blackwell who, despite much serious opposition, had forced her way into the Medical College at Geneva, New York, and was graduated from there in 1849. A young lady who was graduated from Oberlin College in 1847, Antoinette Louisa Brown (shortly to marry Miss Blackwell's brother) preached in Congregational and later in Unitarian churches and obtained ordination as a minister in 1853.

These experiences inspired Miss Bremer upon her return to Sweden to undertake practical work to raise the status of women and organize them for public life. Her sister has written that from that moment Fredrika's predominant thought was "how she might be able to secure liberty and an unrestricted sphere of activity for Swedish women." She thought, in fact, of all the women of Europe. She immediately sent out into the world, printed in all the principal languages, a comprehensive program for women's emancipation. As the response was weak, she made an attempt to unite the women for a special cause. During the Crimean War she published in the London *Times* an "Invitation to a Peace Alliance" of women, but again without result. In Stockholm she had succeeded, during the cholera of 1853, in organizing a women's association for the aid of poor orphans; she became president of that association, and it proved comparatively easy to organize women for such philanthropic purposes, at least locally. When, however, the next year, she made an appeal for founding a national association of women for philanthropic work, her words died away without any echo. Thus her efforts toward rousing women to form an organized movement were temporarily frustrated.

That does not mean, however, that she worked in vain. Indeed, largely as a result of her efforts, the reform movement of the 1850's in Sweden brought considerable progress in the field of women's activities. They were granted access to certain public offices and, as a consequence, several courses of higher education were opened for them. Perhaps most important in this regard was the fact that women obtained appointments as teachers in public schools. At the same time they were enabled to dispose to a certain extent of their fortune and incomes, and the enactment of this reform led up to the granting of municipal franchise to women taxpayers in 1863.

The voice of Fredrika Bremer was heard outside of Sweden as well. In particular it influenced the brilliant Norwegian authoress Camilla Collett who, with her great novel *Amtmandens Døtre* (The Daughters of the Prefect) in 1855 inaugurated a lifelong activity on behalf of a women's movement in Norway.

During these years one of the "emancipated ladies" of America tried to convey to the women's cause a kind of symbol of their emancipation by a costume that was at the same time more convenient and healthy than the traditional one and more similar to men's clothing. She was Amelia Bloomer of Seneca Falls, New York. Inspired by the women's convention at that town in 1848, she started the next year a weekly paper dedicated to the promotion of women's rights and of temperance, and at the same time she introduced and advertised a new style of dress, consisting of a skirt reaching a little below the knee and a pair of Turkish pantaloons secured by bands around the ankles. This costume was probably called "bloomers." For its history it will suffice to quote the *Encyclopedia Americana*:

Though adopted rather extensively in America, it was unable to hold its ground against the united strength of prejudice and ridicule, and abroad it scarcely made further way than furnishing a favorite subject of burlesque on the stage and of ridicule in the pages of the comic papers. One or two "strong-minded" women who ventured to brave public opinion by donning the new costume were persecuted by the mob. This movement, however, led the way to more rational dress, and until the advent of shorts, bloomers were popular with women gymnasts and athletes.

An American lady who came too late to attend the international Peace Congress in London in 1851 gave instead a lecture on "Bloomerism." She made her subject, according to the ironical report of the *Times,* "a rallying or central point, round which to group long disquisitions, medical, legal, political, and moral" and, in particular, pictured "the degraded position a woman held in the eye of the law." She was hailed by an audience who came to amuse themselves; they laughed mercilessly at her most serious points and merrily cheered the most touching stories. Her only successful hit seems to have been her reference to the misfortune of Mrs. Mott in 1840; at that many of the audience cried "Shame!" Otherwise she was simply ridiculed.

Thus even such a modest departure from ladylike tradition was defeated at this early date. The victorious advance of women was destined to bring with it much more radical devices for the external equalization of the sexes. For a couple of decades, however, bloomers were conceived as the last word in emancipation.

Only after 1860 did feminism in Europe develop into a movement of considerable dimensions. In 1866 women's associations for suffrage were founded in England; in 1869 they were organized into the National Association for Woman Suffrage. In 1867 John Stuart Mill presented to the House of Commons a petition for suffrage signed by 1,499 women, headed by Harriet Martineau, Florence Nightingale, and others; and in 1869 the British Parliament granted municipal franchise to women taxpayers. No doubt the example of America was still a stimulating force. There, in that year, were formed at the same time two separate national Woman Suffrage associations. The territory of Wyoming organized itself in 1869, giving votes to women as well as to men, and it was imitated the next year by the territory of Utah. Simultaneously in another field came an impetus from America in the moving of Elizabeth Blackwell from New York to London, where in 1869 she assisted in founding the National Health Society and the London School of Medicine for Women.

In the same remarkable year, 1869, Mill published his famous book *The Subjection of Women,* written several years before.

Partly a product of conversations with Mrs. Mill before her death, it was essentially an elaboration of the arguments of her article of 1851. There he remarked:

> Though there are not in this country, as there are in the United States, periodical Conventions and an organized party to agitate for the Rights of Women, there is a numerous and active Society organized and managed by women, for the more limited object of obtaining the political franchise. Nor is it only in our own country and in America that women are beginning to protest, more or less collectively, against the disabilities under which they labor. France, and Italy, and Switzerland, and Russia, now afford examples of the same thing.

This book evidently came at a moment when the soil was well prepared for its reception. It had an immense success and was translated into many languages—in Denmark by no less a personality than Georg Brandes. From that time on the women's movement in Europe could act and develop by its own force. It is, however, significant that the international organizations of women—the International Council of Women in 1888, and the International Woman Suffrage Alliance in 1904—were formed on American initiative. And the first instances of woman suffrage were offered by an increasing number of American states from 1890 onward; Europe followed only in the twentieth century.

❋ ❋ ❋ ❋ ❋

The story of the peace movement and of feminism demonstrates clearly that Americans were far ahead of Europeans in the art of organizing large associations to agitate for special causes. Their superiority in this regard was evidently a fruit of their early democracy. The ideas were rarely, or perhaps never, original. But in the history of nations it is far more important to convert ideas into realities than merely to throw out a number of ideas.

In still another movement of the first half of the nineteenth century the Americans formed the vanguard. That was the temperance movement. In this case they may even claim a certain originality of thought.

Temperance, of course, has always been regarded as a virtue.

One of the old Norse Eddic poems warns against hard drinking, and there is preserved a speech by a famous Norwegian king of the twelfth century which has justly been defined as a sermon on temperance. He looked askance at the German merchants who brought wine to the country and tempted the people to riotousness, and he ordered them to be off as quickly as possible, while he praised the Englishmen who imported useful goods like flour.* Didactic poetry of a later age could, and did, choose moderation in all its forms as a subject for teaching, even going to the length of recommending moderation in truth-telling. Pietistic theology used the sixth commandment as a springboard for condemning all kinds of carnal lust, including gluttony and drunkenness, and many of the pietistic sects of the eighteenth century demanded of their members complete abstinence from all intoxicating drinks. In such a profoundly Christian nation as the American there would be a fertile soil for preachings of this kind.

The first impetus, however, for a temperance movement came not from a man of pietistic disposition but from one of a broader humanity. He was the celebrated physician Benjamin Rush of Philadelphia, a friend of Franklin's, a man of wide social and political interests, a nationalist, a liberal, an abolitionist, in short a champion of reforms, educational, penal, and whatever you can think of. Practising among the poor, he became intensely aware of their hygienic needs. As early as 1772 he published *Sermons to Gentlemen upon Temperance and Exercise* which were printed in London as well as in Philadelphia. In one of these sermons he treated of the use and abuse of wine and strong drink; such beverages he would not allow to people under forty years of age. In particular, he advised all statesmen, legislators, and others who labored for the public good to abstain from wine, and he asserted that there was "the same inseparable connexion between intemperance and vice that there is betwixt vice and punishment." He commented not only on the physical

* Because of this speech the saga of the king mentioned was very popular with Norwegian readers during the German occupation of 1940–45; a modern translation was sold out and had to be reprinted.

but even more on the psychic consequences of consuming spirits; and he pointed out the social evils caused by intemperance: "A people corrupted by strong drink, cannot long be a *free* people." And he proposed laws to lessen the use of liquors. Some fifteen years later he published a pamphlet which was really a pioneer work in its field: *An Inquiry into the Effects of Spirituous Liquors* (or, in later editions, *Ardent Spirits*) *upon the Human Body, and Their Influence upon the Happiness of Society*. This pamphlet was reprinted in Great Britain (Edinburgh, 1791) and many times reprinted in America. Its program, however, was not heeded for many years.

In the nineteenth century temperance societies were formed in Massachusetts and the state of New York. The most active of them was the American Society for the Promotion of Temperance, founded in Boston in 1826. Based on religious principles, it soon started propaganda not only in America but in Europe as well, or more precisely, in Great Britain. The first known temperance societies in the British kingdom date from 1829; they were located in Ireland and Scotland. England followed in 1830. Several local societies were formed, and in 1831 they were organized respectively into the Scottish Temperance Society and the British and Foreign Temperance Society.

News of the American temperance societies gave the stimulus to similar organizations in Sweden in 1830. An American Sunday-school teacher, Robert Baird, who came to Paris in 1834, became interested in starting a movement for temperance on continental Europe, and during the next few years he traveled three times through the northern countries for this purpose. He wrote in French a history of the American societies (1836) which was soon translated into German and Swedish. On the initiative of the King, the Swedish edition was presented to every parish in the kingdom. The movement spread, partly through Baird's efforts, to Germany, Belgium, and Holland. In Norway the first temperance society was formed in 1836, mostly as a consequence of British impulse. In both of the Scandinavian kingdoms "the beautiful, Christian, historic, shining example set by the United States" was frequently referred to, and American propaganda literature was put to use. Letters from American emigrants also had some effect.

A vehement agitation was set on foot in Ireland in 1838 when the Capuchin Father Theobald Mathew started a true revival movement. By his passionate and popular sermons he awakened the oppressed Irish peasants from their drunken stupor and persuaded them by the hundreds of thousands to discard whiskey and join the temperance societies. That virtually brought about a social revolution which had far-reaching consequences in the history of Ireland. From there he was called in 1843 to England to preach his gospel to the industrial workingman; his influence there was considerable, though not so profound as with the more emotional Irish. Finally, in 1850, he was called to America and the movement thus returned to the place of its origin in a more impassioned form than ever.

The program of the movement was originally just what was meant by the word "temperance." It demanded abstinence only from spirits but allowed temperate use of wines and beer. Such a program could not very well evoke passionate enthusiasm. Gradually the demand for abstinence became total, embracing all intoxicating beverages. In England in the 1830's originated the nickname of "teetotaler." Under the influence of Father Theobald there was formed in 1851, in Utica, New York, the Independent Order of Good Templars, which met the craving for solemn and symbolic rites and adopted the uncompromising program of total abstinence in the national as well as in the individual sense. A Good Templar was not allowed to renounce his personal obligation, and the Order demanded general prohibition by law.

This new American organization was destined to become the most active and effective instrument for international propaganda. A couple of decades elapsed, however, before it was strong enough to expand its activities outside America. In 1868 it reached over to Great Britain, in the 1870's to Norway and Sweden, and gradually to most other European countries.

Thus again America organized Europe. At the same time it gave to the temperance, or rather total abstinence, movement not only the impetus to action but also a program of practical reforms. America offered the first instance of a local option law (in Indiana, 1832) and the first instance of state prohibition (in Maine, 1846). The humane spirit that inspired American penal reforms and assistance to all disabled members of society also created the first asylum for inebriates (in Boston, 1857).

One qualification must be made: The temperance movement in Europe gained real power only in a few countries, in Great Britain and above all in Sweden and Norway. It is a significant fact that in the twentieth century first a Swede and then a Norwegian were elected International Chief Templars. But with the Order, American influence went everywhere.

*   *   *   *   *

What can be demonstrated so positively in regard to particular reform movements is not so easily traced with respect to the general advance of democracy. America was and remained, however, a source of inspiration for all democratic efforts in Europe. In the adoption of universal manhood suffrage after 1820's, in the establishment of free public education, in the organization of voters into political parties, the United States led the way. Such institutions were part of the general program of democratic ideas everywhere and needed no American impulses to precipitate them. What America did was to achieve such reforms before the rest of the world, thus providing a practical demonstration that could not fail to have its influence abroad.

V

THE LAND OF OPPORTUNITIES

FROM the moment of discovery, America was to the European nations the great land of opportunities—opportunities of loot or of labor, of a better living for some and a higher profit for others, opportunities to escape from religious, political, or social oppression and to gain a chance to shape one's life according to one's own creed or need. All these opportunities became still more real with the foundation of the free republic of the United States, with the disappearance of established churches, with the ever fuller development of democracy, with the opening up of almost infinite areas of new land.

All kinds of people in Europe thought that across the Atlantic they might be able to realize their social ideals, of whatever brand they might be. Not a few of them acted upon this thought, and this was the origin of many communistic colonies established on American soil. In those innocent days communists were not forbidden to enter the United States; indeed they were welcomed. But it has to be added that they were of another ilk than their modern namesakes. They had no plan to transform the whole national constitution according to their ideas. They were satisfied if they were allowed to achieve their communism among themselves within a closed society. For many of them —especially the first to come—communism was simply a part of their Christian faith; their desire was to renew the original Christian brotherhood by complete community of life and labor.

Such were the Seventh-Day Baptists, an offshoot of the German Baptist Brethren (Dunkers), who formed a community at Ephrata in Pennsylvania in 1732, and the Shakers, who established their first meetinghouse at Mount Lebanon, New York, in 1785. In the next century came several communist groups from Germany—the Harmonists or Rappites, who settled in Pennsylvania

(1803) and later in Indiana, the Society of Separatists of Zoar, who came to rest in Ohio, and the True Inspiration Congregation, who founded a community called Amana in Iowa. From Sweden between 1846 and 1854 came more than a thousand Pietists who set up a community in Illinois which they named Biskopskulla and which enjoyed genuine prosperity for a brief period. These colonies, established by Europeans, played but a slight part in American development. They rather form an aspect of European history, witnessing to the dreams of social perfection that lived in European Christendom and sought realization in the dreamland of unlimited opportunities.

The nineteenth century saw other attempts to practise communism in America, not according to ancient but to new social doctrines. Although they were even less successful than the Christian attempts, they nevertheless offer more historical interest because they led to something new and because we can discern better what their originators expected in America.

Robert Owen, who has been called the father of English Socialism, but may more accurately be termed the father of the English Coöperative Movement, purchased the old Rappite colony in Indiana and renamed it New Harmony. There he set up a coöperative community as a demonstration of his plan for the redemption of the human race from the existing evils of society. "I am come to this country," he proclaimed, "to introduce an entire new state of society, to change it from an ignorant, selfish system to an enlightened social system which shall gradually unite all interests into one and remove all causes for contest between individuals." People flocked to New Harmony from every country in the north of Europe as well as from every state in the Union. Within three years, however, Owen was forced to abandon the venture, convinced by sad experience that the attempt was premature.

Not many years later, Etienne Cabet, a pupil of Owen, but far more of an impractical dreamer than his master, painted in his utopian novel *Voyage en Icarie* a colorful and extremely attractive picture of the happy life in a fancied communistic state. Resolving to attempt the realization of his ideal in America, he sent forth his inspiring appeal *Allons en Icarie!* which resounded through Europe. Land was bought in Texas, and in 1848 a band of enthusiasts set off for the new Eden, singing to the tune of the *Marseillaise:*

> Arise, O workingman, bending to the dust,
> The hour of wakening has sounded.
> Look, on the shores of America,
> The banner of sacred community waves.
> Let us go to found in Icaria
> The happiness of mankind.

When the Texas land proved swampy and unhealthy the Icarian community was transferred to Illinois where a motley assemblage of uprooted Europeans from many nations—Frenchmen, Germans, Swiss, Belgians, Spaniards, Englishmen, and Swedes— came together. They presently found, however, that they could not keep together, and this attempt likewise ended in failure.

A similar fate overtook the Fourierist Phalanstery of Victor Considérant, who came to America convinced that it was, above all other lands, the country of realizations. His purpose was not merely to realize Fourierism in the favorable environment of the New World. His object, he wrote, was more general, for America "affords the opportunity of experiment and of practical verification to every other progressive doctrine." He felt sure of success. "Friends," he cried, "the Promised Land is a reality." Strong in this faith, he collected money, purchased land in Texas, and in 1854 sent out a pioneer band representing, in his words, "the *élite* . . . of European society." These colonists were not, however, fitted for the hard work of founding a settlement on virgin soil, and despite his enthusiasm Considérant had to abandon his experiment in 1863.

His was not the last attempt to practise communism in America, but it was the last effort of Europeans to demonstrate their utopian theories on the American proving ground. Later European reformers were to lose their faith in isolated utopias and to adopt a more realistic platform, addressing themselves to the task of winning the masses with social policies calculated to transform the general economic system. In this struggle America was to give relatively little in the way of inspiration or assistance. On the whole, later European socialism had to work out its own methods.

❋   ❋   ❋   ❋   ❋

The communistic groups that sought to realize their ideas of a new society were not the only ones that listened to and followed the call of America. In fact, they were a small minority. If they crossed the Atlantic in hundreds, thousands of other Europeans every year took the same way. Emigration to America was an uninterrupted stream for more than a hundred years after the reëstablishment of peace in 1815, and formed a constant element of European history, life, and thought.

The general reason for emigration can be stated in very few words: Every person who left Europe for America wanted and expected to find better living conditions. This general idea, however, may include a whole complex of different conceptions of the kind of improvement which individuals had in mind. If we would grasp the reasons for America's appeal to such large numbers of people in Europe, it is well worth our while to examine the question more closely.

There can be no doubt that the first stimulus to emigration after 1815 is to be sought in the economic conditions prevailing at that time. The result of the long wars was a general depression in Europe in industrial as well as agricultural activities. Governments refused to redeem their debts but collected high taxes. Industrialists went bankrupt, workingmen became unemployed, farmers were unable to discharge their obligations. On top of all this, frost and rain destroyed crops, and famines harried large districts. People could not but desire to get away from such conditions, and in those countries where the inhabitants previously had some knowledge of emigration, particularly Great Britain and Germany, the idea of going to America arose spontaneously.

In the summer of 1816 a Dublin newspaper reported:

Great alarm seems to be felt in England, on account of the disposition to emigrate manifested by all ranks of the community. The middling orders, endeavoring to save something from the wreck of their fortunes, are collecting in various parts of the country with a view to *exportation;* nay, we have heard, that three villages, or what we in Ireland, perhaps, might call handsome country towns, have had meetings sufficiently open when the plan of emigration was regularly discussed, and the practicability of its accomplishment unanimously admitted. As they were principally small farmers, agricultural pursuits were those which occurred to them; but as they were aware of the extraordinary value of labor in America, they felt this circumstance as a serious impediment to their project. It was then proposed to article a certain number of laborers out of employment for two years, with their passage free, at a reasonable salary.

The writer goes on to say that the result of the discussion was the election of two deputies to be sent to America to make the proper inquiries and pave the way for settlement. Pointing out the ominous example thus offered, the paper warns: "If it should become systematic, and while distress and taxes continue, there is every danger that it may become so—there is no conjecturing where it will terminate."

To substantiate its considerations the paper printed at the same time a letter from London from which it appeared that seamen in English ships were deserting in American waters to try their fortune over there, that hundreds of workingmen were being discharged from iron works and mines, that many towns were crowded with people out of employ, and that a number of respectable families had sunk into bankruptcy; in brief, "the most horrible distress prevails in England." "Such is the state of the country," the correspondent concludes, "and such are the people whom the well-fed hirelings blame for a wish to change the glorious and expensive constitution of England, for the rude but plentiful democracy of America."

The last sentence of this letter suggests that mere economic reasons for emigration could be strengthened by considerations of a social or political character. Both motives appear intermingled in the letters which the emigrants sent back from their new homes. Many such private letters were published and helped stimulate the emigration. Here is a letter from 1817:

The land is rich indeed, and every industrious farmer may become a freeholder of the United States, by paying eighty dollars, being the first instalment for a quarter of a section of land; and though he has not a shilling left, he may easily gain as much off the land, as will pay the other instalments, before they become due. The land being his own, there is no limit to his prosperity; no proud tyrant can lord it over him; he has no rent to pay; no game, timber, or fishing laws to dread; few and small taxes to pay; no excise laws to harass him; no tythe nor poor's rate; so that the farmers are prosperous and happy.

Other letters from the same time detail the material advantages of the new country: "there is no want of meat and drink here"—"abundance of fruit"—"beef and pudding, tea and rum" —"for breakfast he has coffee, beef, mutton, bacon, potatoes, butter, bread, pickles, etc., etc., and the rest of his living is as good"—"to us, who have long been half-starved in England, it appears like a continual feast."

The new-won independence is also praised: "If a man be industrious and steady, he reaps the fruit of his own labour." Or the equality of men is stressed: "We call no man master here." The same conception reëchoed from Germany: *Kein König dort* —no king over there.

The Pennsylvania Dutch and other Germans in the United States sent circulars to their old home districts in the countries on both sides of the Rhine and described the happy prospects offered by their new Germany. Reports of successful vineyards in Kentucky and Indiana reached Switzerland and encouraged emigration from there. Passenger agencies advertised their transportation facilities on the Rhine and across the Atlantic. Shipping firms spread the news of American prosperity and appealed for emigrants to pay their passage by service under redemptioner terms. Contractors and landowners in America provided prepaid passage for all kinds of workingmen.

As a consequence, emigration to America amounted to some thirty thousand people annually, two-thirds of them British, the remainder mostly Germans, with a couple of thousand of French from the districts nearest to the Rhine. This loss of people, however, evoked much concern among the ruling classes, particularly in England. English industrialists, fearing to see their skilled workers, especially weavers, go to another country and help establish competing shops there, persuaded the government to prevent the emigration of such men. The government tried to restrict emigration in other ways too; for instance, by making conditions difficult for American shipping. In Germany as in England, leading newspapers, generally mouthpieces of vested interests, warned the emigrants against the hazards they would meet in foreign countries. Thus from the very beginning the emigration question became an object of public discussion.

Aversion to emigration was, however, noticeably mitigated by the general acceptance by the upper classes particularly, of the Malthusian doctrine, as finally formulated by the author in the fifth edition of his famous work in 1817. Although employers might find it profitable to have a large stock of proletarians competing for work, they could be brought to understand that a certain emigration was a natural cure for overpopulation. What they wanted was to be safeguarded against a drain of population that would make them inferior to American competition. To the upper classes America appeared as a potential, in some respects already an actual, rival; to the lower class it was a promise and a hope.

The British government made an attempt to combine the need of emigration with the interests of national capitalism by directing the emigrants to Canada, and later to Australia; it even granted financial support to such emigration. For a time this policy was successful; prior to 1840, about half of the British emigrants went to British North America. But in the long run it proved impossible to deflect the natural current of emigration. Canada did not offer such alluring opportunities as did the United States and, what perhaps was just as decisive, it had not yet attained the economic and social development that could convey to newcomers the feeling that they were joining a hospitable and orderly society. Many people who landed at Quebec continued their journey to the United States.

This first boom of emigration actually stopped short very soon. America experienced its first great business panic in 1819. There too, overpopulation made itself felt as unemployment in all branches of industry, and not a few emigrants even returned to their home countries. One of them wrote:

The voice of disappointment will certainly have risen above that of wild and romantic adventure, and made itself heard [before I reach England]. Such is the state of things here, that neither farmers nor mechanics can succeed. The country is inundated with the vast torrent of emigration, that has been flowing into it; and the new arriver must be content to penetrate far into the wilderness, and undergo fatigues, expense, and hardships, which he can badly estimate by his fireside.

      ✿   ✿   ✿   ✿   ✿

In that first period of nineteenth-century emigration, another motive besides the economic one was also active. That was the religious one. We have to remember that at that time full religious freedom existed nowhere in Europe; in many countries there was not even the slightest degree of toleration towards dissidents from the official creed. From Württemberg, though ruled by a liberal king, the emigrants included not only such dangerous people as Christian communists but pure religious Pietists as well. When, in 1817, the King of Prussia enforced a union of the Lutheran and the Calvinistic churches, the "Old Lutherans" refused to obey, and when, in 1824, their churches were "unified" by force, they saw no other way than to flee the country, going first to Australia, then to America. Dissidents in other German states also emigrated. Even in Norway, where the Constitution of 1814 safeguarded the free exercise of all Christian religions, dissidents might come up against the civil laws regarding marriages, burials, and military conscription. A few scores of Quakers or Quaker sympathizers constituted the pioneer band of Norwegian emigrants in 1825.

· The wish to escape from religious oppression remained a motive of emigration even in later times. Further groups of "Old Lutherans" left Prussia for America toward the end of the 1830's, and this exodus continued after 1840, when a more liberal régime was inaugurated; at that time perhaps the wish to join fellow believers was the more impelling consideration, and economic reasons also played their part. At the end of the 1830's, a group of Saxon pietists, the so-called Stephanists, fled from the "Sodom and Gomorrah" of their native land and settled at Stephansburg in Missouri. About 1840, Methodists and Baptists of

Wales, refusing to pay the tithes to the Established Church, sailed for America. So did their fellow believers in Switzerland, and other dissidents in the Netherlands and in Sweden. Anti-Semitic measures in Germany drove out many Jews.

The greatest religious movement of emigration was created by the Mormons. Soon after the establishment of the Church of Jesus Christ of Latter-day Saints in 1830, they began to send missionaries abroad, at first to England. In 1840, when they founded their sacred city of Nauvoo in Illinois, they made it an obligation for all converts to come and settle there. By 1844 their number amounted to twelve thousand, and of them four thousand were Europeans. In 1847 they fled from persecution and established a new settlement by the Great Salt Lake, where they built their New Zion. They invited all Mormons to unite in the new land, and they extended their missionary activities to more and more European countries. They were not allowed to preach everywhere because they were essentially regarded as propagandists of polygamy. But not only their religion but also their glowing pictures of the New Zion, which they really cultivated in a marvelous way, kindled a flaming enthusiasm in thousands of minds. Masses of proselytes followed their call. During the 1850's, Denmark, Norway, and Sweden supplied the bulk of these new emigrants, but toward the close of the decade they were joined by Germans, Swiss, and Italians.

Even a movement like this, which carried thousands of people each year over to America, was, however, only a trickle in the great human tide which was running toward the coasts of America. By the 1840's the annual number of emigrants had begun to be counted in hundreds of thousands.

❋   ❋   ❋   ❋   ❋

Toward the close of the 1820's the depression in America came to an end. New enterprises of all kinds were started, and contractors began to send agents abroad to recruit workers. Idle people in Europe realized that there was a shortage of labor in the New World. In Europe itself the latter half of the 1820's brought a series of bad years, with famines ravaging many poor districts. Many different conditions caused an increasing exodus of impoverished farmers to the cities, and from the cities numbers of them continued their wanderings overseas. Almost everywhere economic and social conditions provoked a general unrest which manifested itself in the revolutions of 1830 and radical mass movements through the following years.

Emigration was a natural accompanying feature of the upheaval. Around 1830 America was receiving annually more than twenty thousand immigrants. In 1832 the number suddenly sprang up to an annual average of almost seventy thousand. In 1842 it passed one hundred thousand; in 1847 it mounted above two hundred thousand; in 1850 above three hundred thousand; in 1854 even above four hundred thousand. The total number of immigrants for the period 1847–1857 was more than three millions and a half. It was a migration of an extent never before known in history. It came almost exclusively from the northwestern countries of Europe—from Germany, Ireland, Great Britain, France, Switzerland, the Netherlands, Norway. From the 1830's on, all that part of Europe was in the grip of what was commonly called the "America fever."

The "America letters" played an increasing part in spreading this fever. They exhibited in a highly intimate and convincing way the wealth, the hospitality, and the new equality of the New World. An emigrated English workingman wrote in a letter in 1830:

A farmer took me one day in his wagon into the country to see a factory, and I dined with him, and he would not have a farthing, and told me I was welcome to come to his house at any time; they had on the table puddings, pyes, and fruit of all kind that was in season, and preserves, pickles, vegetables, meat, and everything that a person could wish, and the servants sat down at the same table with their masters. They do not think of locking the doors in the country, and you can gather peaches, apples, and all kinds of fruit by the side of the roads. . . . I can go into a store, and have as much brandy as I like to drink for three half-pence, and all other spirits in proportion. If a man like work he need not want victuals. It is a foolish idea that some people have, that there is too many people come here, it is quite the reverse; there was more than 1,000 emigrants came in the day after I landed, and there is four ships have arrived since with emigrants. But there is plenty of room yet, and will be for a thousand years to come.

A Norwegian farmer, who emigrated in 1831, wrote in a letter four years later:

> Nothing has made me more happy and contented than the fact that we left Norway and journeyed to this country. We have gained more since our arrival here than I did during all the time that I lived in Norway, and I have every prospect of earning a livelihood here for myself and my family —even if my family were larger—so long as God gives me good health . . . This is a beautiful and fertile country. Prosperity and contentment are to be seen almost everywhere one goes. Even if many more were to come, there would still be room here for all. It is possible for all to live in comfort and without suffering want.

Such letters were freely copied and circulated, sometimes printed in the newspapers, and read in wide circles. They influenced strongly the thoughts of many people and encouraged them to follow the example of their happy countrymen.

From the American side a mighty stimulus was given to immigration by the opening of the West which, from the beginning of this period, took place with increasing speed. The Indians were pushed farther and farther westward. New territories were won for the Union at the close of the 1840's. One territory after the other was organized as a self-governing unit or as a state. The opening of the Erie Canal and the building of roads and railroads facilitated access to the western plains, and new laws and new practices made the settling of the land simpler and cheaper than ever.

The more the country was settled, the more it attracted new immigrants. There were two nationalities which were particularly inclined to settle down in closed groups and organize themselves as local units; these were the Germans and the Norwegians. In other ways, however, they were quite different. The Germans nourished dreams of founding a second Fatherland and of making one or another of the western States—Wisconsin, Missouri, or Arkansas—an essentially German state with the German language dominant even in legislative bodies and courts. The Norwegian immigrants brought along political traditions more akin to American ways, and they were more eager to learn American history and become true Americans. But both nationalities loved to maintain the customs of the old country, and hastened to establish their own institutions, notably churches and schools, where their old language was employed. Just because of such organization their settlements constituted in themselves an invitation to newcomers who would naturally find easier conditions there for starting their new existence.

There was no want of direct invitations either, and settlers often sent passage money to kinsfolk at home. In all the countries from which emigration was extensive, a whole literature for emigrants sprang up; guides for settlers were published in large quantities and filled the windows of country stores, and emigrant journals gave advice about where and how to go. In many places emigrant societies were formed in order to organize the voyage of whole groups.

Crossing the Atlantic was usually a hard experience. The ships were small and overcrowded, the sanitary conditions on board miserable, the food supply poor, and a large percentage of the passengers died on the way. Both the American and some of the European governments tried to improve the transportation facilities by making rules for the numbers of passengers and the room to be provided. Economic considerations worked in the same direction. The increasing migration offered new and unexpected profits to transatlantic navigation. It saved the westbound traffic from being predominantly a transportation of ballast. In consequence, American export goods could be sent at reduced freights and thus be sold more cheaply in Europe and, conversely, the increased shipping of these goods helped to reduce the price of passage from Europe. New and larger ships were continually put into the traffic between the two hemispheres; after 1847 steamships came into regular use. In every way Europe and America were drawn more closely together.

Meanwhile the governments of the European countries were becoming gravely concerned about the large volume of emigration. They looked with misgivings at the insecurity of the emigrants in the foreign countries and wanted to protect them against unscrupulous shipping and emigration agents. But still more the governments were affected by the losses to the national wealth incurred by the exodus of people and the removal of their property. More particularly they were thinking of the desertion by the emigrants of private debts and public obligations—economic as well as military. In many countries public authorities discussed how to safeguard private and public interests against such losses. A Norwegian royal commission appointed in 1845 to study all these questions pointed out that the losses caused by emigration were counterbalanced by gains from increased shipping and trade, but even the small restrictions it suggested on emigration were rejected by Parliament. Liberals and democrats in all countries thought it better to examine the real reasons for people's wanting to leave their native country, and they proposed all kinds of social and political reforms, the accomplishment of full religious liberty, freedom of trade, protection of land and factory laborers, alleviation of taxes. In fact, the 1830's and 40's witnessed a series of such reforms, partly brought about by the impact of emigration.

Neither restrictions nor reforms seemed to have any considerable effect in preventing or reducing the emigration. In discussing the reasons for the "Great Migration" of the decades beginning about 1830, one of the ablest American students of this movement, Marcus Lee Hansen (from whose work much of the information here presented is borrowed) gave the chapter devoted to it the significant heading: "America Becomes the Common Man's Utopia." That was indeed what America at that time had become. This holds true not only with respect to the ideas of material conditions to be found over there, but equally with respect to social and political conceptions. The victory of Jacksonian democracy, condemned by the upper classes, gave new hopes to the lower. Repeatedly we find in letters from immigrants such phrases as this: "It is a fine country and a free country." The same Norwegian farmer who, in 1835, told about his economic progress in America, also praised its perfect democracy:

I do not believe there can be better laws and arrangements for the benefit and happiness of the common man in the whole world. [In the election of officials] the vote of the common man carries just as much authority and influence as does that of the rich and powerful man. [In dress and in privileges no distinction can be noted as between farmers and officials.] The freedom which the one enjoys is just as good as that of the other.

In particular, he praised the freedom to engage in whatever business one wanted to.

Emphasis on such American advantages demonstrates the political motives that could enter the decision to emigrate. A Scotch author who, at the beginning of the 1830's, discussed the emigration from Great Britain, wrote:

The causes of emigration are chiefly poverty, dissatisfaction in respect to public measures, or ambition. The majority of those who emigrate to America are driven abroad by the goadings of poverty; another class is formed of adventurous men, who go to seek fortunes in other countries, with the hope of again returning to their own; a third class is composed of men of genius, whose schemes have been frustrated, or whose hopes have been blighted at home; and a fourth class includes individuals who are not only discontented with their condition in the land of their forefathers, but displeased also with all public measures; these men are not, probably, compelled to emigrate from necessity, but from a spirit of dissatisfaction natural to them.

Such dissatisfaction with laws and political conditions would, of course, be a more powerful motive in countries where real oppression of free action prevailed. Therefore we hear much more of emigration on such grounds from Germany than from other western countries. There in many cases emigration was virtually a necessity, a flight from prison or even death. Such cases are reported from the worst times of reaction in the 1820's and, more particularly, after the failure of the revolutions of 1830 and 1848. Not a few of the men who for such reasons fled to America became prominent citizens of their new country and were influential in carrying American ideas back to Europe; it may suffice to point out such names as Francis Lieber and Carl Schurz.

But even in primarily democratic countries like Norway, people might feel disgusted with the resistance they met in their struggles for the perfection of democracy. Until about 1830 the bourgeoisie, united with the bureaucracy, held sway over Norwegian politics and, though largely liberal, kept the farmer class out of power and out of many social and economic privileges. The first farmer who made the attempt (*ca.* 1815) to stir up organized opposition to the ruling classes, a man by the name of Hans Barlien, was for that reason persecuted with so many lawsuits that at last in 1837 he chose to go to America. From there he wrote with bitterness: "Pickpockets or attorneys, unscrupulous creditors, officials and vagabonds who are morally tainted are without power to harm the people here." And he added: "No one is persecuted here because of his religious faith. No restrictions are set upon freedom of occupation; and everyone secures without hindrance the fruits of his own work, and by wise and liberal legislation the American citizen is made secure from the assaults of oppressors."

The remarkable leader of the Norwegian labor movement that started in 1848, Marc. M. Thrane, repeatedly advised the workingmen of Norway to emigrate to America. For, he wrote in his labor weekly, "it is absolutely certain that everybody who can work and is willing to work can become a well-to-do man there." He affirmed that it was mere aristocratic policy to denounce America and dissuade people from going there and, as a special enemy of the clergy, he found it highly significant that warnings against emigration were uttered even from the pulpits.

Thrane was not completely just in charging all opposition to emigration to upper-class interests. There was much of pure patriotism in it also. The great poet and national leader Henrik Wergeland, who had been a pioneer in asserting the rights of labor, was deeply concerned about the loss of able hands. When he was dying in 1845, his very last work was a song-drama in which he pitted love of the homeland against emigration. But economic needs were stronger than patriotic ideas, and when the labor movement could not carry out its program of economic reforms it was obliged to seek an outlet for its wants by emigration. One of Thrane's assistants, P. Hjelm-Hansen, made himself the leader of an emigration movement which resulted in the Norwegian settlement of the Red River Valley in the West.

The labor movement in Norway was crushed. The government threw a miserable sop to it in the adoption of a law which aimed at regulating the position of the poor cotters on the larger farms, but which in fact did little more than legalize existing conditions. At the same time, in 1851, the government, scared by the revolutionary implications of the movement and encouraged by the general reaction in Europe, put hundreds of the most active agitators, including Thrane, into prison. After long litigation most of them were sentenced to longer or shorter prison terms for their activities. After having served his term, Thrane, heeding his own advice, went to America where he became active in the propaganda of the First International. Other labor leaders followed.

A year after the breakdown of the labor movement, the famous Norwegian violinist Ole Bull, himself an ardent nationalist but above all a staunch champion of liberty, set out to found a New Norway in America. When in 1850 he had opened the first National Theatre in Norway, he had chosen for the first performance Wergeland's anti-emigration drama. The defeat of the labor movement proved to him that Norway was not yet the perfect home of liberty, and he turned his eyes to America. In 1852 he bought land in the wilderness of Pennsylvania forests and settled two hundred Norwegians in a town that was named Oleana. "We are founding," he said to them, "a New Norway, consecrated to liberty, baptized with independence, and protected by the Union's mighty flag." Coming to Independence Hall at Philadelphia, he took the oath as an American citizen, and promised to bring to his settlement "thousands and tens of thousands of my oppressed countrymen."

In his home town of Bergen appeared a book entitled *America, Ole Bull, and the New Norway,* published as propaganda for the enterprise. The climax of it was a poem in praise of him and his plans, so naïve that it came dangerously close to parody. It declared that only in America "freedom and peace had rosy conditions," and pictured it as a country that promised mountains of gold. In the labor weekly which still lingered on, Bull's initiative was hailed in verse and prose. The paper predicted that throngs of emigrants would depart with him, saying good-bye to Norway with the words: "Too long have I lived here a slave!"

In little more than a year the enterprise proved a complete failure, and Ole Bull lost his fortune in it. Oleana lived on in Norwegian tradition as the phantasmagoria of vain illusions. As Bull himself was one of the chief models of Ibsen's Peer Gynt, so was his dream of Oleana mirrored in Peer Gynt's vision of the cloud empire Gyntiana. Already in 1853, just before the collapse, a witty journalist, Ditmar Meidell, had made Oleana immortal with a satirical song that won the life of a real folk-song and still lives in the memory of Norwegians both in the old and the new country. As a merry parody of all the exaggerated notions of the American Canaan, a few verses deserve a place here.*

> I'm off to Oleana, I'm turning from my doorway,
> No chains for me, I'll say good-by to slavery in Norway.
> > Oh, Oleana!
>
> They give you land for nothing in jolly Oleana,
> And grain comes leaping from the ground in floods of golden manna.
> > Oh, Oleana!
>
> The grain it does the threshing, it pours into the sack, Sir,
> And so you take a quiet nap a-stretching on your back, Sir,
> > Oh, Oleana!
>
> And little roasted piggies, with manners quite demure, Sir,
> They ask you, Will you have some ham? And then you say,
> > > Why, sure Sir.
> > Oh, Oleana!

* I have been permitted to borrow from the translation by Theodore C. Blegen, in *Norwegian-American Historical Association Studies and Records*, XIV (1944), 118–21.

The cows are most obliging, their milk they put in pails, Sir,
They make your cheese and butter with a skill that never fails, Sir.
   Oh, Oleana!

Two dollars for carousing they give each day, and more, Sir,
For if you're good and lazy, they will even give you four, Sir.
   Oh, Oleana!

      *   *   *   *   *

The stream of emigrants that swelled so mightily from 1847 received a new impetus from the discovery of gold in the newly conquered land of California the following year. The gold fever that seized all the United States infected Europe too. In 1849 adventurers from all the countries where emigration had become a tradition went out to hunt for fortune in the new and more real El Dorado. The adventure was not always happy, and satirical poets again found a subject for their picture of America as the country of illusions. In fact, the Americans themselves hurried to exploit the new riches of the Far West, and it is rather surprising to notice how few Europeans joined the scramble for gold. In any event, the California gold mines helped to confirm the European idea of America as the land of illimitable opportunities.

In the Scandinavian countries there is a curious poetical reminiscence of this episode. In the year 1848, Stephen Foster wrote one of his most popular songs, the well-known "Oh! Susanna," with the chorus concluding every verse:

   Oh! Susanna! Oh! don't you cry for me,
   I've come from Alabama with my banjo on my knee.

This song, we are told, was often sung by the foreign immigrants to enliven the long hours of travel through the country. From the immigrants it wandered back to the old countries, and there the tune was used for a new song, adapted for the events and hopes of the year of composition. In the new text, the chorus ran (I give it in translation):

   Oh! Susanna! Oh! cry no more for me,
   I am going to California and digging gold for thee.

I have seen a reference to this song in Sweden in the 1860's, and I heard it in my own childhood in the far north of Norway in the 1880's. California had become virtually a symbol of America. There was to be found rehabilitation for everyone for whom life had gone wrong in Europe.

VI

PROGRESS THROUGH INVENTION

PRESIDENT Charles William Eliot of Harvard, ranked by many in his time as the "first citizen" of the United States, gave in 1896 an address in which he listed "Five American Contributions to Civilization." Essentially it was homage to American democracy and its ideals of freedom and justice by which the American nation had set a glorious example to the whole world. Among the expressions of this democracy Dr. Eliot mentioned the "welcoming of newcomers" by which America demonstrated that under favorable conditions people belonging to a great variety of races might prove fit for political freedom. Another trait of American democracy was the diffusion of material well-being among the population, and in this connection he remarked: "It is in the invention of machinery for producing and distributing power, and at once economizing and elevating human labor, that American ingenuity has been most conspicuously manifested." Eliot did not hesitate to count this feature of American genius as one of the true "triumphs of reason, enterprise, courage, faith, and justice, over passion, selfishness, inertness, timidity, and distrust." He found in it "a strong ethical sentiment, a strenuous moral and social purpose." And he concluded: "It is for such work that multitudinous democracies are fit."

Many students, in particular men of science, have defined the progress of mankind as the increasing subjection of nature. So far as such progress has been accomplished by the invention of machines and other means of making man the master of nature, the Americans have achieved, in a brief space of time, infinitely more than any other single nation. In the field of inventions they have easily been for more than a century the leaders of the world.

In the light of modern experience it seems strange to read

what Tocqueville wrote in 1835: "In America, people employ with acumen the inventions of Europe and, after having perfected them, they adapt them wonderfully to the needs of the country. There are able workingmen but few inventors." In 1840, however, he added this prophecy: "The more a nation is democratic, enlightened and free, the more the number of interested amateurs of science will increase and the more the discoveries directly applicable to industry will offer profit, honor, and even power to their authors."

Certainly the specific American conditions, the unique opportunities offered to profitable enterprise, opened a large field to inventive genius, and at the time Tocqueville uttered his prophecy there was beginning an age of inventions unmatched in the history of human civilization and destined to transform the life and activities of man everywhere in the world. When, only a decade later, Fredrika Bremer penned an enthusiastic letter to the great Danish discoverer of electro-magnetism, H. C. Ørsted, about the "land of experiment," she saw the distinct signs of American future greatness in the field of inventions. And the following year, 1851, saw the conspicuous success of American machines in a victorious competition with European contrivances, a success which had far-reaching consequences.

Benjamin Franklin had foreshadowed the distinction that was to be so characteristically American by his invention of the Franklin stove in 1742 and the lightning conductor in 1752. The next American invention noted by history was the cotton gin constructed by Eli Whitney in 1793. Technologists do not estimate his achievement very highly from a professional point of view because it did not include a new employment of natural forces. At any rate, it plays only indirectly a part in the history of American influences on Europe. It never came into use in any European country, simply because in none of them was cotton cultivated. Its effect on Europe rested on the immense increase it caused in the American production of cotton. Exports of cotton from America to Europe multiplied from one year to the next on a fantastic scale and advanced powerfully the industrialization first of Great Britain, and later of other European countries.

Cotton became everywhere the basis of the textile industries. At the same time it became a chief element in American economic relations with Europe, the most important item in the trade balance of America. If in the southern states "cotton was king," it also largely determined European interests in America as a factor in economic life and international politics.

*   *   *   *   *

The first American invention which by itself caused a revolution was Robert Fulton's steamboat in 1807. The idea was not original with Fulton, for many partially successful experiments had been made before him; but he, after all, could say of the steamboat, in the words of Columbus: "I did it." The engine of the vessel in which, on August 17, 1807, he went up the Hudson River from New York to Albany, was made in England in the shop of James Watt. Only the hull was built in a New York yard; but previous experiments had shown that the construction of a suitable hull was a very important part of the invention. Now at last the steamboat was a reality. Designed in the first instance to meet the specific American need for river navigation, the invention was an immediate financial success, and before Fulton died in 1815 steamboats were plying all the great waterways of the United States.

They were slower to win favor in Europe. One reason lay in the great wars which absorbed all interests until 1815; even after peace was established many countries suffered from distress and poverty. In Scotland an engineer, Henry Bell, who had experimented for himself with steamboats, succeeded in 1812 in putting one into service on the Clyde for the short distance beween Glasgow and Greenock. He called it the *Comet*, but it ran at a very slow pace and was more of a curiosity than a practical success. Fulton made repeated attempts to interest European governments and capitalists in his invention, but in vain. English capitalists declared that although such vessels might succeed in America, "they will never answer in our small rivers and crowded harbors." In 1815, however, a steamship line was started between Glasgow and Liverpool, and the next year

Scotch and English steamships began to ply the great German rivers, the Rhine and the Elbe. An English engineer, Samuel Owen, a pupil of James Watt, who had been called to Sweden in 1804 and established a machine shop at Stockholm, put a steam engine into a sailing vessel and operated it on the waters of Stockholm in 1816. It was considered such a wonder that it was fittingly named *The Witch of Stockholm.* Another vessel equipped in the same way he called *Experiment,* and in 1818 he built the first Swedish passenger steamer. Along with Great Britain, Sweden was in the vanguard of steamboat-building in Europe, and later the Motala shops built steamers for all the Scandinavian countries.

American promoters became impatient at the slowness with which Europe adopted this new instrument, and an engineer who was at the same time an able navigator conceived the ambitious plan of crossing the Atlantic in a steamer in order to demonstrate the efficiency of the invention. He was Moses Rogers of Savannah, Georgia. In 1819 he equipped a large sailing vessel with a steam engine and paddle wheels, named it *Savannah,* and took it over to Europe. It reached Liverpool in twenty-five days. To be sure, it went by steam only a small part of this time (no more than eighty hours) but it was a hardy experiment, and Rogers' ship was the first American steamer to show itself in Europe. He was not satisfied with his reception in Liverpool, complaining later that the people he met there were in many instances uncivil and insolent to him. Englishmen had not yet learned to regard the Americans as much more than rebellious subjects, and, Captain Rogers said, "they sneer at us on all occasions."

From Liverpool he went to the Baltic with the plan of offering his ship to the Russian government. At first he stopped at Stockholm, and the American chargé d'affaires there, Christopher Hughes, reported that "all classes and sexes of people here have been on board to witness this wonder of American skill and enterprise." The Crown Prince visited the ship, accompanied by the Swedish commanding admiral and a dozen other dignitaries, and he "was much pleased and surprised at the beauty and neatness of the ship and was very curious about the machinery." The King was too busy to come on board, but he expressed his admiration of the construction and said he was very desirous of buying the ship, but unfortunately had not the money for it. The Captain was eager to extend his propaganda, and on his invitation all the foreign ministers at Stockholm made a trip in the steamer on the neighboring waters. Captain Rogers said to Mr. Hughes: "I know, Sir, that I am spending and losing money in this experiment, but I have satisfied the world that the thing is practicable. As I am in Europe, I wish to circulate the fame of my ship and of my country as far and as widely as possible, and nothing gives me more pleasure than to show my ship to all people and especially to all persons of distinction." Mr. Hughes himself was both proud and happy: "This proud triumph over what has been considered insurmountable difficulties, as well as over the doubts and sneers of incredulous and envious Europe, has really afforded me a most unpayable gratification."

From Stockholm Captain Rogers took his ship to St. Petersburg. But the economic result was no better there than at Stockholm; the Russian Czar did not see fit to buy the ship. So Captain Rogers had to take her back to America; but she had made an invaluable trip of propaganda; the practicability of steamboats was finally understood by Europe.

Denmark was the first country to learn from the experience. In 1819 the government bought a steamer from England. It was the first vessel to cross the North Sea exclusively by steam, and was one of the sensations of the year. The ship was put into service as a packet between Copenhagen and Kiel. France got her first steamship in 1820, and in 1822 steamships began to ply the lakes of Switzerland. A Steam Packet Company was formed in Dublin in 1823, and the next year in London the General Steam Navigation Company, intended not only to provide service in British waters but also to develop trade with the continent. In 1825 an English steamship even went to India. The same year the Norwegian government bought two steamers to run as packets along the whole coast of Norway. The minister of finance responsible for the purchase was impeached for his arbitrary act, but he was triumphantly acquitted and praised for his vision of a new age.

The success of the steamboat was assured. For a long time thereafter, however, it could be operated only on rivers and lakes and along the coasts. Capable of only comparatively short distances, it served mainly for the transportation of passengers and mail. Not until 1838 did another steamer, this one built in England, cross the Atlantic. In 1847 American and English companies built ocean liners in order to serve the emigration from Europe.

Meanwhile the increasing international trade created a demand for ever larger and swifter craft. As early as colonial times America had set the pattern of fast sailing, and in the nineteenth century, particularly in the 1830's, American sailing vessels set records that kept the European nations busy trying to keep up with them. America was literally speeding up the whole world.

It did more than just invent new types of fast-sailing vessels. In the 1840's an American navigator, Captain Matthew Maury, began an intensive study of winds and ocean currents on the basis of thousands of logbooks of American skippers, and, as the first result, he published in 1847 a *Wind and Current Chart of the North Atlantic*. It indicated sea lanes which, if followed, would save many days of sailing and lessen the perils of the ocean. It became highly popular and was used by hundreds and thousands of sea captains. The discovery of gold in California increased the demand for fast sailing around Cape Horn, and again Maury prepared charts by which the average sailing time between New York and San Francisco was cut down from 180 to 133 days.

The success of Maury's undertaking became the talk of nautical circles. Here was a great saving to the commerce of the world. Soon Europe began to take notice, and before a congress of all the leading seafaring nations at Brussels in 1853, Maury explained the principle of his charts. Study and improvement of them was made a matter of international coöperation. But Europe had to thank America for its initiative and perseverance in creating this valuable assistance to navigation.

At the same time, the merchants and the navigators of the world began to consider intently the possibility of making steamboats profitably serviceable for carrying ocean trade. In 1853 Maury published his *Lanes of Steamers Crossing the Atlantic*, which gave promise of increased safety and speed. Charts based on his researches and maps are still used by ocean-going vessels. Still more effective was the improvement of the steamers themselves. From the middle of the 1850's the screw propeller took precedence over the paddle wheel as a means of propulsion; and English and American engineers vied with each other in establishing the best designs for this new type of vessel. The 1860's brought the compound engine, which effected so great an economy in fuel that the steamship was able to compete with the sailing vessel in carrying cargoes on long voyages. That meant the final victory of the steamships. The results of Fulton's invention far surpassed the dreams of its author. Both the speed and the volume of exchange of goods between the nations broke all previously imaginable records. To a large extent this development was due to American enterprise and to the stimulus emanating from America.

      ✱   ✱   ✱   ✱   ✱

From the first decades of the nineteenth century the industrialization of America advanced with giant strides. Especially after the depression following the panic of 1819 was overcome, a period of hustling activities and new enterprises began, causing never-ending excitement. Railroads were built, banks were founded, the West was settled, ever new riches exploited—it was expansion everywhere. Not only the economic but equally the moral forces of the nation were spurred on to a hitherto unknown pace. And Tocqueville's prediction that the progress of industry would evoke an acute interest in science was fulfilled almost before it was uttered. In the 1830's even the pure sciences began to find eminent students. In Philadelphia, the great-grandson of Franklin, Professor Alexander D. Bache, performed famous experiments on the earth's magnetism. In Albany, Professor Joseph Henry, building upon the discoveries of the Dane Ørsted and the Frenchman Ampère, discovered electric

induction simultaneously with Faraday in London, and succeeded in converting magnetism into electricity, thus proving
the identity of the two forces. Together with Bache he went over
to Europe in 1837, visited Scotland, England, and France, and
was everywhere welcomed as an equal by the leading scientists
of the time. He demonstrated electrical experiments not hitherto
seen by them, and the great Faraday became so excited he
jumped to his feet and shouted: "Hurrah for the Yankee experiment!"

The electro-magnetic discoveries of the 1820's and 30's immediately led to practical inventions that laid the foundations of
whole new industries. After 1836 the electro-magnet of Henry
was used for the construction of dynamos and motors, and there
was great rivalry among American, British, German, French,
and other inventors in improving these machines for the rapidly
expanding factory system. In this field there was world competition which might just as well be termed collaboration. Sometimes one nation was leading, sometimes another. America could
boast that it had been active in the movement from the first moment and had given it one of its original inspirations.

On the basis of the same discoveries the electrical telegraph
was constructed, and in this instance America clearly took the
practical leadership. Various forms of optical telegraphy had
long been in use in Europe and elsewhere, and following the discovery of electricity a cumbersome system of electrical needle
telegraphy was worked out and put into use both in England and
France towards the end of the 1830's. But it was an American
invention, made by Samuel F. B. Morse, that really provided a
practical solution to the problem. Setting himself to work on the
basis of the discoveries and experiments of Joseph Henry, Morse
was able in 1837 to take out a patent on a method of transmitting
messages by wire. When his telegraph brought the news of the
presidential and vice-presidential nominations of the Democratic
National Convention from Baltimore to Washington even before
the candidates themselves were notified, it was the sensation of
the day. The pioneer of sensational journalism, James Gordon
Bennett of the *New York Herald*, immediately grasped its signifi-

cance. "The magnetic telegraph at Washington," he wrote, "has totally annihilated what there was left of space." The effect of the new invention, he contended, would be to make journalism a more potent force than ever before: "The public mind will be stimulated to greater activity by the rapid circulation of news. The swift communication of tidings of great events will awake in the masses of the community still keener interest in public affairs." His own paper started to make extensive use of the telegraph as soon as new lines were established, and other papers had to follow his example. In 1845 a commercial company was formed to exploit Morse's patent, and two years later the United States had a wire system of 1,700 miles.

Then Europe began to adopt it. After 1845 Morse's method was tested in different countries, meeting at first with doubts, but gradually accepted with enthusiasm. France was proud of its optical telegraph which had proved, according to the expectations of the times, amazingly efficient in bringing news from Rome to Paris in four days. But an eloquent minister was able to persuade the parliament to appropriate a sum for experiments on the electric system. In Great Britain private companies established telegraph lines. On the continent the first permanent lines were erected by Hamburg and Bremen, the enterprising free cities of Germany, in 1847. In the other countries final acceptance had to wait until after the revolutionary movements of 1848. In most of the continental states the action was taken by the governments themselves, and in many of them the establishment and maintenance of a telegraph was declared a public monopoly. Even where the first telegraph lines were laid by private enterprise, as in Great Britain, Denmark, and Sweden, they were presently taken into government ownership and monopolized. Prussia connected Berlin with all the other important cities of Germany in 1849; Austria followed in 1850; then France, Belgium, and Switzerland in 1851; the Netherlands and Denmark in 1852; Sweden in 1853; Norway in 1854; Spain in 1855; and so on. Soon all of Europe was covered with telegraph wires. A submarine cable was laid between England and France as early as 1851. The great task of connecting Europe with America by a submarine cable across the Atlantic was first tried in 1857 but proved a failure. It was repeated the next year, and this time the connection functioned properly; but after three months the line broke. A new attempt was not made until 1866; then, finally, a permanent line was established by the genius and patience of an American engineer, Cyrus W. Field. That was another gift of America to Europe.

It is not necessary to describe in detail what the telegraph meant to the whole world. It was not only a means of spreading news so that it became possible to know anywhere what had occurred the day before or even the same day at any other place. Newspapers won still more importance than they already had; from now on they really became the fourth estate, equal to the three old political estates or even superior to them because of being the mighty champion of public opinion. The telegraph became just as indispensable to economic life, national as well as international, making it possible to grasp opportunities which otherwise would not have presented themselves and to avoid disasters which would otherwise have been unavoidable. For good and for evil, it put a spirit of swift action into all business. Administration too became more efficient, its power more easily centralized. In brief, in all spheres of life the introduction of the telegraph transformed the habits of men and of nations.

The principles of telegraphy by wire have often been modified and improved since Morse made his invention. But the fundamentals have remained the same, and the Morse code is still in use. That is the triumph of his work, which for more than a hundred years has dominated the world even more than that of Robert Fulton.

✦   ✦   ✦   ✦   ✦

In her enthusiastic letter of 1850 about the accomplishments of the American nation "in the field of experimental humanity," Fredrika Bremer did not refer to the invention of telegraphy; that achievement had not yet sufficiently impressed itself on the imagination of Europe, and Miss Bremer was not aware of its connection with the discoveries of the man to whom her letter was addressed, Professor H. C. Ørsted. What she listed as examples were Franklin's lightning conductor, Fulton's steamship, and the discovery by a "happy man" of the means of mitigating bodily suffering—the method of anaesthesia.

This latter contribution to human progress has peculiar relations to two distinct aspects of American activities. On the one side, it is connected with the general efforts for humanizing life and bringing comfort to invalided and suffering beings which are so characteristic of the America of the first half of the nineteenth century. On the other side, the invention was the result of the development of a particular field of medical science which attained in America a truly scientific standard at an earlier date than in any European country. This was dentistry.

It is not altogether easy to explain why this art should reach so high a development in America where it had a much later start than in Europe. A young German dentist who took up practice in Philadelphia in 1812 and worked there for ten years, Dr. Leonard Koecker, asserted later in his fundamental work on the *Principles of Dental Surgery,* published in London in 1826, that "it could not escape my observation that diseases of the teeth were much more common in America than in any part of Europe." But at the same time he observed that "healthy and beautiful teeth are much more highly valued by the inhabitants of that country than by those of any other." It could not be denied, he thought, that in the profession of dentistry quacks were most abundant in the United States and in England. But he also held "the profession of the dentist to be nowhere in the hands of more scientific and excellent men" than in those two countries. Later in the book, however, he retracted this compliment to his English readers and declared flatly that in no part of the world had dentistry obtained a more elevated station than in the United States. At the time of his writing, the fame of American practitioners in dental surgery was widely spread in Europe. They invented both new methods, such as gold filling, and new instruments. The Baltimore College of Dental Surgery, chartered in 1839, was the first institution of its kind in the world. In the same year was published the first dental periodical. The next year was organized the American Society of Dental Surgeons, which began the publication of works on dental science. In 1841, one of the states, Alabama, adopted a law requiring the examination of dentists by a medical board before granting the license to practise. Thus dentistry was made a truly scientific profession, and it is a remarkable fact that America maintained its leadership in this field for a full century. European dentists came thither to learn. It is interesting to note at this point that one of the important new instruments constructed in America, the electromagnetic mallet of 1867, was based on the same principle as that of the Morse telegraph.

A member of the first class of graduates from the Baltimore College of Dental Surgery, William T. G. Morton of Boston, was the "happy man" who gave to the world the art of anaesthesia. Other medical men in America had tried to find methods of making people insensitive to pain from operations. But European authorities declared categorically: "The abolition of pain in surgery is a chimera." A young doctor in Athens, Georgia, Crawford Long, in 1842 made successful experiments with ether as an anaesthetic, but he did not see the general consequences of his discovery, and did not publish his results until seven years later. In the meantime Morton had established the effectiveness of ether for anaesthetic purposes above all doubt. He worked with the conscious intention of finding an anaesthetic that could serve regularly in the extraction of teeth, the most common operation for all people, and consequently in other operations as well. Having observed the effect of ether, he tested it methodically on his own patients in 1846. Then he demonstrated it at an operation in the Massachusetts General Hospital with the same complete success. The operating surgeon exclaimed to the students present: "Gentlemen, this is no humbug!" One of the doctors declared: "I have seen something today that will be heard round the world." The fact was published in a medical journal in Boston, and the leading English medical journal, the *Lancet*, wrote: "Next to the discovery of Franklin, it is the second and greatest contribution of the New World to science."

In the very same year, Morton's method was put into practice by surgeons in London and Paris. Soon it was being used in hospitals all over the world and even on the battlefields of Europe. Fredrika Bremer might well praise ether anaesthesia as a blessing to humanity. It facilitated the work of doctors, and infinitely lessened suffering for men as well as for animals. Other anaesthetics could also be employed, but the principle of preventing unnecessary suffering was permanently established.

✻ ✻ ✻ ✻ ✻

Perhaps it may be regarded as characteristic of national tendencies that the two most remarkable achievements of American mechanical genius during the first half of the nineteenth century—the steamboat and the telegraph—were inventions serving to increase the speed of communication between people and countries. In the field of purely industrial inventions Great Britain was still the leading nation, and many important innovations came from there to American industry. Many of them might be further improved by the practical Americans, but British supremacy in industrial production was yet undisputed. The discovery of the art of employing coke and anthracite in furnaces for smelting iron, formerly tested in Europe and first tried successfully in America in the 1830's, soon put an end to American importation of iron from Europe, and finally made the United States the largest producer of iron products. The most important independent industrial invention made in America in this period was the method of vulcanizing rubber, patented by Charles Goodyear in 1839; it laid the foundation for a whole new industry, but had to compete with a British patent of 1843. The American invention won its complete victory only at the Universal Exhibition in Paris in 1855.

Europe had not yet learned to look to America for the most surprising products of inventive genius. In this regard the decisive change came with the first World's Fair in London in 1851.

At that time, the American most spoken of in Europe was the great showman P. T. Barnum. He had first invaded Europe in 1844; he had taught the world the art and power of publicity and had made himself the most advertised man living. He realized the truth of the old slogan *mundus decipi vult*—people desire to be deceived—and he proclaimed it frankly as his principle of life long before Ibsen declared the lie necessary for weak human beings. He became the embodiment of humbug and as such was regarded by the Europeans as the true incarnation of America. All travelers in America had brought back tales of American boasting. The sensationalism of American newspapers was already proverbial. Why, then, should all American marvels be taken seriously? No, Mr. Barnum was the irrefutable demonstration of the true character of American self-advertisement. Humbug was the word.

The great exhibition of 1851 brought a surprise—the revelation of an America in many ways in advance of Europe. Old Europe had to sit up and learn.

The first Exhibition of All Nations' Industry was opened in the Crystal Palace in London on May 1, 1851, and was kept open to the public until October 11 of the same year. It was planned as the expression of a new age, that of free and friendly competition among all people, and it aimed at stimulating the universal spirit of friendship and peace. Whether it reached this goal may be disputed. Nevertheless it was in many respects a great success. The world had never seen such a magnificent exhibition of products and of producing instruments, from the king of diamonds Koh-i-noor, recently acquired by the British Crown, to tools for the daily life of simple people. It was the triumph of human genius. The exhibition was seen by more than six million visitors, as many as a hundred thousand coming on a single day. Even financially the enterprise was a success. Exultantly the *Times* recalled that the Americans, who certainly were not afraid of great numbers, had scoffed at the idea that entrance fees might bring in an income of two million dollars; that amount was reached six weeks before the exhibition closed. Litigation ultimately arose over the use of the excess income.

The true historic importance of this World's Fair lay in the victorious arrival of America on the stage of industry. One would not grasp this fact by studying the list of medals awarded by the thirty special juries. Unwilling to graduate their awards, the juries concluded to grant a simple bronze medal to every exhibit which might from some point of view be called "excellent," and the lion's share of these medals naturally fell to the British exhibitors, because they displayed as much as all the other nations together. In addition, the juries had reserved a higher, so-called Council medal for objects that gave proof of real originality of design. One hundred seventy such medals were awarded. Of these, seventy-seven went to British, fifty-six to French, and only five to American exhibitors. When the *Times* reported these awards it was mildly critical of the distribution, but found an excuse in the difficulty of the task and in the superior quantity of British displays. It remarked on only one specific omission: it could not understand why the American revolvers constructed by Mr. Colt had received no medal.

The Council medals awarded to Americans were: to Gail Borden, Jr., for the preparation called "Meat biscuit"; to D. Dick for various engineers' tools and presses; to William Cranch Bond & Son for the invention of a new mode of observing astronomical phenomena, etc.; to Charles Goodyear for India rubber; to Cyrus McCormick for a reaping machine.

Six weeks before the publication of the official awards the *Times* had carried an editorial on the result of the exhibition. Since the paper had the reputation of being rather unfriendly to the Americans, its homage to the American achievements must have seemed all the more impressive. The article started with an ironical mention of the ominous presence of Mr. Barnum. Several paragraphs were devoted to Mr. Colt's revolver, which evidently had impressed the editor more than it had the jurors. The author, however, could not restrain himself from observing that, according to reports from America, the principal effect of the new weapon hitherto had been to promote murder. But the article concluded:

It is beyond all denial that every practical success of the season belongs to the Americans. Their consignments showed poorly at first, but came out well upon trial. Their reaping machine has carried conviction to the heart of the British agriculturist. Their revolvers threaten to revolutionize military tactics as completely as the original discovery of gunpowder. Their yacht takes a class to itself. Of all the victories ever won none has been so transcendent as that of the New York schooner. The account given of her performances suggests the inapproachable excellence attributed to *Jupiter* by the ancient poets, who describe the King of the Gods as being not only supreme, but having none other next to him. "What's first?"—"The America." "What's second?"—"Nothing." Besides this, the Baltic, one of Collins's line of steamers, has "made the fastest passage yet known across the Atlantic," and, according to the American journals, has been purchased by British agents *"for the purpose of towing the Cunard vessels* from one shore of the ocean to the other." Finally, as if to crown the triumph of the year, Americans have actually sailed through the ithmus connecting the two continents of the New World, and, while Englishmen have been doubting and grudging, Yankees have stepped in and won the day.

Manifestly the American triumphs at sea loomed most overwhelmingly in the eyes of the English public. It was at the regatta at Cowes on August 28, 1851, that the American yacht *America* beat the British *Titania,* creating, according to another English newspaper, "a positive *furore* in England." It covered the course in five hours and a half, leaving its rival fifty minutes behind. That was a feat that was celebrated both in speeches and in poetry. The *New York Herald,* always picturesque, wrote that the victory "caused as much talk in all circles here and in England, as did the first appearance of the Pacific and Atlantic steamers of the Collins line."

It was a sensational triumph, and well deserved. It was one manifestation of the consistent efforts of American navigators to speed up sailing. More far-reaching effects, however, came from the American achievements at the exhibition itself. There is some exaggeration but a fundamental truth in the statement of an American author who, the next year, published a book on *American Superiority at the World's Fair.* He wrote: "The most important inventions, those which confer the greatest amount of power on mankind, in the ways of industry, were unquestionably furnished by American citizens. In this opinion, the whole world concurs. . . . In this friendly rivalry among the nations of the earth, although a young people, we have held up our heads proudly." The mythological reference of the London *Times* lured the author into adducing another classic simile to express his pride and his hopes: "What we have achieved, however, is but the foot of the coming Hercules—*ex pede Herculem*, etc.; the future is big with other and greater triumphs."

The author, to confirm his boast, then proceeds to enumerate all the excellent American exhibits—Goodyear's vulcanized India rubber, Professor Bond and Son's clock and spring governor, Cincinnati-cured hams, Dick's anti-friction press, Borden's meat biscuit, Colt's repeating pistol, Woodbury's planing machine, patent bank locks, pianofortes, iron bridges, safes, etc., etc. They were not all of the same high order, and even one of those that received the highest prize awarded by the juries, Gail Borden's meat biscuit, soon proved a failure—although Mr. Borden soon rehabilitated himself by giving condensed milk to the world in 1856. Both of his inventions, it may be noted, were natural products of American conditions, of the effort to relieve the difficulties experienced by pioneer settlers on new land.

But most important of all the American inventions were the agricultural machines. There was Prouty and Mears's center draught plow, which, in the trial on July 19, proved better and much lighter than all the British, French, Belgian, and Dutch plows, although the jury awarded to all these the same prize medal that it gave to the American specimen. Above all, there were McCormick's reaping and mowing machines. The author of the work mentioned is fairly transported with pride as he writes:

Of all the contributions toward the matchless collection of aids, auxiliaries, powers, and ornaments of arts, science and industry, within the pellucid, the transparent walls of the Crystal Palace, McCormick's Reaper was perhaps, taken on the whole, the most valuable. Simple in its construction, yet powerful in its *modus operandi*, it revealed itself to the astonished British Agriculturist as an agent of the greatest importance, in the most important of human pursuits.

Cyrus H. McCormick had taken out his first patent for a reaping machine in 1831. His was not the first attempt to construct a machine of that kind; it had been tried by many both in Great Britain and in the United States. But McCormick's machine was beyond doubt the most practicable. He took it to the west in 1847, built a factory in Chicago and made a mass product of it for agriculture on the Great Plains. The principle on which it was based made the construction of mowers possible, and such machines were patented in 1844. Now both of them were tried for the first time in Europe. The trial of the reaper on July 24, 1851, was a complete triumph, though the wheat was still green and heavy from rain.

Horace Greeley, the editor of the *New York Tribune*, who happened to be on the agricultural jury, wrote that in what was thought to be the last sitting, the British chairman of the jury said:

"We have, this week, been testing reapers, and one of the American machines surprised us by the efficiency and the excellence of its operation. But the day was rainy and the grain unripe; so we do not feel sure that its triumph was not owing to those circumstances. We require another trial on a fair day, with ripe, dry grain; and, should this machine then do as well as it has already done under our eyes, we must ask for it the very highest award."

The request was granted, the trial repeated under the conditions required, with a success fully equal to that previously achieved, and a Council medal was awarded to the machine. After these trials we are told that the reaper "had more visitors than the Koh-i-noor diamond itself."

On the list of Council medals for agricultural tools the Mc-Cormick reaper was placed alongside a Norwegian harrow (made in England), British corn and seed drills, and a two-horse and four-horse plow. But none of those other tools had such a lasting success as the American reaper.

The English had the comfort of seeing their machines prove superior in other fields. The day after the *Times* had acknowledged the general lead of the Americans, it was able to tell of a competition in which victory came to the English. It was won by Mr. Appold's centrifugal pump. On September 3, the *Times* told the story:

His hydraulic display was of so remarkable character that no one doubted his superiority, though it was known that there was an American in the field as an opponent. We had been beaten in yachting, and some of our best locks had been picked; we had been taught to reap corn by machinery, and even to admire the destructive merits of Colt's revolvers. It only remained for our cousins to pump us dry by centrifugal force in order to return home from the Exhibition with a song of unqualified triumph. ..

Happily, at the trial Mr. Appold's pump won easily, and the *Times* gave the Americans credit for showing themselves "nothing loth here, as elsewhere, to try conclusions with us." It might have added that the Americans were ready to admit British superiority wherever it existed. When Horace Greeley came home to the United States, he stated in a public lecture that in the World's Fair "the immense manufacturing capacity and aptitude of Great Britain were . . . abundantly represented." Unambiguously he declared Britain superior in iron and its multiform products, in steam engines and force pumps, looms and anvils, etc. The American victory was primarily in the agricultural machines of McCormick.

Their victory at the exhibition was one of the great events of the year. It became a European victory. The fame of the American agricultural machines flew through all countries, and they were rapidly taken into use one after the other, first the reaper and the mower, later the binder, the hayrake, and other American machines. They virtually transformed European farming. They made it ever more profitable to concentrate on fewer crops, and thus advanced the commercialization of agriculture. They limited the need of manpower and made thousands upon thousands of agricultural laborers idle, an ulterior consequence of which was an increasing emigration to America. American agricultural machines were, in fact, a potent factor in the economic and social changes and problems of Europe in the second half of the nineteenth century.

There was at the exhibition of 1851 a machine of another character that won a popular victory almost equal to that of the reaper. That was Lerow and Blodgett's sewing machine. It steadily drew a staring crowd to its operation, and the wondering physiognomies revealed the questions that filled the spectators: What would such a machine mean for the daily life of women?

The invention was new; the first American patent dated from 1846. The machine demonstrated in London was not yet a perfect model. But in 1851 a new patent was taken out by Isaac M. Singer which proved to be the final and victorious type. Singer was not only an able designer, he was at the same time a clever and foresighted salesman. His slogan was: "A sewing machine in every house!" He introduced the installment plan of buying in order to bring the machine within reach of the poor. "The sewing machine agent," a historian of American inventions has said, "with a machine or two on his wagon, drove through every small town and country district, demonstrating and selling."

That holds true of Europe as well as of America. The Singer machine conquered innumerable homes in every European country and it facilitated life for millions of women who now became able to sew and mend clothing in a fraction of the time previously needed. It liberated much woman power, particularly in the middle classes, which could thus be used (and which demanded to be used) in the public life of the nations. On the other hand, the sewing machine laid the foundation of the system of garment manufacture which caused it to be one of the worst sweating industries of the nineteenth century, in which the work of poor women was exploited in long hours at low wages. Thus this machine too created great economic and social problems in all the European countries.

*　*　*　*　*

On the whole, the American inventions of the first half of the nineteenth century helped to promote the industrialization of Europe which had begun in Great Britain in the eighteenth century. Of course, they were only one of the forces in this development. But they were real forces, and they inaugurated what has been called the Americanization of Europe.

VII

AMERICA ENTERS WORLD LITERATURE

'Mid pleasures and palaces though we may roam,
Be it ever so humble, there's no place like home;
A charm from the skies seems to hallow us there,
Which sought through the world is ne'er met with elsewhere.
Home! Home! sweet, sweet home!
There's no place like home, there's no place like home.

WITH this song the first bit of American poetry conquered
Europe. Of course, it was a help that it was written and first sung
in Europe. It was produced by the American playwright John
Howard Payne in 1823, after he had been living in England and
France for fully ten years. He wrote the song as a part of an
opera libretto, and as the libretto was adapted from a ballet he
had seen in Paris, called *Clari, or the Maid of Milan,* so the text
of the song was inspired by a poem written essentially to the
same tune by an earlier author, the young English poet Thomas
Bayly. It must, however, immediately be stated that, apart from
the meter of the first four lines and the general subject of the
poem, the work of Payne was totally different in poetical expression from that of Bayly; above all it was much simpler, and
therefore more genuine, and it has been able to live on while the
verses of Bayly are totally forgotten.

The tune was composed by an Englishman, the director of
the Theatre Royal at Covent Garden, Sir Henry R. Bishop. He
had published it the previous year, with the text by Bayly, as a
"Sicilian Air" in his collection *Melodies of Various Nations.* How
much there really was of Sicilian in this tune may fairly be doubted. At any rate, as remarked by the learned historian of the
song, Mr. Carl Engel, it had much of the character of folk-song,
like many other compositions of the age, both English and others.
In adapting his composition to Payne's text, Bishop had to
change the latter half of it to fit the short chorus with which

Payne had ended each verse. This was doubtless an advantage and helped make the song the hit it turned out to be. It was, in fact, the center of the whole play and the reason for its success. The critics did not rate the opera very highly, but it was greatly applauded by the audiences, and the central song especially moved them to tears. It was published not only as part of the opera score but also by itself, and one hundred thousand copies of it are said to have been sold in England and America the very first year. The most popular singer of the day, the darling of the British public, Miss Kitty Stephens, made it a part of her concert program and sang it throughout the country. It became the property of the whole nation.

The words and the tune appear nowadays so inseparable that we generally forget that the tune was composed by an Englishman. We conceive the whole song as an American production. As such it has passed from one country to the other. It has satisfied the sentiments of many nations, and it has been translated into many different languages; as late as 1945 a new Norwegian translation appeared. Everywhere the song has been felt as typically American. Both text and tune are filled with the frank melancholic nostalgia that became characteristic of American song during the following century.

It was a long time, however, before other American songs reached Europe. The songs of Stephen Foster, so genuinely American both in their sentiments and in their melodic forms, remained largely unknown to foreign nations. In a previous chapter it has been noted that Scandinavian emigrants carried his song to Susanna of Alabama back to their old country with a new text shortly after it had been composed (1848). Fifty years later, in the 1890's, the Danish poet Holger Drachmann, who had many ties with the West, took the tune of *Gentle Annie* for his sweet May-song "See the sun is buzzing o'er the meadow," where the ingratiating melody makes us truly feel that the heart of the poet "is becoming wax in his bosom." I have seen no other sign of acquaintance with the Foster songs in Europe.

How unknown he was until quite recent times may be illustrated by noting how late his name appears in European encyclopedias. The first notice I have found of him in such works appears in the middle of the 1890's in the seventeenth volume of the French *Grande Encyclopédie;* the next in the Danish *Konversationsleksikon,* called "Salmonsen," in 1897. He is mentioned only in the eleventh edition of the *Encyclopedia Britannica* (1910), in the great Spanish *Enciclopedia Universal* (1924), and finally in the German *Grosse Brockhaus,* 15th edition (1930). In other German works of the same kind he is still not noticed, nor does he appear in modern encyclopedias of other countries.

American literature could easily draw the attention of readers in England since it was written in the English language. But, even apart from the political grudge harbored against the American rebels and the patronizing feeling natural to the parent nation, Englishmen could not be expected to appreciate much of the work produced by young America. Most of it seemed to consist of imperfect imitations of English style.

One of the poets of the American Revolution, Joel Barlow, mentioned in an earlier chapter as a revolutionary propagandist in Europe, had some of his poems printed both in London and in Paris, and, according to American tradition, his *Vision of Columbus* (1787) was "read and admired" in both countries. No doubt the reading and admiration were limited to narrow circles, such as could manage to swallow the bombastic rhetoric of the poem. Columbus's "vision" was the great future of the new world, and when the author elaborated this idea with more details and more rhetoric in a new edition (1809), dedicated to a representative of the new future, Robert Fulton, his work, now called the *Columbiad,* certainly attracted more attention, but less admiration. It was remembered in England as "the unreadable Columbiad," characterized by a "curious intermixture of extreme homeliness and flatness with a sort of turbulent and bombastic elevation." In a contemporary review it was charged with "an utter disregard of all distinction between what we should call lofty and elegant, and low and vulgar expressions."

This latter objection leads us to one feature which, in certain respects, represented an advance in American writing over the traditional modes of poetry. The same reviewer unconsciously gave notice of it when he remarked quite generally: "These republican literati seem to make it a point of conscience to have no aristocratical distinctions—even in their vocabulary." Barlow, and most of his fellow countrymen, made the error of implanting simple and direct expressions of human sentiment in an otherwise unctuous and affected style. But such use of natural speech pointed the way to more truth and genuine vigor in poetry.

The English poet Robert Southey stated curtly in 1809 that in America "no work of distinguished merit has yet been produced." Essentially that was true. Histories of American literature may point to the novels of Charles Brockden Brown, published at the turn of the eighteenth century. His somber tales and his studies in tormented states of mind offered samples of a probing of souls that might be taken as the distinguishing mark of the nineteenth century. In America he is remembered as the first man who devoted his life exclusively to authorship, and he is said to be the first author to win an international hearing. This latter assertion, however, is not borne out by the facts. Two of his novels were early reprinted in England, *Clara Howard* in 1807, and the most important, *Wieland,* in 1811. They were unfavorably received by the critics, however, and the author was dismissed as (what he was) merely a follower of William Godwin. Only in the 1820's did he win any attention worth mentioning from the English public. On very questionable authority it has been said that he made a strong impression on Shelley. Walter Scott is said to have called him America's greatest novelist, but that was as late as 1824 or 1825. French translations appeared, as far as I have been able to find, no earlier than 1841, German translations only in the 1850's. In fact, interest in Brown's works came only in the wake of the first American books that had a real success in Europe, those of Washington Irving.

❋   ❋   ❋   ❋   ❋

In 1820, the *Edinburgh Review* scornfully asked: "Where are the great Americans? Who reads an American book?" The same year brought the answer, at least to the latter question. In that year an American book appeared which made a great hit and was read by everybody in Great Britain who cared for literature. It even conquered all of Europe. It was the *Sketch Book* by Washington Irving.

It was not his first book to be published in England. His *Knickerbocker History of New York* had had a London edition in 1809. This satire upon American boasting had a natural appeal to Englishmen, and it was possible to enjoy its humor without any reflection upon American character. The book became popular, was many times reprinted, and was translated into several foreign languages. Its success, however, occurred only after the triumphal reception of the *Sketch Book*.

This book gave Irving almost the position of a naturalized English author. It offered sketches of English as well as of American life, and Englishmen had to marvel at his intimate understanding of their character and customs. He had come to England, originally on business, immediately upon the conclusion of peace in 1815, and he stayed in Europe for no less than eighteen years. During that time he became a close friend and even a collaborator of that other American author in Europe, John Howard Payne. He traveled and lived in many European countries—in France, Germany, and Spain; he felt most at home, however, in England. But he never allowed it to be forgotten that he was an American, and the sketches upon which his lasting renown rests are the American ones.

His *Sketch Book* was in continuation of the line of European literature. In particular, it was most immediately inspired by Walter Scott. Scotland had given to the whole of Europe the most vigorous impulses of national tradition, and Irving, who was by descent a Scotchman (or more specifically an Orkneyan), had imbibed these traditions from his childhood. They became vividly alive to him when he met the great Scotchman. Irving and Scott literally and mentally fell into one another's arms. Irving was able to give motifs to the elder friend and master; Scott had chuckled at the reading of the *Knickerbocker History of New York,* and he encouraged the younger man to continue writing.

The *Sketch Book* by its light and gracious style proved Irving the equal or almost the master of English authors, and he was ungrudgingly acknowledged as such by English critics. His sketches came to be recommended in British schools as a model of excellent English. They won the acclaim of contemporaries by their pictures of England and America in the romantic spirit of the age. If later critics were to charge the author with superficiality, he was rescued by his deft handling of a gentle humor that made his readers smile sympathetically—and no reaction is more agreeable to human feeling. In addition, the most successful of his sketches were stories that had the flavor of something foreign and nevertheless well-known, the Hudson River legends of Rip Van Winkle and Sleepy Hollow.

No wonder that he was admired and loved. He became the darling of the English public. In one review he was called "the Goldsmith of our age." He could speak for America because he evidently was a friend of England, and he became the unofficial but highly successful American envoy to England. His *Sketch Book* appeared at a moment when international politics were beginning to impel a close coöperation between the two Anglo-Saxon powers, and it assumed the importance of a message of friendship from the one nation to the other. Hostility had to give way to the recognition of common interests, and Irving helped make the coöperation not merely one of interests but one of sentiments as well.

The *Sketch Book* was published in two parts, in 1819 and 1820, and it was printed in England in many editions. It was immediately translated into one foreign language after the other. Often there were editions with illustrations by renowned artists. Fancy such a title as *Beauties of Washington Irving*, illustrated by George Cruikshank, published in London, 1835. Literary men were just as friendly as the general public. Pushkin, the founder of modern Russian literature, was enraptured by the new American author and borrowed from him the subject of one of his tales. When the first novels of Fredrika Bremer appeared (1831) the leading Swedish critic of the time knew no higher praise for them than to compare them with Irving's sketches. He pursued his success with other books in the same vein, and they, too, were cordially received. But the *Sketch Book* retained its charm after all the others were forgotten. It was reprinted and translated again and again throughout the whole nineteenth century.

If in this book Irving could be said to have followed the highway of contemporary European literature, he became a pioneer in another field where American authors would naturally take the lead. That was the study of the discovery of America, which extended to the study of the history of Spain. Irving went to Spain in 1826 and was deeply interested in the world of romance that revealed itself to him there.

He had a predecessor there in a younger countryman, George Ticknor, who had gone to Spain as early as 1818 and concentrated upon Spanish literature. Ticknor was a scholar by nature, and became the helpful adviser and teacher of many other students. He inspired Irving too. Not until 1849 did he produce the result of his own studies in his *History of Spanish Literature*, the first comprehensive work on this subject. In Spanish, German, and French translations it was for several decades the commanding guide for all who ventured into the maze of Spanish poetry, fiction, and drama. It could never be a popular work. But long before it was published, Irving and later Prescott had made Spanish history a popular and almost an exciting element of European life.

Irving's material was supplied by Spanish scholars. He was the man who knew how to breathe life into it. In 1828 he was able to publish his *Life and Voyages of Columbus,* a serious work, which really laid the foundation of scientific treatment of the history of Columbus. In addition, it was written in the light and attractive style of which Irving was the master, and it became highly popular. It was immediately translated into French, German, Dutch, Italian, Spanish, and probably other languages, and it increased the fame of Columbus. Irving followed it up with the *Voyages and Discoveries of the Companions of Columbus* (1831) which was more in the nature of an editing of the reports of others. In Irving's rendering they became popular reading in many countries.

He continued the same kind of work in still another field. After he had gone back to America in 1833, he started a series of publications about travels and explorations in western America, partly his own and partly those of others. These books too were translated into foreign languages. They brought the romance and the allurements of the wild West to the hearts of pent-up people who longed for adventure.

Finally, shortly before his death he published a *Life of George Washington*. It was the first work on American history to become truly popular in Europe, and it had a task to fulfill in European thought. It appeared at a time when the United States had fallen into conflict with more than one European nation and was in need of comprehension and sympathy. By raising George Washington up as the hero of all freedom-loving people, Irving won wide understanding for the proper position of his nation in the world. From that time on George Washington was given a place in European primers and textbooks that was a kind of everlasting publicity for the best of America. Thus once more he had acted as the envoy-at-large of America to Europe. When Washington Irving died in 1859, his nation could feel that he had done more to win respect for America than almost anybody else.

*   *   *   *   *

In 1822, the *New Edinburgh Review* wrote: "The *Sketch Book* has roused us, on this side of the water, to a new interest in the progress of transatlantic talent, taste, and genius." The words were written in the review of a new book by another American author, James Fenimore Cooper. Obviously he benefited by Washington Irving's fame. Indeed, he conquered the European public in an even more lasting way than Irving had done, and in a still more impressive way he brought America to Europe. If Irving's popularity was confined mainly to the cultivated classes, Cooper was the favorite of the masses.

Cooper too was strongly influenced by Walter Scott. What novelist at that time could have escaped the influence of the great Scotch author? He was the master of both Europe and America. But perhaps just because Cooper was less of an artist than Irving, he did not conform so completely to the artistic rules set by the authors of Great Britain. He was of a harder, less flexible character, and he had something truly American to give.

Only a year after Irving's *Sketch Book* appeared, Cooper published his novel *The Spy* (1821), and it was an immediate success in England as well as in America. It has justly been called "the first outstanding American novel." It had an English-American subject, the story of an English spy in the American War of Independence. It was told with an ardent patriotism, but yet without debasing the English character. Thus the thrilling story could be enjoyed equally on both sides of the Atlantic. It revealed Cooper at once as the fascinating narrator that he always remained. Within a year the book was translated into French and thus started his conquest of all of Europe.

His next great success took its subject from the same period, but was otherwise of a different character. It was the sea novel *The Pilot* (1824), whose hero was modeled after John Paul Jones. Cooper had begun writing because, in discussing some bad books, he had said he could easily write better books himself. *The Pilot* was written to show that he was able to produce a better sea novel than Walter Scott's *Pirate*. He had the great advantage of having been a naval officer and of having sailed many seas. He knew everything about ships and navigation, and he could tell the story of a sailor with the true freshness of salt sea better than any landlubber, even though he were the greatest novelist. In fact, *The Pilot* came to set the model for all later stories of the sea. It was translated into all European languages, and became part of the reading of boys everywhere. It created the romance of the sea. Cooper himself followed it up with other sea novels, and all later authors of similar works, the Englishman Captain Marryat, the Norwegian Jonas Lie, the Polish-English Joseph Conrad, were indebted to him. They had read and devoured his books in their youth and from them had imbibed the atmosphere of true seamanship and sailors' speech.

Even before the publication of *The Pilot*, Cooper had started the series of works which became the foundation of his greatest world fame, the Leatherstocking Tales. It began with *The Pioneers, or the Sources of the Susquehanna* (1823), and continued with *The Last of the Mohicans* (1826) and *The Prairie* (1827), later with *The Pathfinder* (1840) and *The Deerslayer* (1841). Every one of the titles suggests to an adult reader in any country some of the highest excitements of his early youth. These books had a marvelous success. Translations swarmed, in particular after *The Last of the Mohicans* had appeared. *The Pioneers* came in French in the same year as the original, then in German in 1824; in Swedish and Spanish in 1827; in Danish in 1828, and so on. *The Last of the Mohicans* came out in French in 1826, in Swedish in 1828, in Norwegian in 1830. There was no end of editions and translations. The complete series, and even the complete collection of Cooper's works, appeared repeatedly in England, Germany, Denmark, France, everywhere. The "American novels" were translated into Asiatic languages, Turkish and Persian; they were read in Russia and in Italy. When Longfellow traveled in Scandinavia in 1835, he found them in the cottages of simple peasants. The twenty pages of bibliography in Sabin's great *Bibliotheca Americana* give only an incomplete picture of the worldwide popularity of these novels.

When, in January 1831, the prominent English literary journal, the *New Monthly Magazine,* carried a review of new American books, it recalled that Americans used to complain that "the tone of criticism adopted towards all productions of American literature by British reviewers is captiously and abusively severe, more indicative of the spiteful spirit of a step-mother than of the kindly feelings of a natural parent, anxious to foster the infant efforts of her offspring." The magazine thought such notions obsolete. It praised Cooper above all others, it recalled that he was honored by the name of "the Walter Scott of the New World," and for itself it proclaimed him "the wizard of the sea." "Indeed," it said, "this author, so long as he keeps to the sea, or to the forest, is unrivalled for the force, felicity and truth, with which he always describes nature, whether animate or inanimate."

Three months later, the same magazine included him in a series of "Living Literary Characters" which was opened with

Walter Scott and continued with Bulwer-Lytton. Here was re-
counted the sensation roused by Cooper's first books: "An Esqui-
maux poet could hardly have excited more wonder than the
'great American Novelist,' when he made his first appearance in
Europe. The world fell into a fit of admiration at the first sign
of genius on the barren waste of America." (The magazine seems
to have forgotten the previous success of Washington Irving or
perhaps did not rank it at the same level.) Now, the magazine
said, it became impossible to extend to these specimens of American literary perfection the ridicule formerly spent on the laws
and institutions of the young republic. It stated that Cooper's
works were "received and read in England as the productions of
a man of a very remarkable genius," and it explained the reason:
"No writer of the times has taken a wider range in his view of
human nature, or looked more deeply into the heart. Few know
better how to seize the strongest point of interest, and no one
can work it out more judiciously. . . . We never met with novels
of a more absorbing character. Every word of Mr. Cooper's
narrative is effective, or appears so while you read. All is action,
character, and poetry." Therefore, the article continued, you
could not close his books "until you had read the last line of the
last page." It praised his "entire originality of subject," and it
could not decide which book was best, *The Spy, The Pilot,* or
The Last of the Mohicans.

The article was quoted in the French magazine *Revue
Britannique* where the praise was even reinforced. This magazine
declared directly that Irving was simply an imitator of English
literature while Cooper was the first author of a truly American
color. It decided for *The Last of the Mohicans* as the best of all
his novels: there all was picturesque and vigorous, there the
truth reigned together with the grandiose.

These quotations from the early reception of his books convey an idea of why they impressed contemporary readers so profoundly. The five Leatherstocking Tales in particular maintained their power over the world public for generations to come.
One reason was their subject: the clash between primitive
people and so-called civilization, between the wilderness and the

settlements, the vivid picture of frontier life. This life was personified in the unforgettable portrait of Natty Bumppo, the typical frontiersman, formed in the likeness of the celebrated pioneer Daniel Boone, pictured in his successive appearances as Hawkeye, the Pathfinder, or the Deerslayer, the "philosopher of the wilderness." And at his side the noble Indian, the equally unforgettable last Mohican, Uncas. Cooper had an almost unconscious skill at making his persons live and act so as to become real people whom we know and understand. He was a born storyteller, he had a richness of invention, and when he led his characters through their actions, their victories and their defeats, we had the illusion of true life. At the same time he made his heroes the bearers of lofty ideas, and in their fight for such ideas they attained heroic stature. Their defeats became genuine tragedies, and our hearts bled for them.

There came a time when the more refined novels of Bulwer-Lytton pushed those of Cooper into the background. But when taste returned to more substantial reading, Cooper's works again won ground. Always they maintained themselves as the dearest reading of boys, rivaled only by the books of Captain Marryat and Walter Scott. In all countries, adaptations specially made for boys were published, and innumerable imitations appeared. There grew up a whole literature of "Indian novels" appealing to boys. In Germany they became a regular branch of the book industry; in the 1890's we are informed that, after the more serious authors had left the field, "the obscure books of German fiction still swarm with Indians and adventurers whenever America is concerned." No imitations, however, could match Cooper's originals. They became a part of the education of boys all over the world. To "play Indian" became a beloved sport in which the boys wore Indian dress with feathers and moccasins and learned to cry "ugh" (on the continent pronounced *hoogg*). Still more important were the ideals of noble-mindedness and justice absorbed from these books; they meant something for the future life of the boys, nowadays perhaps replaced by the Scout movement which certainly has adopted some of its features from the Leatherstocking Tales.

People may question whether it represented a degradation or a promotion for Cooper's novels that they became the favorite reading of boys instead of being admired by the more sophisticated public. At any rate, in that way they were lasting forces in the life of the nations. In the twentieth century they seem to have lost this prominent place in the hearts of boys; they have had to compete with so many other and more modern "boys' books." But many generations of men in the nineteenth century received from Cooper some of their strongest and dearest childhood impressions.

* * * * *

In the wake of Irving and Cooper came a historian, William Prescott. He wanted to be nothing but a historian, and he was a scholarly one, working directly on documents and firsthand reports. But he belonged to that school of historians who conceived of their task as one of creative literature. That meant that their writings were likely to reach the general reader. Prescott demonstrated the close relationship of history and the novel by writing the biography of Brockden Brown. He knew even better than this pioneer novelist how to construct and write his books so as to make them really exciting reading. Like Cooper, he was a most convincing narrator. His subject—Spanish and Spanish-American history in its most brilliant period—had a color of romance that naturally appealed to the taste of an age of world expansion. Starting with the *Reign of Ferdinand and Isabella* (1838), he continued with the *Conquest of Mexico* (1843) and the *Conquest of Peru* (1847), and finished with the *Reign of Philip the Second* (1855–58). All these books went through a long series of reprints in London, and from the beginning of the 1840's they were translated into one language after the other— German, Spanish, French, Italian, Dutch, Danish. The author himself was honored with membership in the Royal Academy of Berlin and the Institute of France, and when he came to England to receive a doctor's degree from the University of Oxford, he was celebrated as one of the foremost men of the time. Most indicative of the popularity of his works was perhaps the fact that they were condensed and adapted for the use of schools and the reading of boys in many languages. That holds true for the two books on Mexico and Peru; they took their place by the side of Cooper's novels in numbers of boys' libraries, and they taught the young readers the same lessons—admiration of courage and noble acts, detestation of cruelty and treachery.

Prescott's fame prepared the way for other American historians. Bancroft's *History of the United States* now came within the horizon of a larger European public, and was reprinted in London and translated into continental languages—German, Danish, French. His three volumes on the first phase of the American Revolution, published in 1852–54, preceded by a few years Washington Irving's *Life of Washington* and derived advantage from the popular success of that work. Just as Prescott finished his work he was followed by Motley, who, after having begun rather unsuccessfully as a novelist, by long, strenuous work achieved his *Rise of the Dutch Republic* (1856) which attained almost the same popularity as the stories of Mexico and Peru. It was translated into Dutch, German, French, and Norwegian, and it was adapted for schools and for youth. It helped to spread the idea of freedom and to encourage the small nations in their aspirations for independence.

❀   ❀   ❀   ❀   ❀

American poetry was much slower than fiction to win a European public. In 1822 there appeared in London a collection of *Specimens of the American Poets*. The British magazines were interested and they printed many reviews of the books; interest in America was mounting, and the critics were, on the whole, friendly. Evidently, however, they felt a little uncertain in regard to the new samples of American literature offered to them, and they varied widely about whom they should consider as really worth of access to the English Parnassus. Generally they agreed with the judgment pronounced by one of the reviewers that "in point of literary dependence America seems to be still a British colony," and that to the Englishman the imitation of English style and sentiment was "vapid and uninteresting."

The man who in America was soon to be proclaimed as the first true poet of the nation was represented in the collection by the poem *The Ages,* which, appearing here amidst the heated discussions of the South American revolutions, presented to Europe both the challenge and the promise of the American concept of freedom. This poem (written in the ambitious meter of Byron's "Childe Harold's Pilgrimage") was called by one of the English critics "a masterly sketch" which "ought to immortalize" the author. Others gave their preference to other poets. Bryant's later work made his prominence indubitable; he was not only a master of poetical form, but he commanded a world of beauty, fine sentiments, and noble ideas. Yet he never won great fame or a wide reading public in England.

Washington Irving, who acted as a literary as well as a political envoy to Great Britain, had a collection of Bryant's poems published in London in 1832. He wanted to impress upon the British public the fact that here they would meet an American poet; on the title-page he added to the name of the author the designation "an American." He dedicated the book to Samuel Rogers, a rather negligible poet but a man of taste and wit, generally regarded as a potentate in the republic of letters, a protector of young talents. In the dedication to Rogers, Irving tried to stress the American character of Bryant's poetry. He wrote:

> The British public has already expressed its delight at the graphic descriptions of American scenery and wild woodland characters, contained in the works of our national novelist, Cooper. The same keen eye and fresh feeling for nature, the same indigenous style of thinking and local peculiarity of imagery, which give such novelty and interest to the pages of that gifted writer, will be found to characterise this volume, condensed into a narrower compass and sublimated into poetry.

> The descriptive writings of Mr. Bryant are essentially American. They transport us into the depths of the solemn primeval forest—to the shores of the lonely lake—the banks of the wild nameless stream, or the brow of the rocky upland rising like a promontory from amidst a wide ocean of foliage; while they shed around us the glories of a climate fierce in its extremes, but splendid in all its vicissitudes. . . . Neither, I am convinced, will it be the least of his merits in your eyes, that his writings are imbued with the independent spirit, and buoyant aspirations incident to a youthful, a free, and a rising country.

It is said that Samuel Rogers appreciated highly the works of the American poet. Probably he subscribed to Irving's opinion that they were "characterised by a purity of moral, an elevation and refinement of thought, and a terseness and elegance of diction, congenial to the best of your own genius and to your cultivated taste," and even to the further judgment: "they appear to me to belong to the best school of English poetry, and to be entitled to rank among the highest of their class."

But it may be that just for these reasons the poems did not catch the ears or the hearts of the English public. As one of the critics said of the book: "perhaps its chief fault is that it is not sufficiently American." Another critic expressed the same idea in other words: "He may be the first, or one of the first, of his race at home, as Bryant is said to be; but as soon as he comes here to contend with our Byrons, our Campbells, or Moores, to say nothing of our elder poets, he sinks into insignificance." A graver objection to Bryant's poetry was worded in the simple but telling statement: "He wants fire."

Now it seems a general experience that pure lyric poetry rarely attains great popularity, and, despite his democratic profession of faith, Bryant's poems have a proud and cool aristocratic reserve that does not appeal to the masses. So it should not be wondered at that his star paled under the hot rays of passion in Byron's or Shelley's poetry. Nor should it cause wonder that a younger American poet who was in possession of more expansive warmth was able to conquer the public that left Bryant unnoticed, and even for a time to be the most widely beloved poet of the English language.

He was Henry Wadsworth Longfellow. Later critics have been busy pointing out all the qualities in which he was wanting—true originality, profoundity of thought, psychological subtlety, the inspiration of passion. It seems, however, more important to grasp the reasons why he won such universal admiration and love. They are, indeed, manifest. He expressed noble sentiments in beautiful verses, he spread over life a romantic charm that was just what the age wanted, he allowed people to weep agreeably over distant sorrows, feeling themselves in

sympathy with everything good and fine, and at the same time
he preached to them healthy, edifying morals in words that made
their modest strivings acquire the luster of high ideals. In all
his poetry there was the simplicity of a warm heart, and it went
to the hearts of simple people. None of his single poems was so
widely and so often quoted as his *Psalm of Life* (1838), the
poetical transcription of the good American slogan, Go ahead:

> Not enjoyment, and not sorrow,
>   Is our destined end or way;
> But to act, that each to-morrow
>   Find us farther than to-day.
>
> ....
>
> Lives of great men all remind us
>   We can make our lives sublime,
> And, departing, leave behind us
>   Footprints on the sands of time.

A British Tory might call such exhortation a "democratic
fallacy." But it strengthened and comforted the common man.
John Ruskin stated in a letter in 1851, and repeated it in another
letter in 1860, that this poem had more beneficial influence on
men's minds than any other modern composition whatever. "It
has been," he said, "a kind of trumpet note to the present generation," and he added: "It is now known by heart by nearly all
the reformers and agitators, good and bad, but *does good* to all
of them."

In England, Longfellow began to win favor as early as the
1830's. His world fame was founded by his two long epic poems,
Evangeline (1847) and *Hiawatha* (1855) which both attained
an unexampled vogue. The former was evidently inspired by the
Swedish poem of Esaias Tegnér, *Frithiof's Saga,* and by Goethe's
great idyll *Hermann und Dorothea,* whose classical meter it imitated. The latter took both meter and other inspiration from the
Finnish *Kalevala.* But the work of Longfellow surpassed in popularity all predecessors. Despite the foreign character of the subjects there was in these poems no search for the extravagant
or superhumanly heroic. They were just sufficiently exotic to

awaken the curiosity of the reader; their tragedy and heroism had an appeal to all human hearts. They were translated into all European languages, *Evangeline* eight times into German, four times into French; *Hiawatha* five times into German. Authorized and unauthorized editions in English were innumerable and were sold in millions. In England, Longfellow was so popular that when his *Courtship of Miles Standish* was published in 1858, ten thousand copies are said to have beeen sold the very first day.

He lived to experience the decline of his immense popularity. In the course of the 1870's, the minds of the reading public underwent a change. The desire for realism pushed romanticism aside. Still throughout the whole nineteenth century, and even later, Longfellow's verses were read and re-read by thousands of people, and were translated into new languages. But they no longer had the effect of their first appearance. In their time they had helped interpret America to Europe, in continuation of the work of Washington Irving. What was more, they had carried a sense of beauty to masses which had lived for long without such joy. They had cast sunshine over a world whose clouds people desired to forget. One generation was grateful for this performance. Another wanted to arm itself for battle against the powers of evil.

*   *   *   *   *

At the time when Longfellow's star rose high on the firmament of Europe, there died in America another poet, Edgar Allan Poe, a genius of undoubted originality, who never attained the same popularity either in Europe or in America, but who retained his fame when that of Longfellow faded, and exerted a profound and lasting influence upon all later literature. He was not original in the sense that he broke away from everything in past or contemporary literature; on the contrary, many roots connected him with previous authors, some of them still active during his whole lifetime. Like Brockden Brown he knew and was influenced by William Godwin, the pioneer in the psychology of crime, and he received impulses from the German Amadeus Hoffman, from Victor Hugo, from the English Gothic

School. Briefly, he was an offshoot of Romanticism with all its interest in the extraordinary and the terrible. By his intensity of feeling and form, by his artistic sensibility, he became one of the most brilliant representatives of this movement, certainly the most brilliant fostered by America.

Most of his life, Poe produced his stories and poems relatively unnoticed by his countrymen and by the whole English-speaking world. He became in some measure known to English readers by the publication in London in 1838 of his *Narrative of Arthur Gordon Pym,* which ran through several editions there. When Charles Dickens came to America in 1842, he promised Poe to try to find an English publisher for him, but nothing came of it. In 1846, however, *The Raven and Other Poems* appeared in London, but failed to draw any considerable immediate attention. It was the publication of Poe's *Tales* in 1845 that created his European fame. And that began in France.

In October 1846, in the *Revue des deux mondes,* one of its editors, E. D. Forgues, better known as "Old Nick," devoted an article of twenty-six pages, under the heading *Etudes sur le roman anglais et américain,* to a review of Poe's *Tales.* What had struck this Frenchman most strongly in the *Tales* was the consistency and concentration of their construction. He defined the author as a "logician, a pursuer of abstract truths, a lover of the most eccentric hypotheses and of the most arduous calculi." He explained the technique of the author as taking firm hold of an extraordinary situation and, from this starting point, leading the story onward to the last and most extreme consequences, with, he said, "a truly American tenacity." The method was, in a way, very simple, but it attained a sure and powerful effect. M. Forgues might have a little fun with the author's errors in the topography of Paris in the stories located in that city; but he understood that they were laid in foreign places in order to make the most incredible things credible to the American reader. The review did not do full justice to the genius of Poe, but certainly served as a good introduction to the French public.

French translations of his tales began to appear in magazines and newspapers, and were collected in books, beginning in 1853. Translations multiplied during the following years. The most celebrated and most effective were those made by the poet Charles Baudelaire, and he translated the poems as well. He wrote his first enthusiastic study on Poe in the *Revue de Paris* in 1852, and he made a steady propaganda for the American master poet. Théophile Gautier has told us how Baudelaire's translations made a real sensation. Victor Hugo declared that they gave a "new thrilling chill." In the beginning there was opposition. But gradually authors and critics of all generations —Barbey d'Aurevilly, Villiers de l'Isle-Adam, Emile Zola, Paul Bourget, Jules Lemaître, Remy de Gourmont, Jean Richepin, and innumerable others—came to express their admiration for Poe. He became the great model for many of them. His poetry was a powerful influence with Baudelaire, Paul Verlaine, Stéphane Mallarmé, and many others.

He taught the French poets that true poetry must not imitate or explain, but suggest and impress a sentiment, a mood of mind, evoke an echo in the soul. It should not attempt to paint nature, but to make nature a symbol of poetic feelings. One school of his followers called themselves Symbolists. To all of them the infinite longing for beauty and for artistic enjoyment was common; they cultivated the fantastic and the mystical. They would live only for their art, and they adopted for themselves the name of Bohemians. As early as 1858, one of them called Poe *le roi des Bohèmes*. When they started a cabaret for Bohemians in Paris, they named it *Chat noir* for one of Poe's stories.

Poe himself was a perfect artist, and he made the most severe demands on the craftsmanship of authors. He became the prophet of *l'art pour l'art*. The true significance of this slogan may be disputed. At any rate it commanded the highest efforts towards making all literary creation true art. To Poe this demand embraced two fundamentals: the style and the construction of every piece of art. In both matters he set an example that profoundly influenced all literature after him.

One of the foremost students of Poe, Hervey Allen, has said that this style was "unusually effective when used by him, but

not to be imitated." And another eminent scholar, Van Wyck
Brooks, has stated that "Poe was to leave no followers behind
him." Nevertheless it must be said that no author in any country has escaped the influence of Poe's example. His own style
was not completely identical in all his work; it runs the whole
gamut from the cool matter-of-fact style of his detective stories
to the musical phrasing in many others and in his verses. But
the fundamental aim of his style, maintained in all his writings,
was perfect precision and pregnancy of expression, every word
and every sentence formed according to the intention and the
effect of the whole work. He allowed no mere clichés, no negli-
gence or looseness in the choice of words; every single expression had to evoke the sentiment or the conception desired by
the author. This rule has come to be accepted as the obligation
of every writer. Edmund Gosse has said that, of modern English
poets, "there is hardly one whose verse-music does not show
traces of Poe's influence." The most fastidious stylist of modern
Norwegian prose, the leader of the neo-romantic school around
the turn of the last century, Tryggve Andersen, declared frankly
that Poe was his great model.

In the same way his ideal of construction triumphed everywhere. His fundamental demand was for unity within every
single work, whether novel, story, or poem. That was what struck
particularly the French authors—the single-mindedness of all
Poe's stories, what Zola called his "mathematical logic and de-
duction." And it became a lesson to all authors. At the close of
the nineteenth century Camille Mauclair wrote in an article on
Edgar Poe idéologue: "To all of us he remains a powerful modern-
ist, the first who has conceived the application of experimental
methods and the adjustment of scientific elements to art." In
particular, this holds true of the short story, which he first
brought to perfection in its modern form. Concentration upon
one significant incident was the ideal which he set and which
remained after him. In verse as in prose composition, concentration meant intensity, and that was the alpha and omega of his
creative work.

More particularly he is celebrated as the originator of the

detective story. A connoisseur of this branch of literature, "Ellery Queen," has recently said that Poe's *Murders in the Rue Morgue* (1841) was "not merely a pioneering effort or an experimental incunable, but an acknowledged technical and artistic master-piece." From him descend all the modern authors of detective stories, from Anna Katharine Green and Conan Doyle onward. His pioneer stories in this field even gave impulse to works of authors in other fields, such as Victor Hugo, Charles Dickens, Dostoievski, and Robert Louis Stevenson.

France always was the center of the cult of Poe. From there it spread to the rest of Europe. It reacted even on England; there his *Poetical Works* were published in 1852, and later in new, sometimes illustrated editions. A collection of all his works, with Baudelaire's study of his life and writings, appeared in London in 1873. They were translated into many languages, into German in 1853–54 (*Ausgewählte Werke*), Spanish, Italian, Russian,* Danish, and others. Everywhere they were an influence for heightening the level of literary taste and the sense of poetic beauty. His most famous poem *The Raven* was included in most English language readers. Perhaps no other author of that language has enjoyed a more lasting admiration than Poe.

*   *   *   *   *

During the first half of the nineteenth century not a little American literature was read in Europe, even apart from such authors as Irving, Cooper, Prescott, Longfellow, and Poe. Most of it, however, simply served as entertainment reading and had no serious impact on the mind. In the 1830's and 40's, Nathaniel P. Willis was a frequent contributor to British magazines and almost the best-known American writer in Great Britain. This entertainment literature from America was so popular that an enterprising German publisher started, in Leipsic in 1852, an *Amerikanische Bibliothek* to supplement the *Europäische Bibliothek* that had appeared since 1846. The American series in-

* Two small sketches by Poe were translated in a Russian magazine as early as 1838 and 1839; but only in the 1850's did a more comprehensive work of translation begin in Russia.

cluded during the 1850's some sixty volumes, or about fifteen complete works annually. Then the interest apparently was satisfied, and after 1859 very few volumes appeared. In 1871 the enterprise was given up. To judge from the selections for this publication, the most popular American author would have been Mrs. E. D. E. N. Southworth, who not only opened the series, but was later represented by ten more works. After her the most popular were (in the order here given): William G. Simms and Mayne Reid, the two lady authors Mrs. Ann S. Stephens and Miss Susan Warner ("Elizabeth Wetherell"), Emerson Bennett, Charles W. Webber, and Nathaniel P. Willis. Of all these authors, only Simms and Willis play an appreciable though not very vital part in the development of American literature. But it has to be admitted that the others, in their time, were also most popular with the American public. Captain Reid was the "boys' novelist" *par excellence,* Bennett and Webber imitated Cooper with their novels of frontier life, while the three ladies made more women weep than anyone previously had. Miss Warner's first book *The Wide, Wide World* (1850) even rivaled *Uncle Tom's Cabin* which was also included in the series, as the most popular novel published in America during the whole nineteenth century. Thus it is apparent that European and American readers were in happy harmony as to literary taste; on both sides they preferred the lighter literature.

Simultaneously with this series of German translations, another publishing firm in Leipsic started a *Collection of Standard American Authors* in the original language, and in the course of fifteen years (1854–69) about eighty volumes were brought out. In this case too, the interest obviously decreased after the first ten years, and the series was stopped. The books included in this collection were on the whole on a higher level than those of the *Amerikanische Bibliothek.* It ought to be mentioned, however, that among the first volumes in this latter series were works by Poe and Hawthorne. When the latter, early in the 1850's, published *The Scarlet Letter* and *The House of the Seven Gables,* he caught the immediate attention of serious minds in Europe. Along with their romantic atmosphere they had a fine and deep psychology, united with a warm human sympathy, that gave them a high place in the hearts of men as well as in the admiration of leading critics. They really were in the vanguard of the new literary movement that was beginning just at that time to transform romanticism into realism.

But nothing from America, in the middle of the century, created such a general sensation as a novel which, from a purely literary point of view, would not seem to be entitled to the highest praise, but which appealed to the noblest sentiments of love and mercy with a pathetic tale so passionate as to sweep aside all other considerations. The book was *Uncle Tom's Cabin* by Harriet Beecher Stowe.

It appeared in the United States in 1852. The same year it was reprinted in England, followed by a couple of scores of other editions, and in the same year was translated into French (both in Belgium and in France), German, Flemish, Swedish, and Italian. The next year translations appeared in Danish, Norwegian, Dutch, Czech, Polish, Slovenian, Hungarian, Rumanian, Spanish, Portuguese, and Welsh. They were shortly followed by translations in Serbian, Armenian, Finnish, Russian, Greek, and Hindustani. All these translations, sometimes many different ones in a single language (for instance, twenty-four in German) went through many and large editions. Besides the complete translations there were many special adaptations for children and young people. It would be impossible to calculate even approximately how many millions of copies of the book have been sold in all countries of the world; it would certainly be very conservative to guess at fifty millions. In the course of the first half year after its publication in England one million copies were sold in that country, and its success was on the same scale in several other countries. The bibliography in Sabin's *Bibliotheca Americana* which fills twenty-five pages, though it gives nothing but the mere titles and registers only first editions, offers but a partial picture of the worldwide triumphal march of the book. Remarkable a piece of work as this bibliography is, it is not complete; for instance, it does not mention a new Norwegian adaptation that appeared as recently as 1908.

This is not the place to discuss the mooted question of the truth of the picture Mrs. Stowe presented of the conditions of the Negro slaves in the South. The people of the South have protested vigorously against the implications and allegations of general cruelty that could be drawn from her book. Very few people in Europe had any opportunity to test the reliability of its presentation as to conditions in general, and, as a matter of fact, I doubt whether they formed any broad conclusions in that regard. They were certainly much more impressed by the merciful girl Eva than by the cruel slave driver. But, no doubt, at the same time they were fortified in their opposition to slavery. At that time, all European people were aroused against the system of slavery as contrary to all considerations of humanity; even the serfdom of the Russian peasants was on the verge of abolition. The most friendly European observers of American institutions were unanimous in condemning slavery. Europeans could hardly understand the arguments of Americans in favor of it. But they did not for that reason imagine the Southerners more cruel than other people. They read and accepted *Uncle Tom's Cabin* as an expression of warm human feelings. They were not primarily interested in it as an attack against slavery. They could not be, simply because the problem of slavery or the colored problem did not exist in their own countries. Therefore the book maintained its appeal and its interest long after slavery in America was completely abolished. It continued to be the most moving sentimental novel about suffering and mercy, simple but genuine in its call for kindness and goodness toward all people of any station or race. That was the reason for the immense popularity of the book.

On the other hand, it fixed the attention of the European nations more than ever before on the acute internal conflict that was rising in America and threatened the very existence of the Union. That was a wide conflict involving mental as well as social questions, and it affected profoundly the European appreciation of America's position in world development. *Uncle Tom's Cabin* was one of the factors that determined how Europeans sided in the new battle of and in America.

VIII

INTERNATIONAL POLITICS AND CIVIL WAR

In the middle of the nineteenth century the European nations and governments manifested a new interest in the United States. They no longer asked merely whether they could make use of American experience as an incitement to or a warning against democratic progress. They became curious about the country for its own sake. American literature became a mass article on the European book market; the year 1852 witnessed the unprecedented success of *Uncle Tom's Cabin* and the start of the *Amerikanische Bibliothek* in Germany. The many editions of Alexander Mackay's *Western World* from 1849 on gave proof that, at least in Great Britain, a large public really wanted factual information about the new power. The wide circulation in many countries of Bancroft's *History of the United States* was a demonstration of the same earnest desire.

There were several reasons for this broad and lively interest. The passionate political discussion about American democracy, combined with the revolutionary movements of 1848, was one of the reasons. Another was the immense increase of emigration to America. Still another reason, which particularly influenced the governments, was the ever more clearly recognized appearance of the United States as a power in international relations. It could not escape attention that, in simple numbers of population, the United States in the course of the 1850's had passed Great Britain. Even before that time, American policies were marked by the consciousness of increasing power.

Obviously, the government and the people of the United States were primarily interested in the peaceful development of commerce and international intercourse. Therefore, it may perhaps be regarded as natural that just at this period an American scholar should become the universal teacher of international law.

124

He was Henry Wheaton, American minister first to Copenhagen, later to Berlin. His *Elements of International Law* (1836) and his *History of the Law of Nations* (1842) were translated into several European languages—French, Italian, Spanish—and remained for half a century the classical textbooks in their domain, as such superseding even more completely in Europe than in America the old Swiss work of Vattel. In particular, Wheaton was an authority on the questions of neutrality which were shortly to attain a prominence in European politics.

Because nobody expected anything but modest and peaceful action on the part of the United States, all of Europe sat up in surprise when its government in 1845, without asking anybody for permission, annexed, or rather accepted, Texas as a member of the Union. Neither Great Britain nor France looked favorably on the act, and the British government even asked the French to join in preventing it. But France refused to go to war for that purpose, and so both powers had to put up with American expansion. Nor did they see any way to interfere in the American war with Mexico which was to terminate with the conquest of California in 1848. "The embarrassments of domestic affairs here will forbid al lBritish or French interference in Mexican affairs"; so reported the historian Bancroft, newly arrived in London as American minister in 1847. The British newspapers, he said, growled savagely at the American military success out of "their own inability to interfere." "It was a hard lesson for England to learn," the Minister concluded, "but she has learned it, that America means to go her own way."

During the same years the American government considered many plans for acquiring Cuba, and when, in 1852, France and Great Britain proposed a joint declaration by which all three governments should disclaim any such intention and even discountenance all attempts by other powers for the same purpose, the United States refused because it would allow of no European intervention in American matters.

During the 1840's and 50's many questions and controversies arose between the United States and Great Britain, and the British government was made to feel that it could not decide them by its own will. The Oregon territory was divided by peaceful settlement in 1846, and when, thirteen years later, upon a disagreement relating to the exact borderline, Lord John Russell on behalf of Great Britain declared that the British proposal for the solution of the question would have to be accepted without compromise, President Buchanan answered that no discussion could be conducted "except upon terms of perfect equality." Finally Great Britain accepted arbitration, and the matter was decided according to the American contention.

In the same way Great Britain was compelled to negotiate with the United States about the limits of British possessions in Central America and to compromise on the question of the construction of a neutralized international canal.

The troubles concerning Central America produced a short exchange of views in the House of Commons one day in 1856. The Prime Minister, Lord Palmerston, said that he wanted to avoid conflicts with the United States, but he could not persuade himself to omit a reference to the naval power of Great Britain. Thereupon the leader of the opposition, Disraeli, expressed his regret at the frequently recurring misunderstandings between the two countries. He warned against the hostility manifested by Great Britain to the legitimate development of American power. It would be wise in England, he said, not to regard with such extreme jealousy the natural expansion of the United States, and "it would be wise if England would at last recognize that the United States, like all the great countries of Europe, have a policy, and that they have a right to have a policy."

In this whole period the United States had no abler and more vigorous Secretary of State than William L. Marcy (1853–57). With Americans generally he has not won the reputation he deserves, but since the days of John Quincy Adams and Henry Clay no maker of American foreign policy maintained with such consistency and energy the independent position of the United States in world politics. He was at the same time an efficient administrator who began the task of organizing a stable foreign service for the country. The most remarkable gain he won for America was that by successive treaties (1854, 1856, and finally

1858) he opened Japan to foreign commerce—an event of universal importance. The European powers followed his lead.

Shortly after he had been appointed Secretary of State, he took up a European question which for a long time had vexed many nations, having been ventilated frequently before by both American and European governments. That was the question of the Danish Sound dues, exacted since the Middle Ages from all ships on their way into the Baltic and maintained by treaty with the European governments even after Denmark had been forced to cede the coast lands east of the Sound to Sweden. The United States had taken over the payment of the dues as a heritage from colonial times, and when, at last, it concluded a treaty of commerce with Denmark in 1826, the continuance of payment was presumed. Now, in 1853, Marcy instructed the American representative in Copenhagen to urge the abolition of the Sound dues; and when the Danish cabinet hesitated and delayed to act on the matter, he, in 1855, denounced the treaty with a term of one year. He took the position that the United States was not legally bound to pay the Sound dues, and he threatened to have American ships pass the Sound without paying where the term of the treaty had expired.

That put Denmark in a precarious situation. Obviously, if it agreed to cancel the Sound dues for the United States it could not easily stop other maritime nations from claiming the same privilege. That would mean a great financial loss to the small nation which, apart from this question, was in a difficult situation owing to the large debts incurred in the recent war with Germany for the preservation of the Slesvig-Holstein Duchies. Denmark thought itself entitled to a substantial compensation for the abandonment of the Sound dues. Accordingly, the Danish government hurried to invite all the interested nations to a congress for the discussion of the whole question.

Unfortunately the letter of invitation stressed the political import of the Sound dues, the part they had played in the politics of the North of Europe and in the balance of power in that part of the world. The question, the Danish government thought, should not be considered merely as one of commerce or money, but as a political one. That gave Marcy the opportunity to declare that "the government of the United States will never consent to the pretension that the *new* world is to be appropriated to adjust the political balance of the old." The United States, he said, had seen enough of the operations of the European theory of the balance of power to be firmly determined "to avoid being brought within its vortex."

At any rate, he would not accept the invitation to the congress because he could not admit the liability of his country to pay any kind of contribution. On the other hand, he did not want to use the legal strength and the superiority of power of the United States to the detriment of a small friendly nation, and he authorized the minister in Copenhagen to promise a liberal allowance from his country as a compensation for what Denmark did for the improvement and safety of the navigation of the Sound and Belts.

It is not necessary here to describe the transactions that followed, the meeting of the congress in 1856, and the final conclusion of an international treaty for the commutation of the Sound dues into a capital payment once and for all, in 1857. The United States kept its promise to pay a voluntary contribution on the same scale as the other nations concerned. All of them were happy that the question had been brought up by American initiative and action. Unhampered by old diplomatic notions and, in particular, unhampered by considerations of balance of power, the American government had taken the lead in this case just as it had done forty years before, without any comparison in other respects, in the matter of tributes to the Barbary States of North Africa.

✿　✿　✿　✿　✿

The negotiations regarding the Sound dues happened to commence just as a new European war, the first between the great powers of Europe since 1815, brought disturbance to both political and commercial relations in the world. The so-called Crimean War brought to the fore again all the questions of neutral rights at sea which had been so burning during the Napoleonic wars and for which the United States had fought so persistently.

This time it was again the American government which sought coöperation with other neutral nations in maintaining the principles of the freedom of the seas for neutral commerce and navigation.* In July of the same year the United States concluded a treaty with Russia regarding the rights of neutrals at sea, founded on the principle that "free ships make free goods," and immediately after, in September, Marcy proposed to other neutral governments an international convention based on the same principle. This proposal, however, did not appear opportune to the countries it was addressed to, and they treated it dilatorily. While it still was under discussion, Marcy had to protest against British violations of American neutrality. The British minister in Washington had used several consulates as recruiting offices for the British army. When Marcy's protests in London were not heeded, the President without further ceremony dismissed the British minister, and the guilty consuls were convicted.

Such occurrences made it urgent for the peace conference in Paris to define the rights of the neutrals and, on April 16, 1856, it adopted the famous declaration that embodied the essential claims of the neutral powers. It contained four articles, two of them confirming the freedom of neutral flags and neutral goods, one requiring blockades to be effective in order to be binding, and one abolishing the use of privateers.

The United States could well regard the three former articles as a victory for principles it had asserted from its foundation. But the fourth one seemed contrary to its traditions and its interests. During the War of Revolution, American privateers had proved highly effective in hampering British commerce, and in treaties of commerce, such as that with Sweden of 1783, renewed in 1827, the United States had obtained recognition of

* As a matter of fact, the Scandinavian kingdoms preceded the United States by their declaration of these principles as a basis of their neutral policies. They relied, however, much on the influence of America in this matter—"a source of proud reflection to an American representative," wrote the chargé d'affaires at Stockholm with a modesty that nowadays appears surprising. The foreign secretary of Sweden and Norway, "delicately," says the same chargé d'affaires, suggested that the United States might support the views of the Scandinavian government in London. American assistance did not become necessary.

the right of its privateers to bring their prizes into the neutral ports of the other country. Marcy was a hard-headed realist, and the chief consideration he now put forward as an objection to the abolition of privateering was based on a hard reality of his country's position—its inferior naval power. Rivalry with Great Britain was one of the main elements in American foreign relations, and if privateering should be forbidden, the commerce and navigation of all smaller powers would be at the mercy of the British navy. This Marcy saw and it was the reason why he would not accept this one article of the Declaration of Paris— except on one condition, namely the addition of an amendment that all private property that was not contraband, even when belonging to belligerents, should go free at sea and be exempt from seizure by armed vessels. This radical proposal, which would have transformed all prevailing principles of warfare, was not accepted by the great Powers of Europe. As a consequence, the United States did not adhere to the Declaration of Paris.

Thus it might appear that the United States remained out of the development of international law. But the American government solemnly declared that it would in future, as previously, conform to the three other rules of the Declaration. A few years later, at the outbreak of the Civil War in 1861, the United States even renounced the right of privateering. Secretary of State Seward tried again to have Marcy's amendment adopted, but did not make it a condition of compliance with the whole Declaration of Paris. The European Powers thus could not complain of wilful obstinacy on behalf of exclusive American ideas. Nevertheless, they did not welcome America very heartily among the great Powers of the world. They looked at it as a disturbing element, and were not at all displeased when internal conflicts seemed to presage a serious weakening of American strength.

*　*　*　*　*

At the moment when the war between North and South claimed all the energies of the United States, Europe was in a period of ardent struggles for liberal ideas. The Crimean War had been generally felt as the final defeat of reactionary tyranny.

It was followed in Russia by the emancipation of the serfs (1861) and by other liberal reforms. Great Britain and France sealed the victory of free trade by their commercial treaty of 1860 which became the model for new treaties between other countries. The National Liberal Party rose to power in Prussia, and national agitation set all of Germany in motion. This made the Slesvig-Holstein question a burning issue again, and threatened the integrity of the kingdom of Denmark. In Sweden the old constitution of Four Estates was staggering towards its downfall; in Norway the forces of democracy were gathering force for new advances. In Southern Europe the thrones of Greece and Spain were tottering before the pressure of revolts. The kingdom of Italy was just established on the basis of a liberal constitution. But still some provinces awaited annexation, and when the government in Washington invited Garibaldi to join the Union army, he refused because he planned to fight for the liberation of the *irredentas*. A labor movement was beginning to raise its head in several countries, particularly in Great Britain, Belgium, Germany, and France, and together with British trade-union friends Karl Marx was planning an international organization of labor. The movement for universal suffrage was soon to become powerful.

Nevertheless the powers of reaction were strong in many parts. When Bismarck took the reins of government in Prussia (1862), he haughtily defied the liberal majority, and after his military triumphs he had the greater triumph of seeing his opponents pass over to his side: in German politics it has always proved more true than anywhere else that "nothing succeeds like success." The Polish rising for freedom in 1863 was defeated, and the confidence in Czar Alexander's liberalism expressed by State Secretary Seward failed to meet the expected response. On the contrary, the battle of Poland inaugurated a new period of reaction in Russia. In Western Europe, however, enthusiasm for the Poles gave new stimulus to popular movements, and it created the opportunity for the founding of the first Workingmen's International.

The Civil War in America appeared to Europe a part of this

universal fight between freedom and oppression. The prospect of victory for the North was conceived by all those interested in the existing state of things as a disturbance of the balance of power both of ideas and of international relations. In January 1862, the American minister sent by Lincoln to St. Petersburg, Cassius M. Clay, pictured the whole political situation produced by the events in America in these words:

The monarchies of Europe have always regarded our republic with jealousy and distrust, because it was an ever-living protest against any other than self-government. They are injured by us, because the immigration to us of men, money, and the arts, is to them a great and increasing loss. They have just cause to fear us, because of our expansion by the acquisition of territory. They say our republic, by "annexation," by which other nations or fragments of nations are united to us, by consent or partial force—by our sharing with them a common liberty—is an advantage which monarchies and aristocracies cannot avail themselves of; that by this means we have already greatly increased our domain; that we threaten the absorption of the isles of the western Atlantic and the Pacific, of Canada, of the Isthmus, of Mexico, and of South America; that our mercantile aptness equals that of England and surpasses that of France and the other nations; that this gives us the power, and they fear the inclination, to interfere at no distant day with European governments, which threatens their ruling classes, and, perhaps, their national existence; that the great European system of the balance of power must now be extended to America; that, perhaps, it would not have been expedient to have made war upon us to weaken us, but that now, we having divided ourselves, self-interest, if not self-preservation, demands that that division should be made permanent. This would give a fatal blow to the prestige of republicanism, and by compelling the two republics to keep up, by onerous taxation, an extensive system of fortifications and standing armies, they would both be too well balanced and too much weakened to disturb others, either by the force of their example or the power of their arms. These are the views and avowals of the European aristocracy, and especially those of England.

Naturally powers who felt themselves injured or endangered by the British dominion of the seas would not deem it an advantage for the United States to become weakened. Even before the outbreak of the war, in January 1861, the American minister in St. Petersburg defined the situation clearly: "Those governments on this side of the Atlantic, who have looked to our republic as the only maritime check in the world upon Great Britain, will not be quite satisfied to see the counterpoise disappear, and that haughty power restored to its old position of mistress of the seas." In fact, after the armed conflict had started, both Czar Alexander and his foreign minister Prince Gortchakoff frankly upheld this view and expressed their hopes for the preservation of the Union. The same was the position of the Prussian government both before and after the accession of Bismarck, and that of the Austrians as well. Of course it has to be taken into account that none of these governments could have any sympathy with rebellion. In Germany, moreover, the aspirations to national unity were felt to be kindred to the American efforts for maintaining the Union; there, a victory for secession would be taken as a blow to national ideas. In both countries the liberals sided with the North; in Russia the emancipation of the serfs appeared to be a close parallel to the struggle for the emancipation of the slaves in America. When Simon Cameron, who had been Lincoln's Secretary of War, came as minister to St. Petersburg in the summer of 1862, he reported home: "There is no capital in Europe where the loyal American meets with such universal sympathy as St. Petersburg; none where the suppression of our unnatural rebellion will be hailed with more genuine satisfaction."

On the other hand, jealousy of American power was manifest in the governments of Great Britain, France, and Spain. In January 1861, the Russian ambassador in London reported that the Englishman "at the bottom of his heart desires the separation of North America into two republics." All three governments declared their neutrality, but they recognized the Confederate States as a belligerent power and watched for an opportunity to acknowledge or establish their independence. It was a serious blow to British trade when, immediately upon the outbreak of hostilities, President Lincoln proclaimed the blockade of the South. The British minister at Washington declared to Seward that it was "a matter of the greatest consequence to England to procure cheap cotton," and the South relied upon "King Cotton" to compel Great Britain to grant full recognition to the Confederacy. By the time the blockade had lasted a year, there was already a cotton famine. The American minister at

The Hague reported on April 30, 1862: "Europe groans daily more and more under the growing dearth of cotton . . . . the cries of England, France, and Belgium are sufficiently audible to attest the severity of the calamity." Hundreds of textile factories closed their doors, hundreds of thousands of workingmen became idle, wages went down, in some departments of Belgium to as little, we are told, as twenty-five centimes (five cents) per day.

Nevertheless there was no unanimity of public opinion in these countries regarding the blockade or the war in America generally. More important than such immediate commercial or economic considerations was, in fact, the political ideology of the parties and classes. Even on the cotton question differences of political ideas manifested themselves very clearly. The historian Motley, who toward the close of 1861 came as American minister to Vienna, after having stopped on his way for some time in England and France, wrote in a report of August 1862: "As the American government is supposed to withhold the cotton which keeps the European mills going, the sympathy of European governments is mainly against the blockading power. A cotton famine is supposed to portend possible popular European commotions." The last sentence reveals the social element in the complaints of the blockade, the fear of a revolution from below. And the truth is that the division of opinion in Europe concerning the American Civil War was largely determined by the political and social affiliations of the persons involved.

American historians have discussed and have presented different views on the true meaning of the conflict between North and South. To contemporary Europe the question presented itself in a very simple form. There it was reduced to the battle between freedom and slavery, for or against democracy. The North stood for freedom and democracy, the South was against both —that was the general idea. Both of the European parties watched with anxiety the outcome of the struggle, expecting victory or defeat for their own ideas. Now as never before there was truth in what Longfellow in poetical presentiment had couched in the majestic lines of his poem, "The Building of the Ship" (1849):

> Sail on, O Union, strong and great!
> Humanity with all its fears,
> With all the hopes of future years,
> Is hanging breathless on thy fate!

The frontiers of the parties could be somewhat blurred by special considerations. There were liberals, such as Gladstone, who thought that the Confederate States must be entitled to secede when they so wished and that it would be neither right nor beneficial to the other states to force them to remain within the Union. On the other hand, there might be people who for purely moral or religious reasons were enemies of slavery. In the spring of 1862, some of the Catholic bishops of France instructed their clergy to pray for the emancipation of the slaves, and in February of the next year, about eight hundred Protestant pastors of France sent an address to all Evangelical pastors in Great Britain against giving support to the partisans of slavery.

In Great Britain the fight against slavery was so recent that memories of it were still living in the minds of the people. Motley, who himself shared the simple conception of the conflict as one between slavery and free labor, tells us in January 1862, that antislavery feeling in England was so strong that it had been necessary for the Southern partisans to persuade the British public that slavery had nothing to do with the American Civil War. "It is gravely asserted," he writes, "by many who pass in the world for reasonable beings, that the secession was brought about by southern opposition to tariffs and by the love of free trade!" He thought at that time that what he calls "this ridiculous notion" had found many believers in Europe. He discovered soon that in this regard he was mistaken. Both his and other reports from Europe demonstrate clearly that democracy, in all senses of the word, was the dividing factor.

The minister at The Hague, an experienced journalist by profession (James S. Pike) wrote in 1862:

Our case in Europe is a very plain one—democracy everywhere supports the federal government; anti-democracy everywhere opposes it. If there be exceptional cases, it is where policy temporarily dominates principle. The rebellion of the slave-holders being a bloody protest against the progress of free principles, it finds itself in union with the reactionary party of Europe, and with its entire aristocracy.

When the new minister appointed by the Lincoln administration came to Madrid in the summer of 1861, he found that the prevalent idea of "the aristocratical and governing classes" was "the notion of an aristocratical and chivalrous society in the south of the United States, armed to resist the aggression of an under-bred, *sans culotte* democracy at the North." But, he said, "aside from the governing classes, the people of Spain are liberal or democratic in their political sentiments and aspirations," and to them the United States was "the model and example of all that is desirable in government." He added that the editors of popular and liberal journals came to him for information, and reproduced in their papers the ideas and statements he conveyed to them. Some time later, he was able to send an address from a large number of citizens of Barcelona in support of President Lincoln.

From Vienna Motley wrote:

To expert aristocratic or royal governments to feel as the American people in regard to this conspiracy of a slaveholding oligarchy against the sovereignty of the people would be unreasonable. The populations sympathize with our cause, and so do the great thinkers and publicists; but politicians would prefer that the great republic should dismember itself quietly in order that Europe should be put to no further inconvenience.

About England in particular he wrote:

Nothing can exceed the virulence with which the extreme conservative party regard us, nor the delight with which they look forward to our extinction as a nation. They consider such a consummation of our civil war as the most triumphant answer which could be made to their own reform party. The hatred to the English radicals is the secret of the ferocity and brutality with which the Times, the Saturday Review, and other tory organs of the press have poured out their insults upon America ever since the war began.

The London *Morning Post*, generally regarded as the mouthpiece of the Prime Minister, Palmerston, declared in February 1862 that "if the Government of the United States should succeed in reannexing them [the Southern States] to its still extensive dominions, Democracy will have achieved its grandest triumph since the world began. . . . And who can doubt that Democracy will be more arrogant, more aggressive, more levelling and vulgarizing, if that be possible, than it ever had been before?"

In words that sound strangely similar to twentieth-century Fascist oratory, the same paper admitted that "many thoughtful Englishmen who have watched, in the policy of the United States during the last twenty years, the foreshadowing of a democratic tyranny compared with which the most corrupt despotisms of the Old World appear realms of idyllic happiness and peace, have gratefully recognized the finger of Providence in the strife by which they have been so frightfully rent asunder."

Almost all the influential papers of England were on this side. But the *Daily News*, a low-priced paper that addressed itself to the broad masses which were not reached by the more fashionable papers and were not represented in Parliament, stood firmly for the North. Harriet Martineau wrote articles for it. John Stuart Mill also came out for the North, and the *Westminster Review* was on the same side. The most active friend of the North was John Bright's *Morning Star*, and during the whole year of 1862 Bright devoted himself almost completely to stirring up labor and radical sentiment in favor of the North. He toured the country speaking for this purpose. After hearing him, a mass meeting in London in January 1862 adopted this resolution:

That in the opinion of this meeting, considering the ill-disguised efforts of the Times and other misleading journals to misrepresent public opinion here on all American questions . . . [and] to decry democratic institutions under the trial to which the Republic is exposed, it is the duty of the working-men especially as unrepresented in the National Senate to express their sympathy with the United States in their gigantic struggle for the preservation of the Union. . . .

Goldwin Smith, a follower of John Bright, and a prominent publicist, appealed to the moral and religious sentiments of his countrymen in his forceful pamphlet *Does the Bible Sanction American Slavery?* John Eliot Cairnes, a friend of J. S. Mill's, published the book *The Slave Power* which has been called "the most powerful defence of the cause of the Northern States ever written." Gradually, public opinion in Great Britain came round to the side of the North.

Perhaps the most remarkable feature of popular opinion in this case is that not only the English working class in general but particularly the textile workers of Lancashire unanimously favored the cause of the North in spite of the sufferings which the war, with the blockade of the South, brought upon them. It is one of the most striking demonstrations of the Marxian doctrine according to which class solidarity is the most decisive factor in shaping parties and opinions, contrary to that false materialism that seeks the reason of all action in narrow economic interests.

The climax of Bright's speaking tour was a meeting called by the Trades Unions of London on March 26, 1863. It was, states the historian of Britain's attitude in this crisis, "the greatest, most outspoken, and most denunciatory to the aristocracy, of the meetings held to support the cause of the North." After Bright, a succession of the leading trade unionists spoke, and young Henry Adams, sent by his father, the minister to London, to cover the meeting, says that with their speeches the real affair began; for it was the true aim of the meeting that the working class of England should announce "by an act almost without precedent in their history the principle that they make common cause with the Americans."*

Such was the general situation in Europe. From all quarters the reports are almost unanimous in contrasting the "ruling classes" to the "masses," the former in sympathy with the Confederacy, the latter favoring the Federal government. The official representatives of the Union felt handicapped by the fact that throughout the whole of Europe English newspapers were dominant while American papers were almost unknown, and news from America came mostly by way of England. According to the rules of diplomacy, the ministers could not easily apply themselves to influencing the press in favor of their government, but they often made the consuls attempt the task. Thus in 1862 a

---

* Ephraim D. Adams, in his *Great Britain and the American Civil War*, II, 291, hesitates a little to accept the tradition that the call for this meeting was really inspired by Karl Marx. This tradition, however, receives strong support from the fact that the first speakers after Bright, the bricklayer Howell and the shoemaker Odgers, were close friends of Marx. Odgers was, some months later, elected the first president of the First International.

Swiss-born consul at Elsinore, Denmark, who had been a journalist in St. Louis (Charles L. Bernays), constituted himself a press agent to furnish German, French, and Swiss newspapers with articles representing the Unionist views. The American government continued to send its consuls for Denmark to Elsinore even after the place had lost its importance by the abolition of the Sound dues, but Bernays soon discovered that Elsinore was "at the very end of the world," and after half a year there he went back to Missouri to work for the Republican party at home. In other places, however, American consuls were more successful and counteracted the English newspapers to their heart's content.

The dissension among the parties was most dynamic in England because there public opinion largely determined the attitude of the government. More than once there was actual danger of conflict between Great Britain and the United States. In the fall of 1861 American naval officers committed the blunder of taking two Confederate delegates from an English mail steamer. The British government requested that they be delivered up, and for a while all Europe was excited over the prospect of war. But Secretary Seward wisely acknowledged the error and complied with the British demand. The incident, which had threatened to range even liberals against the United States, ended by strengthening its prestige. The surrender of the Confederate delegates, wrote the minister at The Hague, "will vastly elevate and improve the position of the United States at every court in Europe. It paves the way for a genuine sympathy in its efforts to subdue the rebellion. . . . Everywhere has it been believed and avowed by ruling classes that at such a crisis a headlong democracy was sure to drive the government into the broad road to national ruin." "The tones of European governments are greatly changed," reported Clay from St. Petersburg. "If England now seeks a quarrel with us," he added, "we will have all liberal Europe on our side."

The many reverses of the Union army during the first two years of the war discouraged the friends of the Federal government, and many European governments began to suggest that it might be wise to make peace. In 1862 the Emperor Napoleon formally proposed to the British government a joint intervention by an offer of mediation, and in the British cabinet a strong party was in favor of accepting the proposal. Palmerston, however, with his strong realistic sense, was not inclined to act upon the impulse of the moment. He wanted to wait and see the further development of the war. He would not risk bad relations with the United States in case of victory for the Union party. The French proposal finally boiled down to a suggestion of armistice, and in order to make it appear less hostile the Russian government was asked to join the action. But Russia refused to join except on the condition that such a suggestion should be agreeable to the United States. A resolution by Congress made it indisputably clear that such would not be the case. And the whole idea had to be abandoned, much to the chagrin of Napoleon, but to the secret delight of his opponents at home. It was one of the signs of his declining power.

Many considerations kept the European powers from interference with the conflict in America. The journalist-diplomat at The Hague, Minister Pike, felt that "in fact, the rulers of Europe may be said to have, more than ever, their hands full of their own concerns." He dramatized the European situation by stating: "There are a number of governments in Europe just now whose stability is reckoned considerably below par." In another report he wrote: "Events are looming both in the north and south of Europe that tend to divert attention from America. . . . So far as the future is concerned, the condition of things in the United States, bad as it is, seems to be stability itself when compared with the rickety state of the political system of Europe. The whole continent is but a pent volcano, with only here and there a standing ground not torn with threatening fissures."

That was in the spring of 1862. And that year saw both revolution in Greece and Garibaldi's march against Rome. Next year the Polish insurrection broke out, and the Slesvig-Holstein question came to a head, ending with the German invasion of Denmark at the beginning of 1864. In both these crises the increasing estrangement between the recently allied Western Powers was publicly demonstrated. That was one feature of a general development that characterized these years—the dissolution of previous alliances, the disturbance of the balance of power by which the peace of Europe was conditioned. Two particular factors had made international relations unstable. One was within Europe itself—the rise of Prussia. Another was the rise, outside of Europe, of the United States. Besides, the ambitious young kingdom of Italy might prove a quantity to be taken into account. In such a situation every power had to be careful not to raise new enemies. Motley was right when he wrote:

> There is a vague idea prevalent that foreign powers, by intermeddling, can put a stop to what they are pleased to call our "wicked and causeless" war. Governments, however, are pretty well aware that foreign interference will only be adding another war to the one already existing.

France was the only power that steadily chafed under the constraint of inactivity. Napoleon felt the ground trembling under his feet, and he had to do something to maintain his prestige. He sought a gain for himself and a loss to the United States by his Mexican enterprise—his expedition to Mexico and the establishment of a puppet emperor there. But the adventure ended in defeat and was abandoned in shame. It proved just another step on his road to decline, and it finally strengthened the position of the United States.

During the first years of the Civil War there were intermittent difficulties with both Great Britain and France, and also with Holland and Spain, regarding privateers armed by the Confederate government. These ships were mostly built or bought in one of these countries; then equipment was sought in one or another of them, or they might seek harbor for repairs in neutral ports. The American government protested vigorously against all protection of such traffic as being contrary to the rules of neutrality, and, somewhat reluctantly, all the governments concerned yielded to the American protests.

Liberal opinion in Europe was brought wholeheartedly over to President Lincoln by the proclamation of emancipation for the Negro slaves within the Confederate States on January 1, 1863. The act was hailed with enthusiasm by all the friends of the United States. It proved to them that the war was really being waged for freedom, and they saw in the act the expression of the determined will of the Federal government to persevere in the war until the goal was reached. It made all plans of interference from abroad impossible. "I doubt," Motley wrote, "if there is a government in Europe that would dare to confront the strong anti-slavery feeling which is entertained by a large majority of the European population."

Then came, in the summer and fall of 1863, the military successes that made the prospects of victory ever more certain, and everywhere liberals and democrats exulted. All those who had felt doubts about the ability of a democratic government to conduct firm policies and keep up the constant efforts needed for a long war were profoundly impressed by the achievements of America. The minister to Berlin, Norman B. Judd, wrote in January 1864:

> The development of the power and strength of republican government as shown in our history for the past two years, and the successful issue of the financial demands attendant upon the enormous expenditure occasioned by the war, surprises all of those who have been accustomed to theorize and form opinions based upon the resources of countries already fully developed, as most of the European states are. Theirs are the theories which always look up to the rulers as the fountain of all power, honor, and emolument, instead of, as with us, looking to the people as the great fountain of power. Our experiences will not only restore, but greatly increase, that confidence in republican institutions that was so rudely shaken in the early part of our struggle with the rebellion.

The year 1864 did not bring victory as early as had been hoped. Again the enemies of the republic began to scent the possibility of its defeat. Still more they felt a malicious satisfaction when, later in the year, they saw the parties in the North split on the election of a president. They pointed to this internal dissension as a sure sign of the natural weakness of a democracy, and they anticipated the defeat of Lincoln which, they thought, would cause the abandonment of the war. His reëlection confounded them. From The Hague wrote Pike:

> Nothing could do more to silence cavillers on this side than the re-election of the President. The moral impression produced by the spectacle of

an orderly and free election in the heat of a great war does more for us than any triumphs in the field. The value to us of the political lesson it teaches to those in Europe who have seen in the apparently confused and conflicting warfare of opinion among the press and public men of the loyal States only the discord of a Babel is not to be overestimated. The civil and military prestige of the nation is to-day at a greater height than it ever was.

The American minister at Madrid expressed himself similarly: "The effect of this event upon Europe can hardly be overestimated." The minister at Brussels, H. S. Sanford, developed the same theme more explicitly in his report of November 25, 1864:

The news of the almost unanimous election of the Union ticket reached here on the 21st, and has made a profound impression here and throughout Europe. It is received and commented on by the public press and in political circles in accordance with sympathies for or hostile to republican institutions. While the organs which represent the latter feeling consider and deplore this result as giving assurance of a prolongation of the war, the representatives of more liberal sentiment hail it as a triumphant vindication of the principles of self-government, and an assurance that the Union has passed safely through its greatest trial, and is to stand as their great exemplar through ages.

All European liberals felt greatly encouraged by this proof of republican strength. From it they expected to gather new forces for their own fight. Sanford reported what they said to him:

The safe issue of the "grande république" from this tremendous struggle would, they assert, have a profound and far-reaching influence in the world; that from it would date a new era of progress and reform in Europe, while its fall would be likely to have a contrary effect, and to cause a reaction from the present liberal tendencies of the age.

Their opponents, on the contrary, seem to dread our success as likely to prepare the way for trouble and revolutions in Europe, as did the successful result of our revolutionary struggle in 1776, and to think that no effort should be spared to avert it; and hence the bitter, unscrupulous, and mendacious course which their organs in the public press have pursued toward us.

A few months later the Confederate army surrendered and the war ended. Liberal and democratic Europe received the news as a victory for itself, and the political speculations founded on the cleavage in the United States were definitely at an end.

But scarcely a week was allowed for enjoying and celebrating the happy event. Closely upon it came the tragic news of the assassination of Lincoln on April 14, 1865.

"Few events of the present century," so reported Charles Francis Adams from London, "have created such general consternation and indignation." And a perusal of newspapers and letters from those days fully confirms this statement. The news came as a terrible shock to Europe as well as to America and everywhere brought consternation and horror—these are words recurring again and again in public and private utterances. The great French monthly *Revue des deux mondes* wrote: "One universal feeling of stupor, indignation, and affliction has followed upon the announcement of this tragedy. . . . We have been, as it were, thunderstruck by the sudden contrast which places such a catastrophe on the morrow of the great and decisive victories obtained by the American government." The word "thunderstruck" reappears in the reports from other countries as well.

At the present date it is difficult to conceive that a political murder could rouse such general commotion. Our times have experienced too many much worse crimes, nor were similar deeds unknown before 1865. But there was a glaring and profoundly felt contrast between the cheerful news of the first week of April and the sad report of the middle of the month. People in Europe had identified themselves so completely with the contest of universal ideas in America as to be equally afflicted by losses as cheered by successes. "Lincoln represented," it was said in a French newspaper, "the cause of democracy in the largest and most universal acceptance of the word." And then his murder seemed so unreasonable, so senseless. The words his assassin had shouted: *Sic semper tyrannis!* appeared such a cruel caricature as applied to this mild and modest man. People had read and admired Lincoln's magnanimous speeches of reconciliation. They had imagined that a man who amid the conflict could speak "with malice toward none, with charity for all" would be the best hope of the Confederates for the future and could be hated by nobody. When his murder was announced, many people at first could not believe it, so incredible did it seem. John Bright's *Morning Star* wrote:

The appalling tragedy which has just been perpetrated at Washington is absolutely without historical precedent. Not in the records of the fiercest European convulsion, in the darkest hour of partisan hatreds, have we an example of an assassin plot at once so foul and so senseless, so horrible and so successful, as that to which Abraham Lincoln has already fallen a victim, and from which William H. Seward can hardly escape. Only in such instances as the murder of William of Orange, of Henri Quatre, or of Capodistria, have we any deed approaching in hideous ferocity to that which has just robbed the United States of one of the greatest of their Presidents.

When Lincoln had first been elected president, he was even more unknown to Europe than to the American nation, and, like the Americans, Europeans looked to Secretary of State Seward as the leading man of the new administration. In English newspapers in particular, Lincoln had steadily been caricatured as the uncouth rail-splitter, a man without genteel manners and higher culture. Only after the proclamation of emancipation did people become aware of his true personality, and more and more they came to see him as the great leader. At his death his real worth suddenly dawned upon the whole world.

Perhaps no one was ever so widely and so profoundly mourned as this American president. The greatness of America seemed embodied in this single man. Truly the *Revue des deux mondes* stated that the spontaneous burst of sorrow that occurred "is not only an imposing homage rendered to a noble victim; it is a pledge of sympathy given by the world to the United States." It was even more: another French publication said that the demonstrations in all parts of Europe "show how extremely popular the ideas of liberty and equality have become, as they are represented by the United States. Over the ashes of the President of the American republic the whole of Europe has come to confess her democratic faith."

Governments and diplomats hurried to express their sympathy officially—that was a matter of course. But they were joined by the representatives of the peoples. Speeches of homage and grief were heard, resolutions of sorrow and indignation were adopted by the parliaments and legislative assemblies of Great Britain, France, Spain, Portugal, Belgium, the Netherlands, Prussia, the Hansa cities—wherever such institutions were assembled. The liberals of France, headed by Jules Favre, sent a special address of sympathy on their own behalf. American legations and consulates everywhere were flooded with calls of individuals and delegations, with letters and addresses from private people, from civil and religious societies, from freemasons' lodges in France, from municipal boards in all parts of the British Empire, from liberal and democratic organizations, from chambers of commerce, from workingmen's associations in England and Italy, from the International Working Men's Association (signed, among others, by Karl Marx), from students' and women's organizations in Italy. Poems were written in many languages, even in Latin. It was a world in grief.

Among the poems was one of an especially noteworthy character by Henrik Ibsen. It was not a tribute to Lincoln; its subject was rather the movement that followed upon the murder and the impact of the event on the future of Europe.* Ibsen asked:

> Thou Europe old, with order and law,
>   With maxims that never fail,
> With an unstained name, without blemish or flaw,
> With a virtue that keeps all meanness in awe,
>   Why grew'st thou so strangely pale?

He recognized the hypocrisy and fear behind the moral indignation. He saw how Englishmen, Frenchmen, and Germans —personified as "the cotton magnate, *gloire's* proud son, the men from the land of lies"—had taken the peace for granted, but then were shocked out of their assurance by the shot over in America. He scorned them for trying to make believe that such a crime was foreign to them—didn't they remember the Prussian assault on Denmark, their own callousness at the rising of the Poles?

* I quote from a translation by Thorkild A. Schovelin in the monthly *Scandinavia*, published in Chicago (July 1884).

In fact, he said, the Great Powers themselves had prepared the ground for murders and bloody deeds:

> With promises broken, with faiths betrayed,
>   With contracts that naught secure,
> With last year's oaths this year gainsaid,
>   You did History's ground manure.

Thus the guilt was partly theirs:

> You placed with your most gracious hand
> Martyrdom's blood-red badge on the grand
>   Abraham Lincoln's breast.

Ibsen had no mercy for them. On the contrary, he desired the progress of the forces that were undermining the existing political system. He was the prophet of catastrophe. He thought that only a complete revolution could clear the ground for a new society, and that such a revolution would not come before the evil consequences of current politics showed themselves in their full horror:

> Let the worm gnaw on;—till he empties the shell,
>   Nor walls nor roof will decay.
> Let the "system" but work its ruin well;
> The sooner Revenge will its judgment tell
>   On Falsehood's latest day.

Ibsen was not the only theorist of catastrophe at that time; Karl Marx proclaimed the same idea on the basis of historical philosophy. History has not accepted it except with many qualifications. At any rate, Ibsen's contemporaries did not want to see the "system" work itself out to its ultimate consequences. On the contrary, they united their forces as strongly as possible in the fight for freedom.

No doubt the Civil War in America influenced and encouraged political progress in Europe, not only by what was conceived as a triumph for democracy, but by sharpening the conflict between the ideas of freedom and servitude. As early as the summer of 1862, Pike wrote from The Hague that it appeared to him natural that the attitude of the reactionaries towards American events should "engender a new stimulus to the revolutionary temper of these old countries." In Holland he witnessed the over-

throw of a long-lived conservative regime by a new liberal majority and the appointment of a liberal cabinet. Then the bill that
abolished slavery in the Dutch colonies finally carried.

In Sweden, where the question of constitutional reform, the
replacement of the Diet of Four Estates by a modern Riksdag,
had been sleeping through the 1850's, it was raised again before
the Estates of 1862–63, and the royal cabinet laid before them a
proposal for the establishment of a two-chamber system, formed
partly on the Danish, partly on the American model. Some pre-
paratory reforms of a democratic character were voted in 1863,
but the new Riksdag plan came to a decisive vote only in December 1865. Then it was adopted in spite of strong resistance.
The American minister in Stockholm wrote in his report: "Who
shall not say that the great example of our own beneficent institutions has not had much to do with this, and other liberal efforts
in various directions?"

If, in this case, the direct influence of the American struggles
may be doubtful, it certainly exerted itself with full power in
Great Britain. There the pressure for democratic reform, and particularly for universal suffrage, mounted together with the movement for friendship with the United States. The parliamentary
elections of July 1865 spelled victory for the one as well as the
other. They not only gave the liberal government a much larger
majority than expected, but increased to a great extent the radical
element within this majority and compelled the cabinet to pro-
pose a much broader extension of the suffrage than it had originally planned. When Charles Francis Adams reported on the
issue of the elections, he pointed out that all the former members of Parliament who had frankly professed their friendship
for the American democracy were reëlected (John Bright, for instance stood without opposition), and new members of the same
orientation had been added, the most distinguished of them
being John Stuart Mill. As to the importance of the result and its
connection with American affairs Adams made these reflections:

It is not unfair to infer that the termination of our struggle has not
been without its effect on this result. At the time when I first reached this
country, in 1861, the character of the elections, then taking place, to fill

casual vacancies, was such, in consequence of the general impression that the "bubble of democracy had burst in America," as to fill the conservatives with hopes of what they denominated a strong reaction. It was this feeling which really lay at the root of all their views of our struggle. Had the Parliament been dissolved at any time prior to July, 1863, there can be little doubt that it would have had a considerable effect on the issue. As it is, I cannot resist the belief that this period marks an era in the political movement of Great Britain. Pure old-fashioned conservatism has so far lost its hold on the confidence of the country that it will not appear in that guise any more. Unless some new and foreign element should interpose, I look for decided progress in enlarging the popular features of the constitution, and diminishing the influence of the aristocracy. Already the great increase of wealth in new hands, outside of its limits, has much diminished its relative importance in the social scale, and driven it to the necessity of husbanding its accumulations to keep pace with this late competition. The extraordinary deference formerly paid to mere rank, without regard to personal qualities, is much worn away. It is impossible not to perceive traces of the influence of our institutions upon all these changes. Hence the deep interest which has been taken in all quarters in the events that are happening in America.

In a later report he observed:

The bugbear held up on all occasions is the Americanizing the old English institutions. Nevertheless, it is tolerably evident that to a certain extent Americanized they will be, if the proof continues to flow in that America furnishes the best example of a successful application of the true principles of government to the advancement of the human race.

A clear evidence of the part America played in the new British reform movement is offered by the fact that Tocqueville's work on American democracy was on this occasion again vividly discussed in Great Britain. The opponents of democracy tried to employ the book for their purposes, but, no doubt, the democrats had the better of the argument.

On the whole, it may be truly asserted that the fight and victory of the democratic forces in America conveyed new strength to the democratic movement in Europe. Liberals and republicans in France found new support for their ideas. Democrats in Norway learned to direct their energy to the consolidation of their demands into firmly planted institutions.

Minister Adams was animated with a strong consciousness of the responsibility which in this situation rested on the American nation. "The progress of the liberal cause," he wrote, "not in England alone, but all over the world, is, in a measure, in our hands." America, he thought, must show itself worthy of the trust and hopes of liberal Europe and not give reasons for disappointment.

It has to be admitted that American government during the next years after the Civil War was not such as to evoke admiration and call for imitation. Fortunately by this time European democracy was mature enough to bear such disappointment and to continue its fight even without encouragement from America. After a while, however, this came back again.

Incidentally, the Civil War in America produced an important change in naval warfare. The famous duel between the Confederate *Merrimac* and the Federal *Monitor* in 1862 convinced the maritime powers and all naval men that the days of the old sailing warships, frigates and ships of the line, were numbered. From now on, the superiority of steamers and ironclads was clear. It was fitting that Sweden, the homeland of the builder of the *Monitor*, John Ericsson, was the first European country to start the building of new monitors. Other countries followed and even improved on the original model. Within a few years all the navies of the world were modernized on the new pattern.

Perhaps still more far-reaching in its consequences was an aftermath of the Civil War affecting the peaceful relations of all nations. It grew out of the strife that followed the American claims to damages for the ravages inflicted by the famous privateer *Alabama*, Captain Semmes, built and equipped in England for the Confederate States. It was a resounding triumph for law and justice in international affairs when this matter finally was left to arbitration and Great Britain bowed to the finding of the court in favor of America. No case of arbitration had ever evoked such a world-wide sensation, and it gave an immense stimulus to the idea of international arbitration. The same treaty (concluded in Washington on May 8, 1871) that decided the arbitration of the *Alabama* claims also materially extended the laws of neutrality during war. Thus, by the efforts of America new hopes were created for the establishment of a system of international justice.

The vivid effect of the news of the *Alabama* judgment is perpetuated by one of the stories of the great Swedish author August Strindberg, included in his *Utopias in Real Life*. There it is made the dramatic climax of the battle of a soul who has gone through war; it suddenly appears as the ray of light that breaks through the dark night of hate, bringing the welcome tidings that war is no longer inevitable.

IX

ECONOMIC POWER

THE Civil War led the United States into new economic policies which, supplementing the immense economic progress of the nation, brought with them considerable changes in the economic life and policies of Europe.

American production and commerce had played a considerable part in the world's economy in colonial times. Even then the British colonies in North America had been in many respects an independent economic power, not merely a dependency of British capital. The shipbuilding and sea trade of New England were in the hands of a domestic commercial and industrial class. The tobacco and cotton growers of the South gradually made themselves masters of their production. After 1815, when the long period of war was at an end, a steady progress went on in all economic fields, in agriculture and manufactures, in commerce and shipping. At the middle of the nineteenth century the United States was the third nation in the world's commerce, ranging behind only Great Britain and France, and its merchant marine was second in the world, having come close to that of Great Britain.

With political independence, one of the first tasks of American government became the establishment of economic policies. As a matter of course, the old mercantilistic system was quashed. But, after 1815, the young manufacturing interests demanded protection, and the tariff was consistently used for protectionist purposes. The southern states, which based their economic life mainly on exports, reacted vigorously against this development, and in 1846 succeeded in enacting a tariff that would put an end to protectionism, at least in its more extreme forms. This was simultaneous with the abolition of the Corn Laws in England. Both events seemed to inaugurate an age of free trade. The United States immediately followed up the new tariff with commercial treaties founded on reciprocity, and Secretary of State

Buchanan was justified in affirming that this was "the commence-ment of a new era in our policy in this particular."

This statement is to be found in instructions sent in 1847 to the recently appointed American *chargé d'affaires* at Stockholm, Henry W. Ellsworth. Through its representative there the American government made strong efforts to bring Sweden over to the same liberal principles that now had won ascendancy in the United States. During the Riksdag of 1847–48, Ellsworth worked closely with leading Swedish liberals in urging the adoption of tariff reform, and it is strange that Buchanan threatened retali-atory measures if Sweden did not comply. His free trade ideas seem not to have permeated his thought completely, since he could think of employing the principles of the old navigation acts to the detriment of Sweden if that country would not grant ex-tensive privileges to American commerce and navigation. He asserted that there was no true reciprocity established by the existing treaty of commerce, because equality of rights between a big and a small country gave more advantages to the small than to the big one. He meant that the "superior advantages" which trade with the great and rich United States offered ought to be compensated for by "fair equivalents" in reductions of the Swed-ish tariff rates. Although the liberal forces in Sweden were not yet strong enough to achieve the desired reductions, Buchanan's threat of abrogating the treaty was not carried out.

It took a long time to bring Sweden over to the liberal line in economic policies. Both the pressure and the example of America, however, exerted their effect. When finally the last remainders of mercantilism were swept away from the Swedish regulations of commerce on January 1, 1864, the merchants of Gothenburg, who had been in the vanguard of the battle for economic liberalism, celebrated the victory by a festival at which they "rejoiced that Sweden could now take her place side by side with America in the march of free trade."

At that moment, however, America had swung over to the other side. But for a decade and a half it had stood with Great Britain for free trade and had influenced all of Europe in the di-rection of that policy. Under British leadership the 1860's were the heyday of economic liberalism in Europe, while America returned to a protectionism more thorough than ever before. That, too, came presently to influence Europe.

The change in America occurred in 1861 when, under the pressure of war demands, Congress voted a high tariff intended to increase the public revenues. Several European governments, particularly those of Great Britain, France, and Belgium, complained because of the impediments put in the way of the exportation of their manufactures. Secretary Seward answered in 1862 with a note in which he affirmed that the new tariff rates were occasioned only by the necessities of war. The American government itself, he said, seriously regretted that it had been compelled to adopt this measure. He even tried to turn the tables against the European governments who had encouraged the war of "the slaveholders" by giving them the privileges of belligerents and persuading them to expect armed alliances and intervention. "Thus," he said, "the European states have morally upheld the slaveholders in the destruction of the whole system upon which the policy of low tariffs in this country was built." And in speaking of this "system" he hinted at considerations that might lead to the introduction of a new system. He wrote:

> For half a century we maintained a low tariff on foreign imports. Why? Our slaveholders employed themselves and their slaves in producing surplus cotton for exportation, and a low tariff enabled European manufacturers to purchase that surplus, while we received payment for it in their productions.
>
> A year ago the slaveholders abandoned their peaceful practice of producers of cotton, relinquished the cultivation of it and devoted all their own energies, with the labor of their slaves, to civil war, designed to overthrow this government and betray the country to the rule of foreign powers. As a military policy they destroy the cotton already in hand and cover their fields with Indian corn instead of cotton. Of course we can send much less, practically no cotton to Europe. How then could we pay for European products? Certainly only in gold and grain. We do this cheerfully, but we acquire the ability to do it only by manufacturing whatever we can make for ourselves.

Although Seward maintained that the increase of duties was "a purely revenue measure" and that with the defeat of the insurrection, which the European governments could advance by changing their attitude, America would "return, so far as is now possible, to the habits it heretofore pursued," he had notwithstanding pointed to the possibility that America might feel compelled to pay for its importations by doing its manufacturing itself. This idea became paramount after the end of the war. The tariff not only was not lowered again, but was steadily raised over a long period of years. America became the leading protectionist country of the world.

*   *   *   *   *

Obviously the rise of America as an independent economic power could not but mean a great deal to the world at large and to Europe in particular. The economic ties between America and the other nations would naturally become strengthened and multiplied. During the first half of the nineteenth century, American commerce was largely bound up with Great Britain; a full half of the American exports consisted of cotton, mostly shipped to the English textile factories. Around the middle of the century, however, many facts demonstrate that America was becoming a considerable factor in general European economic life. It is significant that while the panic of 1837, which was so violent in America, was set off by bank failures in England, the panic of 1857 started in the United States and spread to Europe. It is noteworthy too that the first great private banks founded in the Scandinavian countries in the 1850's were organized on the American pattern.

In the 1860's the development of American wealth and production was so gigantic as to make the country one of the greatest determining forces in the world's economic life. It was a development of immense extent in almost all domains of economic activity. The only remarkable exception was the decrease in the part American shipping took in the world's commerce; American capital found more profitable employment in other fields of investment and left much of the shipping business to other nations, such as the British and the Norwegian. The full exploitation of domestic natural wealth became the task of American energy. By virtue of natural wealth and human energy alike, America rose to be the leading nation in all the main branches of production.

First in agriculture. The chief event in this field was the speeding up of the conquest of the West. To a great extent this was the work of immigrants from Europe, and starting with the 1860's immigration was immensely accelerated. It was indeed demanded by America. It is at first sight a startling fact that, amid the Civil War, the American government should begin to call for immigrants. It was simply the easiest way of solving the manpower problem. The immigrants were wanted to replace the men called to the colors. In 1862 the State Department sent instructions to the American consuls abroad to go in actively for the promotion of emigration from the countries where they were stationed. They were authorized and directed to make it known in all quarters that "nowhere else can the industrious laboring man and artisan expect so liberal a recompense for his service as in the United States." The Department presumed that the knowledge of "this truth" would be sufficient reason to persuade such people to come.

The most effective reason was the Homestead Act adopted that year. The origin of this law was to be found in the demand of the laboring classes in America itself for the opening of land for them, and it resulted in a considerable movement of people from east to west. Still more did it appeal to the laboring classes abroad, particularly in the north of Europe—Great Britain and Ireland, Germany, and the Scandinavian nations. When, after the Civil War, the Federal government abandoned its direct efforts for immigration, several of the individual states continued the work. And the Homestead Law remained in force as the strongest encouragement of all. Many consuls proved active in procuring land and work in advance for intending emigrants. Thus, as consul in Birmingham, Elihu Burritt was largely instrumental in forming the International Land and Labor Agency for the assistance of emigrants.

In 1863 the number of immigrants began to mount after a decrease which started in the middle of the 50's, and after the end of the war it averaged during the 60's more than 300,000 annually; during the 70's a little less; during the 80's more than 500,000; during the 90's more than 350,000. The great mass of all these millions went to the West and helped build up the prairie states. The cultivation of wheat and corn grew to such an extent as to rival cotton in the exports of the country.

The freedom and opportunities of the United States began at this time to attract people from nations who previously had thought little of emigrating—Russian Jews, Poles, Czechs, Hungarians, Italians. Toward the end of the century some of these nations sent the largest numbers of immigrants ever to migrate to America. They were not, however, so predominantly agricultural as were the immigrants from northern and western Europe. They settled down mainly in the urban centers and increased the industrial population of the country or went in for business enterprise. They helped make America a business nation.

The new wave of emigration provoked further discussion in the European countries concerning the causes and the measures to take to remove those causes. At the moment the Civil War was closing, the American minister in Stockholm reported:

> The subject has created alarm among landed proprietors and governing classes. In the country meetings have been held by employers complaining that young laboring men are leaving the Country, and insisting that Government should take steps to prevent an exodus of the people so detrimental to landed and productive interests. . . . Again political partisans seize the occasion to turn the feeling to their own account. Those who may be styled Liberals insist that the cause of the immigration is to be found in the laws of the country which, they urge, among other things, oblige the citizen to pay taxes to support a state religion his conscience does not approve of, and that while the Country is poor, and wages low, public burdens are onerous.

Five years later another minister at the same place wrote:

> It seems to me the emigration is beneficial to Sweden in arousing increasing attention to the condition of the poorer class of people, in fixing responsibility for the same, and in raising inquiries as to the means of improving their condition. As evidence of this I would mention that a convention of working men is to meet in Stockholm the 30th instant [June

1870]; and among its announced topics for consideration are an increase of wages, and the means of arresting the emigration to the United States.

Evidently the discussion by degrees reached deeper down into the true causes of emigration, and all the different aspects of labor and land questions came up for consideration. The chief reasons why these questions at that time became so burning lay in the internal development of the countries, particularly in the advancing industrialization. The 1870's and 80's, therefore, witnessed the first comprehensive measures of labor legislation and the establishment of social security. Certainly the emigration helped lay the social evils bare to public opinion and emphasized the urgency of state action. Clearly, however, none of the measures adopted was able to stop the emigration; in that regard, they appeared to be mere palliatives without serious efficacy. The simple fact was that the opportunities offered by America were infinitely more favorable than the conditions to be found in any European country. And for a long time yet the emigration itself contributed to increase the difference in favor of America by developing the rich natural resources of that country.

*　*　*　*　*

The manufacturing industries of America experienced a growth parallel to, or even surpassing, that of agriculture. Again the natural wealth of the country was the basis of this rapid rise. It became manifest that in the production of raw materials for industry America was leading all other countries. That had long been true as to cotton; now it proved true as to such basic materials as coal, iron, and copper. Besides this natural wealth it is again necessary to stress the spirit of ruthless enterprise prevailing in the American society. It was not hampered by many old traditions, and it need not consider much the human aspects of labor as long as the country was so open for all able-bodied and industrious people. Here prevailed a habit of thinking in terms of machinery; here it was natural to seek all kinds of labor-saving devices. The Civil War had made many new demands for organizing industry, for instance in the establishment of shoe factories and garment shops. The settling of the West required increasing numbers of agricultural machines. Ever larger quantities of domestic cotton were consumed by the country itself. By 1860 the capital invested in manufactures was calculated to amount to one billion dollars. At the close of the century it had risen to ten billions. The value of manufactured products was by 1860 estimated at two billions of dollars. By 1900 it was thirteen billions, and it exceeded by far the value of agricultural products.

This immense growth in production made possible a large expansion of foreign trade. It must be noted that during this period the commerce of other countries was also rising, in many cases even relatively more than that of the United States. As a consequence, America's proportion in the world's trade remained about the same, amounting to about one-tenth of the entire exchange of goods. That was by itself a very large proportion, only surpassed by two and occasionally three other nations (Great Britain, France, Germany). But in America's portion exports exceeded imports very considerably. American articles were in increasing demand everywhere, and the economic power of America was steadily rising.

The growth of American trade made it urgent to improve the conditions of shipping goods across the Atlantic, and the improvements achieved accelerated the growth of trade. In the 1870's ocean freight costs were greatly reduced because steam was substituted as a motive power for sail, bigger ships were built, and iron construction replaced wood. Furthermore, trade was stimulated by the vast quantities of gold that came from the new mines of California and Australia. The United States had in 1849 exported two million dollars of gold; ten years later it exported sixty millions. Later it was able to keep most of the gold in its own hands so as to strengthen the national economy.

By 1870 American exports reached a total value of almost 400 million dollars. Still, more than half the exports consisted of articles that would serve as material for foreign manufacture. Chief among them was cotton, but iron ores and other articles played an increasing part. The exportation of such articles was steadily mounting during the following decades, but much more slowly than that of other goods, so that by 1900 they constituted less than a fourth of the entire exports.

Foodstuffs, in crude form or to some extent processed, were in 1870 exported to a value of a little more than 70 millions; wheat and meat were the main articles under this heading. Only ten years later the exportation of such articles had mounted to 460 millions. Although prices went down, the value of these exports in 1900 was about 550 millions. It is to be noted that, during this later period, the proportion of manufactured food-stuffs was increasing more than that of crude stuffs. That was a sign of the mounting importance of American manufacturing.

Manufactures in the strict sense of the word were almost without importance in the exports of America during the first half of the nineteenth century. In 1860 they did not amount to more than 47 million dollars, which was 15 percent of the entire exports. Their real growth came only in the 1880's, when they increased from 122 to 179 millions, and almost explosively in the 1890's, ending in 1900 with a value of 485 millions, or 35 percent of all exports. In 1898, for the first time, American exports of manufactures exceeded the imports of articles of the same class. At that time manufactured goods had become the greatest item in American exportation. The entire exports had in 1900 a value of 1,371 millions, more than four times as much as in 1860.

Such an immense exportation naturally made itself heavily felt in the other countries. Consumers abroad undoubtedly bene-fited by cheap American goods—cheap because they were produced in such large quantities and by the use of labor-saving machines. But foreign producers could not feel equally happy, for many of them were ruined by American competition.

The effect first manifested itself in agriculture. From the 1860's to the beginning of the twentieth century, the cost of transportation of a bushel of wheat from Chicago to Liverpool went down from 37 cents to 10 cents. The price of wheat sank gradually from $1.90 per bushel in the 1860's to $1.55 in the 70's, $1.00 in the 80's, and $0.70 in the 90's. The movement was has-tened by the panic of 1873. During the depression that followed, all kinds of cheap American goods were dumped on the European market, manufactures as well as foodstuffs. For European agriculture it ushered in a grave crisis. Only Russia was able to meet the competition of American grains, and she did so only by lowering the standard of living of her peasantry. The grain growers of Western Europe could not hold their own against such an invasion, and, as a consequence, agriculture changed from grain-growing to cattle-raising. That holds particularly true for Great Britain and the Scandinavian countries. In many parts of Germany and France sugar beets replaced grains. These other operations, however, required less labor, and this became a new reason for the rural population to emigrate. From a European point of view this movement constituted a vicious circle: American grain produced emigrants, emigrants produced more American grain.

European governments found themselves driven to protect their agriculture as far as possible. In Great Britain the manufacturing and commercial interests were so strongly entrenched that they could resist the complaints of the farmers; until the new century began, the British government left the farmers to shift for themselves. Seafaring Norway, which could not produce grain enough for its own consumption anyway, kept for a time to the same line. Denmark proved able to make cattle-raising, with the production of meat and butter, extremely profitable, largely by importing American corn and other feeds, and remained a free-trade country. The rest of Europe followed the example of America and passed over to policies of protectionism. Germany was first, raising its tariff duties in 1879. In 1882 France refused to renew the commercial treaty with England and then raised the duties on all farm products. The same year saw the victory of high-tariff policies in Austria-Hungary, Spain, and Portugal. The wave of protectionism practically engulfed the whole continent.

The agrarian interests took the leadership, but very soon they were joined by the manufacturers. In the course of the second half of the nineteenth century all of Western Europe became industrialized. The young industries there suffered under both British and American competition. As early as the 1880's the manufacturers raised the cry for protection. Thus tariff walls again divided the nations of the world.

America did not seem to suffer. It was still able to increase its exports. Its wealth and economic power advanced by leaps and bounds. In the last year of the century, an American historian, Brooks Adams, published a book entitled *America's Economic Supremacy*. All signs, he thought, indicated such a result of the international development.

X

THE AMERICAN TECHNIQUE

In 1902, Brooks Adams wrote in *The New Empire:*

American supremacy has been made possible only through applied science. The labors of successive generations of scientific men have established a control over nature which has enabled the United States to construct a new industrial mechanism, with processes surpassingly perfect. Nothing has ever equalled in economy and energy the administration of the great American corporations. These are the offspring of scientific thought.

Scientific thought consistently applied to every domain of human activity, and especially to industry and business, came to distinguish American life. When Björnstjerne Björnson, the Norwegian poet and prophet of life, was in America in 1880–81, he was particularly struck and pleased by the speed and convenience of everything American. He noticed the innumerable small gadgets for the facilitation of household work and, as a practical farmer, he observed how "everything used in agricultural and daily work surpasses what is used in Norway." "We are mere beggars and small boys compared with people here," he declared.

What was true in 1880 was still more so half a century or more later. American ingenuity had changed and eased daily life everywhere in the world as its creations were adopted by other nations. A hundred years ago it gave the sewing machine to the women. Since then it has given us all kinds of agreeable contrivances—safety pins, refrigerators, vacuum cleaners, elevators, safety razors, fountain pens, cheap watches, phonographs, and what not. That is an Americanization of life which nobody complains of. Besides, there is all the inexhaustible service electricity has been put to. Who would be ungrateful for it?

The chief factor that has made all these good things accessible to all people is the American system of standardization. The idea of introducing this system into the manufacture of machine-made goods was not original with the Americans. But in human progress it is less important to point out who first thought of one or another improvement than to state who first did it. In this, as in so many other cases, the Americans were the first to act on the idea.

It goes back to the very beginning of the nineteenth century, and it was given birth by the severe mother of human resourcefulness: war. Eli Whitney, the inventor of the cotton gin, was the founder of the new system in his shop for the manufacture of firearms in Connecticut. There he instituted the practice of making up in thousands every single part, all exactly alike and therefore able to replace each other whenever needed. This was the principle of interchangeability which was thus introduced into American manufacture. And it was this principle that made all large-scale production possible and could make production cheap. It was the principle of the division of labor, so strongly stressed by Adam Smith as the basis of modern industry, now carried out to its full consequences. It was to give rise to the peculiarly American reliance upon the machine for precision and speed.

For half a century, however, American manufacture was so little developed as to feel no need of adopting this system more generally. It continued, however, and was gradually perfected in the production of firearms. Especially was it developed by Samuel Colt, the inventor of the revolver, in his factory, also in Connecticut. He had his decisive success in the Mexican War (1846–48). Colt was the man who took the system to Europe. At the World's Fair of 1851 he was less appreciated by the experts than by the public. But he gave a lecture on his ideas before the London Institute of Civil Engineers, and was elected the first American member of that distinguished institution. In 1853 he ventured to start a shop of his own in London. The state of arms manufacture in England at that time was still such as described by the *Edinburgh Encyclopedia* of 1830:

The manufacture of a gun is performed by the following workmen, viz.: barrel forger, borer and filer, lock forger and filer, furniture filer, ribber, and breecher, rough stocker, screwer together, polisher and engraver, in all ten different persons, few of whom can execute any branch of the art but one.

All these workmen were artisans and worked by hand. Colt brought over American machines, and in his factory he employed more than fifteen times ten in bringing a single pistol to perfection. In London he found that when he hired skilled men for his work, they were unable to discard their former habits of handwork and adapt themselves to the machines. He had to find intelligent unskilled workers; they conformed much better to the task. He had hardly established himself in London when the Crimean War broke out, whereupon he sent a letter to the British Board of Ordnance to tell them that by his system of manufacture firearms could be produced both better and cheaper than by the old methods. In consequence he was called before a special parliamentary committee on small arms and was thoroughly examined by its members. That was in March 1854, and it was the meeting between old and new ideas. Some few questions and answers from this hearing will illustrate the direction of thinking:

"Do you consider that you make your pistols better by machinery than you could by hand labor?"—"Most certainly."

"And cheaper?"—"Much cheaper."

"Do you consider that the muskets manufactured by machinery in America are as well fabricated as the Minié rifle which has been submitted to you?"—"There is none so badly made at *our* national armories as the Minié rifle shown to me; that arm would not pass one of our inspectors. . . ."

"Are the Committee to understand that the fault which you find with the Ordnance is, that one arm is not like the other?"—"That is the very thing I find fault with in the arms I have seen here; there is more difference between one and another when they are made by hand, than there can possibly be when they are made by machinery. A machine tells better for uniformity than hand labor does; the eye cannot control the hand sufficiently to imitate a machine; it is the uniformity of the work that is wanted. . . ."

The members of the committees were so impressed by Colt's statements that they resolved to visit his factory in America. After having seen it, they were fully convinced of the superiority of his system, and according to their recommendation the British government ordered a full set of American machines for the manufacture of arms in the Royal Small Arms factory at Enfield, England. They even brought American workmen and foremen across the sea to set up and run the machines. That was the start of the system of standardization in European manufacture.

Colt became a famous man in Europe. He received gifts of honor from the Czar of Russia, the Sultan of Turkey, and the King of Sardinia. At the next international exhibition in London, in 1862, he was given an honorary medal. In 1863 President Lincoln sent elaborately ornamented pistols of Colt's revolving pattern as presents to the kings of Denmark and of Sweden and Norway.

More important, the principle of standardization gradually established itself in Europe. There sprang up a demand for American tools and machines, and the exportation of them became an increasing part of American commerce. In almost every new field of manufacture, however, the Americans were in the vanguard of standardization and mass production. It was and remained the truly American technique, and cheap American products flooded the European markets. As early as the 1850's, an American who had watched the methods of firearms construction transferred them to the construction of watches and founded the first factory in that branch, which was followed by many others. After the Civil War, American factory-made shoes found their way to Europe and began to crowd out the old shoemakers. It was still several decades before shoe factories were founded in the European countries, but when they were, they followed the American models.

A British parliamentary committee that went to America in 1854 to study the organization of manufacturing establishments there reported many features in which American industry was superior to British. The committee was struck by the "admirable system," everywhere adopted, in the selection and adaptation of tools and machinery and in the effort to make the special tools and contrivances needed for the most economical and effectual work. "The contriving and making of machinery," the committee wrote from America, "has become so common in this country, and so many heads and hands are at work with extraordinary energy, that unless the example is followed at home, notwithstanding the difference of wages, it is to be feared that American manufacturers will before long become exporters not only to foreign countries, but even to England."

Another point bearing on the same subject, the committee said, was the fact that the Americans were never satisfied by what they had already attained in regard to labor-saving machinery, but were steadily avid for new ideas and improvements —"a spirit occasionally carried to excess, but upon the whole productive of more good than evil." One thing that particularly attracted the notice of the committee was the care bestowed on the comfort of the working man—the clean and ample workshops, the abundant supply of good drinking water, in many cases cooled with ice, etc. In that connection the committee also remarked with satisfaction the morale of the workingmen—their cleanliness, their sobriety, and their regular attendance. In all such matters the committee recommended the American example.

Reports of this kind, whether public or private, doubtless impressed European thinking, and the increasing competition of American manufactured articles on the European market brought rivalry and imitation. In particular, the American eagerness for new contrivances must have been an incentive to competition.

Whether inventions were domestic or foreign in origin, the Americans were always busy improving upon them. Telegraph, locomotives, agricultural machines, printing presses—all such things were incessantly remodeled and perfected so as to serve more easily and more cheaply. The American pattern was one of speed, economy, and consolidation. The whole world benefited from this progress.

The steady efforts to make urban life and work more convenient produced in America in 1852 the elevator and the streetcar. Elisha G. Otis in that year made the elevator practical by his invention of a safety device and other improvements that made it function more quietly. He started the first great elevator business, and his invention, so states the *Encyclopedia Americana,* "probably did more to increase the value of city real estate by making tall buildings possible than any other invention of the century." Its influence in Europe was not so immediate. There the elevator was first introduced in hotels. Later it conquered business buildings and private houses, and gradually it became indispensable in any building of a certain height. The name of Otis will be found in many elevators in Europe. When they became electric they made possible the building of skyscrapers.

A streetcar line, the first in the world, was constructed in New York as early as 1832, but did not pay and was discontinued. A new line in the same city, operated by horsepower, was opened in 1852, and it came to stay. It must, however, be noted that this line was constructed by a French engineer. The same engineer then went back to France and acquired a license to establish a similar line from Paris to Sèvres. This line which was opened in 1855, was called "the American railway" (*chemin de fer américain*). Thus the principle was recognized as American. The narrow streets of Paris did not allow of streetcars within the city itself before many buildings were demolished, and car lines there were constructed only in 1875. In other European capitals and big cities horsecar lines were in use at earlier dates—in London in 1860, Copenhagen in 1862, Berlin in 1865. The American minister to Russia reported in 1864 that "the American system of street railroad is introduced in St. Petersburg, even into the most fashionable streets." Oslo followed in 1875, Stockholm in 1877.

Twenty years later, horses were abandoned for electricity. An experiment in that line could be seen at the International Exposition of Electricity in Paris in 1881, but again it was America that introduced the idea into practical life. The first electric trolley line was built at Richmond, Virginia, in 1887. In the 90's the European capitals began to follow the example, Oslo this time being among the first, in 1894.

At the close of the 1850's the sudden discovery of abundant

oil wells in Pennsylvania brought a revolution in domestic life all over the world. Kerosene, refined from coal oil, had been distilled for some years. But now kerosene lamps—petroleum or paraffin lamps as they more generally were called in Europe— at once became a mass product and reached out to the most remote parts of the world. I have often heard the tale of how my grandfather, a merchant at Tromsoe, far north in Norway, who every year made a trip to Hamburg for his commodities, early in the 1860's brought home a petroleum lamp and at night placed it burning at the corner window on the main street. In a little while hundreds upon hundreds of townspeople crowded around the house and could hardly tear themselves away from the wonder they saw before their eyes. The lamp was of the type called the Moderator, which required pumping up at certain intervals. Later, lamps were constructed with wicks that absorbed the oil and kept burning as long as there was oil in the receptacle. Of course, in the far north where the winters were long and the days short (at Tromsoe the sun is away for two months, and on the shortest day only one or two hours can be without artificial light) a petroleum lamp would mean much more than in more southerly countries. Yet everywhere petroleum brought a light infinitely stronger and clearer than the old candles gave, and far cheaper. The old domestic industry of making candles from tallow at the autumn slaughter disappeared, and some people no doubt regretted that the cozy custom of sitting and talking in the dusk before the fireplace also gradually came to an end. But the new light created new opportunities for work and reading; life grew lighter in every sense of the word. In addition there were the convenient little oil stoves where coffee or tea or a small meal could easily be prepared; they facilitated housework for the women, and could even serve the menfolk out on their working places.

Nowadays the story of petroleum as the brilliant source of light sounds almost like a fairy tale of long ago. Now there are several generations who never have seen a petroleum lamp and would not understand how to use it. For after only two decades it began to be pushed aside by the electric lamp.

The story of that lamp, too, is as exciting as a fairy tale. And it is, at first, the tale of the wizard of electricity, Thomas A. Edison. The day in 1869 when he established himself as a professional inventor inaugurated a new epoch in the history of inventions. Often before they had been provoked by practical needs and even by prizes offered for special machines or devices. But now came the time when science was methodically put to use in the search for new tools and contrivances for the advance of industry and the improvement of living conditions. It was a systematization of efforts that led to the establishment of public commissions and of research laboratories in all large industrial concerns for studying and making inventions.

Edison was the pioneer in this area, and the field of study which from the beginning offered the greatest promise was electricity. He started with such important innovations in the art of telegraphy as the construction of the duplex and later of the quadruplex telegraph. Then he directed his efforts to the problem of the electric light, and in 1879 succeeded in constructing the first really serviceable incandescent lamp. It was the wonder of the International Exposition of Electricity in Paris in 1881. The electric light became the dream of the world. Edison made the dream a reality by his planning of central power stations able to distribute the electric current to all the houses of large districts. That was, indeed, a great constructive idea, one of those that mark an epoch in human history. One of the historians of American inventions, Holland Thompson, says:

> The incandescent lamp and the central power station, considered together, may be regarded as one of the most fruitful conceptions in the history of applied electricity. It comprised a complete generating, distributing, and utilizing system, from the dynamo to the very lamp at the fixture, ready for use. It even included a meter to determine the current actually consumed. The success of the system was complete, and as fast as lamps and generators could be produced they were installed to give a service at once recognized as superior to any other form of lighting. By 1885 the Edison lighting system was commercially developed in all its essentials, though still subject to many improvements and capable of great enlargement.

The first power centers for distributing electricity according to Edison's plans were built in New York and London in

1882, the next one in Milan in 1883, and Berlin in 1884. From the beginning of the 90's the system spread contagiously. The northernmost town in the world, Hammerfest, was the first town in Norway to adopt it. Electric light became even cheaper than petroleum lamps and could throw its rays into homes and workshops everywhere. It also became the general street light, making cities safer than they had ever been before. Then the electric light was taken into use for advertising purposes by stores and shops and places of entertainment along the streets; brilliant signs and window displays became striking features of city streets everywhere. From the closing decades of the nineteenth century, people have learned to live in an illuminated world, the blacking out of which could be endured only in circumstances of total war.

The wide distribution of electric power provided homes with much more than light; it could be used for many other purposes in easing or replacing handwork. Electric heating generally proved too expensive for common people. But electric cooking came much more into use, and moreover, electric current was an economical labor-saver for the operation of washing machines, flatirons, vacuum cleaners, shavers, and what not. In the twentieth century, electricity became everyman's servant to such an extent as to revolutionize daily life. Almost every new practical gain in this field came to Europe from America.

Electric current was a transforming power not only in home life but also in industry and production. Electric furnaces, constructed in America, made possible the commercial production of such an important metal as aluminum (1886), of carborundum, and of calcium carbide. For the full exploitation of electricity, however, it was necessary to transmit electric power over large distances without too much loss. The first successful central station for this purpose was built in Colorado in 1891. In Germany a similar center for transmission came into operation the next year. Nevertheless, most civil engineers waited to see further results before committing themselves to the possible hazards of such expensive enterprises. Before the nineteenth century had closed, however, the principle of long-distance transmission was safely beyond the stage of experiment, and big electric power stations were established wherever natural power was accessible.

The new method was particularly pregnant with consequences for countries rich in water power. Perhaps no country in the world was so influenced and well-nigh transformed by it as was Norway. There for centuries the abundant waterfalls had been driving mills and plants of many types, mostly for the exploitation of the great forests of the country. Now, from the turn of the century, the same waterfalls made it possible to establish large new industries, and Norway suddenly became one of the most highly industrialized countries in Europe. As early as 1892, Björnstjerne Björnson, the great optimist, wrote a marching song for the Norway of the future which concluded with the prophetic line: "Soon, you know, all shall come for electricity from Norway!"

Two years earlier a civil engineer, Gunnar Knudsen, who later became the leader of the great reform party that dominated Norwegian politics during the first three decades of the twentieth century, had suggested the use of electric motive power for railways. Soon afterward he proposed and carried an annual appropriation on the national budget for the public purchase of waterfalls. Fifteen years later, the damming and exploitation of rivers was made a matter of public license, and state and municipalities vied with private corporations to harness the immense quantities of power made available by the new system. Norwegian engineers specialized in electricity, and shops for the manufacture of electrical tools developed to such an extent that they could produce for exportation.

While Edison had thus made electricity the greatest motive power in the world, another American inventor discovered its usefulness in another practical domain with important consequences for all modern life. He was Alexander Graham Bell, the inventor of the telephone. To be sure he was not a native American, but an immigrant from Scotland; and other immigrants, like the Serbian Pupin, played a great part in making the telephone a practical success. The fundamental invention, however, was made in America and was patented by Bell in 1876. The London

Times mentioned it the next year as "the latest American humbug." But a few years later Europe accepted the telephone as a necessary feature of business and increasingly also of private life. From the first it was almost exclusively a city contrivance; it was introduced as far north as Tromsoe, Norway, in 1883. I remember from the days of my childhood the wonderment with which it was received, the sheer amazement at being able to listen to voices of people from other parts of the town. At that time, however, people began to adapt themselves to the ever new wonders of applied science, and what was at first a wonder very soon became an everyday experience. In the 90's, with the invention of the Pupin coil, the long-distance telephone became commercially profitable, and national telephone systems came into existence. America remained the country where the use of the telephone was most generally extended, and also the country from which most of the telephone apparatus of the world came, manufactured by the American Telephone and Telegraph Company. But one after another of the European countries began to approach the American standard, and even a country like Norway could export telephone instruments.

Like the telegraph, the telephone was most important for business transactions. Both of them subserved the American efforts for efficiency and labor-saving. For office work these efforts produced all kinds of practical systems and devices. One of the oldest was the typewriter, finally achieved in America after attempts to construct one in several countries. Thomas Hall, who had earlier invented a sewing machine, demonstrated a typewriting machine at the International Exposition in Paris in 1867. Another machine was patented by Charles Sholes in 1868, and, together with Carlos Glidden, who had seen some attempts in Austria, he finally put a serviceable typewriter on the market in 1873. The manufacture of it was taken over by the firm of E. Remington and Sons and, with improvements made by one of the sons, the Remington became the first typewriter to conquer not only America but Europe as well. After the typewriter came the adding machine, the cash register, and many other contrivances for speeding and facilitating business. Then electricity was employed for the operation of many machines for tabulating, computing, bookkeeping, addressing, etc. America steadily continued not only to initiate all such practical improvements, but also to dominate the world market of typewriters as well as cash registers and similar products; such American methods and creations are imitated and used in all countries.

From the point of view of historical continuity, it is interesting to note the connection between the civil and the military system of production. The Remington firm which manufactured the first typewriter as a mass article was originally a small-arms factory, formed along the principles of Whitney and Colt. The same member of the firm who made the final improvement in the Remington typewriter was the man who perfected the breech-loading Remington rifle which in the 1870's was adopted for use by several European armies, for instance by those of Sweden and Norway (later a Norwegian rifle, the Krag-Jörgensen, was adopted by the American army).

From another point of view one may observe the connection between office methods in business and in public libraries. Many impulses for office reforms came from the Library Bureau, founded in Boston in 1876. And America was the first country to found library schools, where many students from Europe received their first education. The Dewey system of cataloguing books was, entirely or partly, adopted by many European libraries as the most practical in existence.

An invention by Edison along a different line from those hitherto mentioned was the phonograph, which he patented as early as 1877. It was some time before this invention was perfected enough to attain practical importance. About 1885, the Norwegian Department of Education sent a man out to demonstrate the phonograph in the high schools of the country; the students who listened to the explanation and the performance of this talking machine could not but wonder at and admire the scientific ingenuity of the inventor, but they could not conceal the fact that the sounds produced were not very agreeable to the ear. The whole thing seemed more a curiosity than a useful instrument. Edison steadily improved upon his first model, how-

ever, and in the 1890's he created a phonograph in which the wax
cylinder was replaced by a rubber disc. That made the phonograph a musical instrument to be enjoyed by everybody. It
brought music into circles where, until then, the accordion had
offered the highest enjoyment, and by successive improvements
it became capable of meeting the most exacting musical demands.
At first it seemed to vulgarize music, but gradually it proved a
valuable educational instrument.

Somewhat the same thing can be said about Edison's invention of the moving picture. In 1889 he first demonstrated moving
pictures, and they were commercially presented for the first time
in New York in 1894. When I first came to America in 1908, the
"shows" open there were to me a complete novelty, and I was not
much impressed by them. They offered reproductions of rather
low art, and the pictures shown were indistinct and flickering. A
few years later, however, the invention of the multiple-reel feature created the triumphant success of the movies. From that
time on they conquered the world. Like the phonograph, the
movies brought art to wide circles of people to whom the theater
had been nearly inaccessible. And movies could be set up not only
in cities but in villages and in the open country as well.

Both phonograph and movie were a natural outgrowth of the
democratic society of America, and they were powerful forces for
the democratization of art in Europe. On both sides of the Atlantic they effectively furthered the aesthetic education of the people. The movies certainly also reacted upon the art of the theater.
In particular that influence can be observed in Russian drama, in
the tendencies toward mass effect and the swift succession of pictures, and it can be seen too in the works of the German Ernst
Toller and the Norwegian Nordahl Grieg. Following the American pattern, native movies have been made in many European
countries, and the French film dramas are generally regarded as
the finest type of movie anywhere produced. American movies,
however, dominate the world, partly because of the large capital
invested in the movie industry there, partly because they can address themselves to such numerous audiences that they can be
distributed more cheaply than the productions of smaller coun-

tries. After the movies became "talkies," their influence increased still further.

*   *   *   *   *

Of course Americans were not alone in making inventions, although they were leaders in many fields. In the matter of communications, the leadership mostly belonged to Europe. But even in regard to European inventions the American technique was often decisive for their development. That was the story of the bicycle, or velocipede as it was first called. Its construction was the result of the combined efforts of Germans, Englishmen, and Frenchmen. But only after America had entered upon the bicycle industry in the 1880's, and introduced into it the method of standardization, could the bicycle become cheap enough to be a means of getting around for everybody. In flat countries, like Denmark and Holland, it became and remained highly popular. In America, however, it was almost completely crowded out by the automobile.

This was not an American invention either. It was French. But it was an expensive tool. Every car cost thousands of dollars. When the Americans got hold of it, their natural idea was to try to make it cheaper. The first attempt was made by Ransom Olds in Detroit, Michigan, who in 1901 cut down the price of an Oldsmobile to $650. Henry M. Leland constructed a better gasoline motor, which was used for the Cadillac (1903). He insisted more strongly than anybody else upon precision in manufacture. He had worked in one of the federal small-arms factories during the Civil War, later in Colt's revolver factory, and he introduced the complete system of interchangeable parts into auto manufacture. He wanted to show Europeans that the American car was superior to any made in Europe, and in 1906 he went over to England, taking along three Cadillacs. He let them be taken completely apart by officials of the Royal Automobile Club at its race track at Brooklands. From an apparent jumble his mechanics, by means of the simplest tools, assembled the pieces again into cars, and the cars stood the test of running five hundred miles over the track. After that performance the Cadillac was awarded the prize for the most meritorious automobile achievement of the year, and

Europe was obliged to believe in the advantages of the American system.

In 1909 Henry Ford devoted his factory to the mass-manufacture of one single type of car, a lightweight model whose use of gasoline was reduced to a minimum. He made it a slogan that "everyone can afford a Fordmobile," and his car was sold in such immense numbers that he was presently able to reduce the price to $350. The Americans became an auto-driving nation. And they made large conquests in Europe too. The Ford Company established assembly factories in many European countries, and other American firms followed its example. Automobiles opened up remote corners to regular traffic which brought them into close communication with the outside world. People could no longer feel as isolated as many had done before.

Then came the airplane. This time it was an American invention. It was in 1903 that the brothers Wilbur and Orville Wright demonstrated the practical solution of the problem of flying by a conveyance heavier than air. They could not yet fly for as long as a full minute, and only in 1908, in France, did they succeed in producing a plane that was able to maintain itself in the air for a considerable length of time. That was the conquest of the air. The German airships, the Zeppelins, were outdated almost before they were made. The airplane invaded one country after the other and finally encircled the world. Air traffic became a regular part of national and international communications. The plane changed the aspects of life for both peace and war.

This is not the place to tell of the achievements of flying in war. It is both a thrilling and a cruel story, one of heroic self-sacrifice and of terrible destruction. Everybody hopes that there will never again be a need for such feats. In any event, they can never be a part of normal life. The normal thing is peace. Our ideas of what is normal have been profoundly changed by the airplane. It has become a kind of fashion to talk of this "shrinking world." That is an awkward word for designating what should be called our enlarging world. True, distances are crumbling. But horizons have grown wider and wider. By the plane, together with other means of swift communication, the world has been enlarged to every one of us in a way that even Jules Verne could not dream of. It has really become, in Wendell Willkie's phrase, one world.

One other great invention of the twentieth century has affected our thought in a similar way—the wireless or radio. An Italian, Marconi, constructed the first wireless telegraph, and in the first year of the present century he was able to use it for a message across the Atlantic. It was followed by the wireless telephone, and in the development of this invention America played a part (chiefly, to be sure, the work of a Swedish immigrant, E. F. W. Alexanderson, who constructed the alternator that made the first radio broadcast possible). It was the Bell Company that, in 1915, succeeded in sending the first telephone message across the Atlantic. Since the beginning of the 1920's, broadcasting has become an element of daily life, bringing news, information, music, into every home.

A single small fact may illustrate what all these inventions have meant to the world. It is not too much to say that only because of them, from the electric light on to the radio, the remote and ice-locked islands of Spitsbergen (with the significant Norse name of Svalbard, "the cold border") have become inhabitable. For more than half of the year the islands are cut off from any traffic by sea, for almost as long a time there is no sun shining, and only a generation ago it meant almost certain starvation to be stranded there for a winter. Now thousands of people are finding a living there, working in the coal mines, and children are born who live their whole youth on the naked cliffs. The glorious summers, with the sun shining night and day for months, may compensate for the dark winters. Yet how could life have been endurable for people there but by virtue of modern inventions? They don't feel isolated from the world as long as they can hear the news every day and enjoy the finest concerts. Their settlements are brightly illuminated with perpetual light, and the modern canning industry can preserve the vitamins of their food for them. Happiness and well-being can exist even in such a lonely spot.

XI

THE ALMIGHTY DOLLAR VERSUS
AMERICAN IDEALISM

"Mammon is the idol which the people worship," wrote an English traveler in America in 1836. It is a typical pronouncement. Judgments to the same effect are to be found in one after another of the writings of foreign visitors. Almost without exception the Europeans who visited America during the nineteenth century reported that they heard everybody talking about money, discussing ways of earning wealth, appreciating everything according to its pecuniary merits, and valuing people on account of their fortune. It was the reign of the almighty dollar.

With the increasing power of the United States, many Europeans began to fear that the same spirit might conquer their own nations. Indeed the immense emigration from Europe to America demonstrated clearly that large numbers of Europeans were only too susceptible to the American philosophy of economic prosperity.

Most European authors who described and derided this aspect of American life pictured it as a feature of the unlimited democracy of the country. In a way they were right. America was the first country organized without a nobility. Matthew Arnold could say with truth in the 1880's that "the middle class is in America virtually the nation." At any rate, the ideals of the middle class dominated the whole nation, even the laboring classes. The business of such a class and such a nation was, as President Coolidge appropriately stated—business. In a society, on the other hand, which had been educated under the tutelage of a noble class, business was regarded more or less as sordid. By ancient tradition it was indeed placed outside of society. The only honorable social ranks acknowledged were those of the priests and the officers, that is the ecclesiastical and military upper classes. Beneath them were the farmers who performed the work necessary for the life of all. The merchants entered as

179

a kind of parasite. By and by, of course, even noblemen began to do business and think of profit, but it was not good manners to speak of it. In such a society what Walt Whitman said about Matthew Arnold would be generally applicable: "He hated to touch the dirt—the dirt is so dirty!"

No such feeling obtained in America. On the contrary, to the Americans their economic feats were their greatest pride. The task of their life had been to conquer a continent, not by arms but by labor. By necessity their efforts had been so overwhelmingly directed toward material gains that these were uppermost in their thought. They did not feel the least ashamed of talking about such achievements or of praising their successes in this field. In this regard there was a conspicuous difference between American and European manners. Old-fashioned Europeans were hurt by the frank American discussions of incomes, profits, and fortunes.

In 1886 the Scotch immigrant Andrew Carnegie, who had made one of the largest fortunes in America, published a book of more than five hundred pages to demonstrate to the world all the advantages of his adopted country. He called it *Triumphant Democracy* and he opened it with these words: "The old nations of earth creep on at a snail's pace; the Republic thunders past with the rush of the express." What great achievements did he then describe? He had extremely little to say about art, and what he wrote about literature amounted essentially to an account of the mass production of newspapers, magazines, and encyclopedias. What he dwelt upon was the superiority of America in population, wealth, agriculture, manufactures, the application of science for social and industrial purposes—in short, the whole material progress of the nation. He praised the constitution and the laws of the republic because they guarded private property and enterprise more securely than did any monarchy, because there was no income tax and no restriction on the sale of land, because (so he said) the Senate was a house of landlords able to legislate freely in their own interests. Such an appraisal could not but impress Europeans as the idolizing of pure material egotism.

Now, since King Henry IV of France, three centuries and a half ago, proclaimed as his program that every peasant should

have a chicken in his pot every Sunday, it has been generally acknowledged that it must be a vital plank of every political platform to work for the heightening of the standard of living. Such a
program, however, comprises more than merely material advancement for the people. It includes intellectual and moral
progress as well. Instinctively everybody agrees that a certain
standard of economic welfare is needed for the growth of civilization. In modern times, no nation in the world has succeeded
in raising the standard of living to such a degree as have the
Americans, and the very exuberance of American economic
activity had such a contagious power as to instigate a revolution
in societies where material conditions have lagged far behind.
Aristocrats were naturally afraid of the American example and
tried to depreciate it.

Incidentally, it is one of the ironies of history that American
development helped strengthen and confirm the economic interpretation of history, the Marxian way of thinking, which to
the Americans themselves appeared abominable because the
conclusion of Marxism contained an indictment of their ideal of
private enterprise. The economic expansion of America was so
strongly bound up with the free action of enterprising individuals that in no other country was Herbert Spencer's philosophy
of unrestricted personal liberty so profoundly inculcated in the
general mind. But Marxian historians saw in America a clear
illustration of their thesis that economic life determines the ideas
of nations.

In that case it would be necessary to state that the economic
growth of America really had developed an intellectual life of
the same standard. But that was what the critics of America
denied. Or rather, with Matthew Arnold, they affirmed that
American civilization offered a warning example of what a
middle-class society would produce. In England Arnold was
fighting the efforts of the middle class to win leadership and
power, and when a liberal like John Bright praised "the achievements wrought in America by the middle-class industry, the
middle-class energy and courage, the middle-class religion of our
English race," then Arnold felt bound to ask whether all that

created a type of civilization that should be admired and imitated. To build up a truly human life, he felt, there must be a combination of "the power of intellect and knowledge, the power of beauty, the power of social life and manners, as well as the great power of conduct and religion, and the indispensable power of expansion." None of these did he find in America. He saw mediocrity in religion, typified by Methodism. He saw a poverty of serious interests; he saw little of beauty and little of art, very little of distinction, a great want of the interesting. In short, he saw a society leveled down to plain vulgarity, a nation of Philistines.

John Ruskin and Thomas Carlyle expressed similar unfavorable judgments of America. In 1867, when the principle of aristocracy came under attack in Great Britain, Ruskin, the esthetic critic, raised the battle-cry against the substitution of money power for the martial virtues. He feared the danger of the "imminent prevalence of mob violence, here as in America," and "the monstrous forms of vice and selfishness which the appliances of recent wealth and of vulgar mechanical art make possible to the millions." Thomas Carlyle referred to the plans of destroying aristocracy in an American metaphor as "shooting Niagara," and regarded the adoption of complete democracy on the American model as suicidal.

It is worth noting that certain Scandinavian writers tended to lump Englishmen and Americans together and to regard them both as representatives of the commercial mind. In his book "From the Intellectual Life of Modern America" (*Fra det moderne Amerikas Aandsliv*, 1889) the gist of which was that America had no intellectual life, Knut Hamsun wrote:

> In America there has grown up a way of life that aims at nothing but food-stuff and the acquisition of material benefit or wealth. The Americans are so busy fighting for profits that they use all their abilities for this purpose and interest themselves in nothing else. Their brains are weaned on values and numbers; they have no more beloved matter to employ their thoughts upon than what is offered by the various financial operations. The only subject which is taught daily in their common schools is arithmetic; numbers and statistics form the essence of all their discussions; numbers and statistics enter into the sermons preached from their pulpits. . . .

There is, in truth, no end of things whose value the Americans calculate by numbers. . . . The Americans are a business nation; in their hands everything becomes business. But they are very little of an intellectual nation; their civilization is sadly deficient.

An unbridled glorifier of romantic primitivism (who later became a Nazi), Hamsun attacked all modern democratic culture. From his point of view it was quite natural to include the English nation in his condemnation of modern development and to aver that the Anglo-Saxons were spreading the germs of degeneration and vice that would one day carry them to their doom.

The pictures of English and American society and mentality which we find in the writings of Hamsun, Ibsen, and the peasant-born poet A. O. Vinje, make it perfectly clear that the wrath of the authors was primarily directed against the new industrial society which even in their own country was threatening to corrupt and annihilate the old simple farm life. In a poem on the problems of his time Ibsen wrote in 1870: "Our age is hungering for beauty." Estheticists like Ruskin naturally scorned the machine-produced mass articles that were crowding out the creations of individual artisans. American standardization appeared to them the worst demonstration of the decline of art and taste, and it may be admitted at once that during the transitional period factories poured out too many ugly products, possibly because, from the beginning, they endeavored rather to imitate the old handmade goods than to create a new style conforming to the functional character of the products. It was a long time before the world was allowed to see beautiful locomotives or automobiles. History will perhaps acknowledge that, in the second half of the nineteenth century, Germany was the center of bad-taste production. But undeniably America was the capital country of the machine, and consequently it was regarded as the real source of what was called machine-culture or the mechanization of life. The invasion of Europe by this brand of civilization was by many regarded as the greatest danger of modern life. It was an "Americanization" that would have to be resisted by all the forces of the spirit.

Many observers formulated the problem by questioning

whether civilization should accept the substitution of quantity for quality. That too was the expression of the fear that the machine might dominate man. That was what Hamsun meant when he denounced the American intoxication with numbers. In the domain of art and beauty, quantity could certainly claim no priority to quality without serious losses. And in intellectual life, a mass of knowledge could not be equal to well-trained thinking. In both cases, however, it undoubtedly meant progress if art and knowledge were made accessible to ever larger numbers of people. In many other relations of life, quantity by itself might imply a difference of quality. Small business and big business would constitute almost opposite elements of society. A life in need or a life in abundance would influence the character of man in very dissimilar ways.

The Americans themselves were inclined to stress the moral impact of their economic development. In his *Five American Contributions to Civilization* (1896) Charles William Eliot did not hesitate to include the wide diffusion of material well-being among the population as a moral contribution, like the invention of all kinds of machinery, as mentioned in a preceding chapter. One of the happy consequences of the high standard of living he saw in "the habitual optimism which characterizes the common people." Foreigners, too, were impressed by this spirit of courage, independence, and initiative in the American nation, and they saw in it a basis for true progress.

It came as a surprise when Anthony Trollope, son of the famous Mrs. Trollope, brought out two volumes on *North-America* in 1862, giving praise to the American man. In the first volume he presented the American of the young West, presumably the crudest part of the country, in the following way:

This man has his romance, his high poetic feeling, and above all his manly dignity . . . he will stand upright before you and speak to you with all the ease of a lettered gentleman in his own library. . . . He is his own master, standing on his own threshold. . . . He has worked out his independence, and shows it in every easy movement of his body. He tells you of it unconsciously in every tone of his voice. . . . I defy you not to feel that he is superior to the race from whence he has sprung in England or in Ireland!

In his conclusion, at the end of the second volume, the author extended this picture of new-won human dignity to the Americans generally and explained it as a result of the new conditions of life:

Men and women do not beg in the States;—they do not offend you with tattered rags; they do not complain to heaven of starvation; they do not crouch to the ground for halfpence. If poor, they are not abject in their poverty. They read and write. They walk like human beings in God's form. They know that they are men and women, owing it to themselves and to the world that they should earn their bread by their labour, but feeling that when earned it is their own. If this be so,—if it be acknowledged that it is so,—should not such knowledge in itself be sufficient testimony of the success of the country and of her institutions?

It was another surprise when Henrik Ibsen in his first social drama, *The Pillars of Society* (1877) caused the fight against the conventional hypocrisy of contemporary society to be led by a lady who had come back from America. She it was who proclaimed the moral conclusion of the drama: "The spirit of truth and liberty are the pillars of society." During the next years, both in a novel (1877) and a drama (1879), the latter with the significant title *The New System*, Björnstjerne Björnson used the same device of having mental liberation triumph through the agency of a person who had been in America and had learned there to "think American," that is, to acknowledge frankly the truth of things. One of his closest friends, the poet and preacher Kristofer Janson, a man whose mind is measured by the fact that Björnson made him the model of the religious hero in his drama *Beyond Human Power*, visited America during the years 1879–80 and wrote home about the "quickness and fearlessness" of the people. This man, who for a while employed Knut Hamsun as his secretary, spoke in his book about "American Conditions" (*Amerikanske Forholde*, 1881) of "the proud self-respect created by the American spirit," and declared himself warmly enthusiastic about the ennobling influence exerted on people by American democracy. He considered the immigration of inferior Europeans the worst impediment to moral and social progress in America.

Then Björnson himself went over there (1880–81). Meeting the Norwegian-Americans he discovered that life in America had made them more vivid and independent than they were in the old country, and for himself he declared that he should come back "richer in ideas, in faith, and in happiness" than he was when he left Norway. His own fellow countrymen had considered him a highly outspoken character, but living in the American atmosphere he deemed himself a coward and promised that he would be more courageous in the future.

*   *   *   *   *

Such experiences testify to the fact that there was in American life and thought much more than merely the cult of money. Democracy and pioneer life together had fostered a strong conception of the eminent value of man as man, the dignity of man. Thus it was the Americans themselves who first raised the battle-cry against the supremacy of material goods. The spiteful slogan of the "almighty dollar" was created not by a European, but by an American—Washington Irving. In the 1830's began in commercial New England, in the land of the Yankees, the movement called transcendentalism which became not only a power in America but reached over to Europe and exerted a lasting influence there. The fight against the rule of the dollar, as later against corruption and graft, is entitled to be considered an element of American life just as much as the features against which the fight was directed. From the point of view of history it may be still more important.

In fact, the scandals connected with American politics became chiefly known to Europe because they were exposed and condemned by American authors and journalists. The humorous, but nonetheless trenchant satires on the national government in the *Biglow Papers* by James Russell Lowell were the delight of English readers; from 1859 on they went through many editions in London and formed an arsenal of current witticisms at the expense of America. *The Gilded Age* by Mark Twain and Charles Dudley Warner (1873) brought both laughter and scorn on the sad chapter of Grant's administration. Other literary works, too, helped bring American corruption before the eyes of contemporary Europe. The "muckraking" of the press should not be forgotten, either. All of it was clear evidence of a moral force and indignation inherent in the American nation. It was a force with deep roots and wide-reaching influences. Its most pregnant expression was the transcendentalist movement.

As a philosophy, transcendentalism was founded on ideas from Europe, from Plato and Kant, from Goethe and Coleridge. In America it became a movement. The heart of it was the enhancement of the individual human soul. This was a fundamental Christian concept, but it assumed a new orientation by being transferred from the purely religious to the whole social domain of life. It was the idea proclaimed by the Declaration of Independence as a self-evident truth that all men are born equal, endowed with the same right to be taken into account in the consideration of social activities. In no country, during the first half of the nineteenth century, had this idea attained so much of practical achievement as it had in the United States. Beneath what appeared like vulgarity and boasting was a consciousness of the worth of every single man which in Europe was still struggling for recognition. Democracy in that sense of the word was in America a reality, in most of Europe only an ideal or not even that. It was this fact that gave the American nation its immense vigor and its indomitable optimism.

The feeling of acquiring in America a new human dignity is often expressed in the letters sent back from early immigrants, quoted in a preceding chapter. Towards the close of the nineteenth century it breaks through, in playful form, in the scornful lament that the Swedish poet Gustaf Fröding put in the mouth of an immigrant rejected by the girl he wooed in the old country:

> I was so poor a tailor gone
> In Swedish country far away.
> Here I am Mr. Johansson.
> I earn five dollars every day
> And am by law a gentleman.
> You could have been a Mistress now,
> But you have missed becoming so.

If we have to acknowledge the effects on European thought of American conceptions of the superiority of material gains, we cannot omit to observe the influences of the moral and idealistic forces arising in America. They were indeed of many kinds. In a previous chapter I have pointed out movements of moral reform initiated in America in the first half of the nineteenth century and reaching their climax in Europe during the second half. At that time, a series of religious influences from America made themselves felt in Europe, most particularly in Great Britain.

The works of the Unitarian clergyman William Ellery Channing, one of the finest personalities of the century, reached Great Britain as early as the end of the 1830's and were widely read in the 1850's. His *Self-Culture*, we are told, was "in almost every English house not absolutely steeped in ignorance and frivolity." He was followed in the 1860's by the Presbyterian pastor Henry Ward Beecher who spoke to still wider circles. His unconventional language and human realism had an appeal even to the uncultivated, and his theological latitude opened freer prospects to their religious aspirations. He preached in England in 1863, and his sermons came to be among the most conspicuous books on the shelves of laymen and ministers alike.

In the 1870's came the Episcopal clergyman Phillips Brooks, a man rather of the type of Channing. He too was heard in England. His ideal of preaching was "the bringing of truth through personality." He was concerned with life, not with doctrines, and he combined fervent piety with intellectual freedom and breadth of tolerance. He wanted to communicate to his audiences and his readers the joy and abounding life which sprang from faith in Christ. This was the common trait of all three men, the Unitarian, the Presbyterian, and the Episcopalian—they enlarged and enhanced the minds of the people who came under the impact of their teaching. They represented a genuinely uplifting element in English intellectual life.

And not only in English. In Sweden sermons of William Ellery Channing were translated as early as 1845 and attained a wide circulation; they helped create the first movement of religious liberalism in that country. It the 1860's Theodore Parker became a real power in the same movement; books were written to spread the gospel of this "most prominent religious reformer of our times," the new Luther.

He was hailed as one of the greatest and ablest of men, his works were translated, and a collected edition of them in ten volumes (1865–75) was a unique success. In Sweden he was the true leader in the fight for Christianity without dogmas. Strindberg has written about the impressions he received from him in his youth, and the influence of Parker can be traced through Christian socialists and pacifists down to the ethical writings of Ellen Key. All of them bore the stamp of American optimism, the belief in the perfectibility of man.

American Unitarianism was a liberating force in the religious life of other Protestant countries. Kristofer Janson, who had been active as a Unitarian minister in Chicago for twelve years, went back to Norway in 1893 to organize a Unitarian congregation there. In the most fashionable auditorium in Oslo he gave a series of lectures on the Bible, and I remember vividly the profound impact of having the problems of religion frankly aired in public when formerly they had been discussed only in strict privacy. Nevertheless an indiscreet journalist was brought to penance because he exclaimed: "The gilt was taken off the gingerbread." But the people at large breathed more freely.

Of a somewhat different character were the revivalist movements that came from America in the same years. There were the two evangelists, Dwight L. Moody, the preacher, and Ira David Sankey, the singer. Between the close of the 1860's and the beginning of the 1890's, Moody visited Great Britain repeatedly, touring the whole country. He caused a great religious awakening when in the 1870's he brought Sankey along with him. Using the language of everyday life, Moody moved the great masses. Sankey sang his gospel hymns to catchy tunes, often in march- or dance-rhythm. In 1901 W. T. Stead wrote:

Moody in speech, and Sankey in song, exercised a wider influence than any other two men upon the British people of last century. Sankey's hymns still hold the first place in thousands of places of worship throughout the British Empire. They are sung more constantly, and by a much greater number of people, than any other songs, with the exception of the National Anthem.

Indeed Sankey's hymns became popular in many other countries as well. In Sweden they were daily sung everywhere in the country and in the cities, by common people and by noblemen —even in the royal palaces. They were carried far abroad by the Salvation Army. The very organization of the Salvation Army by "General" Booth in England (1878) was at least partly inspired by the revivalist preachings of the American, Charles G. Finney, the President of Oberlin College. All such revivalist movements are likely to produce manifestations unattractive to cultivated minds, and are bound to be objects of criticism and dispute. But this does not detract from the fact that they represent idealistic aspirations of the people, and in so far as they originated in America they testify to the existence of a strong idealistic trend in the people there.

❋   ❋   ❋   ❋   ❋

The finest idealistic influence of America, however, radiated from the man who was the central figure of Transcendentalism —Ralph Waldo Emerson. No less reliable a witness than Matthew Arnold testified to the early effect of his writings on young people in England. Arnold wrote that, while he was an undergraduate at Oxford in the 1840's, Emerson's *Essays* came to the students there as "a clear and pure voice, speaking from three thousand miles away." And when Emerson himself came to England in 1847 to give his lectures on "Representative Men," he found himself already famous. Although his fame at that time was limited to rather narrow circles, his influence grew slowly but surely, and gradually he became a power in England as in America.

From about 1840 onward, his whole life was a never-ceasing battle against all the crude materialistic tendencies of American thought. He attacked them with all the energy of his will and his words, and European critics often only repeated what he had said. Does it not sound like one of the malicious pictures drawn by foreign critics when, in an address in Boston in 1841, we find him saying: "The Americans have many virtues, but they have not Faith and Hope. I know no two words whose meaning is more lost sight of. . . . The Americans have little faith. They rely on the power of a dollar; they are deaf to a sentiment. They think you may talk the north wind down as easily as raise society; and no class more faithless than the scholars or intellectual men." It was Emerson who proclaimed: "The machine unmakes the man." He was, as far as I know, the first to speak of the "mechanization" of civilization.

He employed this word in quite another sense than it was used by others. The human soul, he wrote, expressed itself in different ways in all the activities of man: "Raphael paints wisdom, Händel sings it, Phidias carves it, Shakespeare writes it, Wren builds it, Columbus sails it, Luther preaches it, Washington arms it, Watt mechanizes it." This was no depreciation of what Watt and other engineers did. On the contrary, Emerson discovered the soul in their machines. Perhaps the later phrase, "the mechanization of life," represents a rather confused idea. If it has a definite meaning, it must be the notion of an intellectual life based on ready-made ideas ordered from the outside. In that case I find it most completely typified by Germany, as defined by Thomas Mann's recent words about "the mechanized romanticism called Germany."

The whole movement gathered around Emerson offers the best proof that American thought was not mechanized in that way. And Emerson differed from all the foreign critics in the essential respect that he was full of hope for the future of America and all humanity. "Cheerfulness and courage," said William R. Thayer in his article on *The Influence of Emerson* (1886), "are the supreme virtues after Emerson's heart; they shine through his writings and live in his conduct." Emerson had no static view of society or civilization; he conceived all life as fluid, progressive; he believed in the steady change of laws, religions, customs. Thus he was a liberator and a stimulator. He was a truly American optimist. He identified himself with the mind that animated all the contemporary movements of reform because they were rooted in "the moral sentiment of man" and aimed at the realization of man's idea of the beautiful and the just.

To continental Europe he was first introduced by Fredrika

Bremer in her *Homes of the New World*. In him she saw the true prophet of the future. She found him personally cold, but she was profoundly struck by his ideas, and she gave the reason for his influence when she wrote "this contemner of the imperfect, of the low and the mean, this insister upon perfection in man has an almost magical charm in his writings. Often I disagree with him and object to him, I see that his stoicism is a lop-sidedness, his pantheism an imperfection, and I know what is greater and more perfect. But I am under the charm, I feel myself growing greater through his greatness, stronger through his strength, and in his world I breathe a mountain air that is refreshing beyond description."

In her book she gave translations from several of Emerson's essays. They were, in fact, the first translations from his works in any foreign language.

When a few years later, in 1859, the gentle and spiritual essayist Hermann Grimm, the son of Wilhelm Grimm, attempted to interest the Germans in Emerson, he described him as "the free and republican American," a man who "wrote and thought American," who filled others with "courage and faith." In Europe generally he was received as the "philosopher of democracy." He was not, however, a philosopher in the accepted European style; he did not create a philosophical or metaphysical system. It has rightly been said that his Transcendentalism rather had the character of a gospel. His thoughts were directed to the moral problems of modern society. The aspect of democracy that was uppermost in his mind was not the rule of the masses or of the majority but the worth and the activity of the individual soul. The health of the modern commonwealth must, according to him, be based upon the honest, manly, simple, and emancipated character of the citizen. He was the champion of the individual. Like Ibsen, he preached to the world the ethical demand that Fredrika Bremer had found typically American: Be true to thyself.

Emerson's impact on Europe during the last decades of the nineteenth century was pictured by John Morley in an article in the *Fortnightly Review* at his death in 1882. There Morley said: "In our generation he has already been accepted as one of the wise masters who breathed into other men a strong desire after the right governance of the soul. . . . He is already one of the privileged few whom the reader approaches in the mood of settled respect, and whose names have surrounded themselves with an atmosphere of religion." Morley contrasted him to the perpetually excitant Carlyle; the lifelong friendship of these two men is indeed a proof of the greatness of their minds, and they agreed at least in the respect both of them had for the independent human soul. Morley found in Emerson that "high and transparent sanity" that made him one of the few moral reformers who inculcated serenity in the souls of men and "turned a passing agitation into an enduring revival." Hence, he said, "we have in Emerson the teaching of a vigorous morality without the formality of dogma and the deadly tedium of didactics." And he concluded: "Emerson remains among the most persuasive and inspiring of those who by word and example rebuke our despondency, purify our sight, awaken us from the deadening slumbers of convention and conformity, exorcise the pestering imps of vanity, and lift men up from low thoughts and sullen moods of helplessness and impiety."

Through the spoken and the written word Emerson had a peculiar power to awaken the conscience of man, particularly of youth. He opened large views to them and roused their sense of social responsibility, so that they always concluded that he had given them their task in life. Hermann Grimm, German interpreter of art and literature, said he was unable to explain what it was in Emerson that had moved him so deeply, but that he felt coming from him a unique vitalizing power and discovered through him a world brightened by eternal sunlight. The English scientist John Tyndall, whose greatest efforts were directed towards assimilating religion to modern scientific research, said: "If anyone can be said to have given the impulse to my mind, it is Emerson; whatever I have done the world owes to him."

Hundreds and thousands of individual men and women might have offered similar confessions about Emerson's influence upon them. Many more were brought indirectly under the sway of his teaching through his disciples. In Great Britain he was a power especially in the 1870's. On the European continent his greatest time came in the 1890's. Friedrich Spielhagen and Hermann Grimm had translated essays of his into German as early as 1857, and some volumes appeared in new editions about 1875; but not until 1895 had his popularity grown so far as to cause him to be included in Reclam's *Universal-Bibliothek*.

Toward the close of the nineteenth century, there arose in Europe a general reaction against the cruder forms of naturalistic ideas fostered by the doctrines of evolution and the philosophy of positivism. People began to cultivate the intimate forces of the soul; religion and ethics came to the fore. The grim ethical imperative of Ibsen conquered the world, and the slogan of the age was: Back to idealism! In this movement Emerson became a powerful aid. When, in Germany, in 1905–1906, Friedrich Lienhard published his remarkable magazine with the significant title *Wege nach Weimar* and the equally significant subtitle *Beiträge zur Erneuerung des Idealismus,* he referred in almost every issue to Emerson as the foremost champion of his ideas. Both in Germany and in England ethical societies were formed, and ethical magazines were published, all of them propagating the works and ideas of Emerson. In England an Emerson Club was formed in 1905. Maeterlinck introduced Emerson to Belgium in 1894. The great Swedish moralist Ellen Key preached his gospel in Sweden.

As the hard conflicts that led to the two World Wars of the twentieth century began to embitter the minds and harden the consciences of Europeans, Emerson was gradually pushed into the background. Still he was a power, and as such he even suffered the fate of being appropriated by the Nazis. In Adolf Hitler's *Nationalsozialistische Monatshefte* (1932) appeared an article on "Emerson—a Man of Today" which tried to picture him as an "advocate of our movement for national freedom" by virtue of his denunciation of everything mobbish. As such the author placed Emerson at the side of Nietzsche. But, he added, while Nietzsche ended in misanthropy and a destructive fury, Emerson always remained healthy and optimistic. Optimism, a firm belief in the future of mankind, the author stated (and in this we may grant he was right), was the great message of Emerson to every new generation.

Five years later, under the Hitler regime, a young man took his dòctor's degree with a dissertation on Emerson in Germany. Through his guarded account one seems to feel that the author was more in sympathy with the ethics of Emerson than with those of Nazism. But he had to wind up with a rather tame proclamation of the virtual congruity of Emerson's teachings with the efforts for the establishment of a genuine "Germanic religion." It was, however, impossible to identify the democratic individualism of Emerson with the servile submission to authority demanded by Nazism. Emerson will always remain a power for freedom.

*   *   *   *   *

When, during the last decades of the nineteenth century, Europe discussed the spiritual values produced by America, two men were always pointed out as the foremost representatives of American intellectual life. They were Emerson and Walt Whitman. Books treating both of them were published in Dutch, German, and French. The Austrian literary critic Karl Federn wrote in the leading radical review *Die Zeit* in 1897: "They are the spokesmen of the same concept of life, Emerson philosophically cool and ethereal, Whitman passionately temperamental and soaked by the fire of the earth." If Emerson was called the philosopher of democracy, Whitman was celebrated as the poet of democracy.

Even the enemies of America, the people who despised American democracy, identified the efforts of these two men and united them in common condemnation. In Knut Hamsun's picture of America considerable space was assigned to the portrayal of them, and it was done in the most merciless manner imaginable. As for Emerson, Hamsun had to grant a certain nobility of mind, but going over his writings in more than forty pages he made them out to be nothing but empty, often senseless talk, completely wanting in real thought. According to Hamsun, Emerson represented a curious mixture from three different continents: he was Asiatic in his religious propensities, European in his desire of intellectuality and beauty, American by his democratic narrow-mindedness and his practical Yankeeism. Thus for Hamsun Emerson's American qualities spoiled whatever of good he might have adopted from abroad.

Walt Whitman came off still worse. He was characterized as a pure American, a true native, i.e., an Indian! He was a savage, his poetry a "natural sound in an uncultivated wilderness," written "without meter and rhyme." One might think that Hamsun, the author of *Pan*, would have felt attracted by what he himself calls the primitive in Whitman's soul, "the Indian-wild sentiment of intimate unity with the elements of nature." And Hamsun goes so far as to acknowledge that if Whitman had been born in a civilized country and had received an intelligent education, he might have become "a small Wagner." But born in America, "this remote corner of the world, where everything is but a screaming of hurrahs and where the talent for commerce is the only manifest talent of the nation," in such a country he could become nothing but a changeling, a hybrid of primitive and modern. Hamsun applies all his mastery of insult to depicting the sad literary result of such a product:

His style is not English, it belongs to no civilized language. It is the heavy Indian style of images without giving an image, transformed by the heavy style of the Old Testament which passes all understanding. His words roll ponderous and obscure along the pages of his book, columns of words, regiments of words roaring away, each one making the poem more incomprehensible than the last. There are poems quite magnificent in their unreadability. . . .

The primitiveness of his sentiments is *behind* the common people. And his language has not the calm strength of popular poetry, only the energy of noise. Sometimes it mounts to loud, orchestra-like outbursts, joyful hurrahs of victory which remind the beaten reader of Indian war-dances. On closer examination, all of it reveals itself as only a wild carnival of words. . . .

I have never found his equal in the art of speaking much and saying nothing. His words are warm, there is fire in them, passion, energy, enthusiasm. One listens to this desperate music of words, one feels his heart lifting. But one cannot grasp *why* he is so enthusiastic. Through all his work the thunder is clapping, but the lightning, the spark never comes. One reads and reads, one page after the other, and is completely unable to catch the meaning of anything. These enthusiastic lists of words neither confuse nor intoxicate, they paralyze, they oppress the reader into dull despair, their unremitting, exhausting monotony finally affects his reason. At the last poem he is no longer able to count to four.

Hamsun did not know that in penning this indictment he was simply repeating the most vulgar criticism of Whitman in America and elsewhere. Indeed, Hamsun was not in this respect a true spokesman for his nation. Far more truly Norwegian was Kristofer Janson, who in his book about America praised Whitman as the prophet and most original poet of the country, the singer of the human type of the future, the ideal American type.

Whitman was, as it were, introduced to Europe by a letter from Emerson to Carlyle in 1856 which told of the publication in the preceding year of *Leaves of Grass*, "a nondescript monster which yet had terrible eyes and buffalo strength, and was undisputably American." But there was no response from Carlyle, and the few English newspapers that took notice of the book were evidently surprised at this "new American prodigy," "one of the most extraordinary specimens of Yankee intelligence and American eccentricity."

Rebelling against all literary conventions and authorities, Whitman followed the sovereign rules of his own genius and created his personal form. Well he might do so, he who was at once a cosmos and the son of Manhattan, the poet of the good and the poet of the wicked, the singer of life and death, above all the singer of the free immortal soul of man embracing all animal lusts and all heavenly yearnings. Embodying in himself the largest and highest aspiration of America, he struck up for a New World. Truly he gave the sign of democracy, and what was the sign? "By God! I will accept nothing which all cannot have their counterpart of on the same terms." He spoke the voices of prisoners and slaves, of all the oppressed generations and beings. It was the American program of the equal freedom of all men transformed into the triumphal hymn of infinite expansion. And it was the ideal of universal fraternity, the noble comradeship of men and nations. He was America's greatest message to the world.

Inevitably, it took time before he could be understood and listened to. His conquest of Europe began in 1868, when William M. Rossetti published in London a selection of his poems, a little pruned and purged, but not so much as to smooth over the rugged individuality of the author. Its reception by the British press was mixed; one of the weeklies called Whitman an obscene rowdy and a dirty dog. But he found faithful admirers, and was eagerly discussed. He had the greatest success a prophet could have: he became a storm center of intellectual life.

It was an age of storm and stress, nowhere more so than in Great Britain, the home of Darwin and other revolutionary scientists. Old dogmas were falling, people were looking for new foundations of life, for a new religion. Walt Whitman brought American optimism, the unfailing faith in human progress and the promise of democracy. Rossetti declared: "I conceive Walt Whitman to be beyond all compare the greatest of American poets, and indeed one of the greatest now living in any part of the world." The Scotch poet Robert Buchanan hailed him as the coming America, the English poet Swinburne sang of him as the prophet of liberty. Another English poet, Alfred Austin, on the other hand, ridiculed the idea of his bringing "the poetry of the future." He said that Whitman's "grotesque, ungrammatical, and repulsive rhapsodies can be fitly compared only to the painful ravings of maniacs' dens." When it was proclaimed that Whitman was Democracy, Austin answered: "I really think he is,—being, like it, ignorant, sanguine, noisy, coarse, and chaotic." In contrast, the Irish Shakespeare scholar Edward Dowden wrote in the *Westminster Review* a serious analysis of Whitman's poetry. Referring to Tocqueville and using the methods of Taine, Dowden set out to demonstrate how Whitman was in truth a product of the soil and climate of America, the first genuine and great poet of the democracy of the New World. Around his chair at Dublin, Dowden gathered a whole group of Whitman devotees.

The poet himself entered, as it were, into the midst of the battle by the publication of his *Democratic Vistas*, written more or less in answer to Carlyle's *Shooting Niagara*, defending in prose his political views, and incidentally attacking many aspects of actual American democracy, for instance the "pervading flippancy and vulgarity, low cunning, infidelity" and other vices of American cities. He demonstrated that he did not approve everything American though he was sure of the great future of America. Some years later, in 1876, vehement polemics engaged both British and American newspapers when Robert Buchanan raised a great cry about America's neglect of its great poet whom it left half starving. By the efforts of Rossetti a thousand dollars were collected in Great Britain and sent to the assistance of the needy author—an episode, it has been said, "unparalleled in Anglo-American relations."

The Rossetti edition of 1868 had cleared the way for Whitman's works in Great Britain. The poet of the German revolution, Ferdinand Freiligrath, who was at that time living as an exile in London, translated specimens of Whitman's verses and had them published in a Munich newspaper. Freiligrath's friend Adolf Strodtmann, who had lived for some years in America during the early 1850's and was the German translator of Byron and Shelley, of Ibsen and Brandes, included poems by Whitman in his *Amerikanische Anthologie* (1870).

An author in the *Revue des deux mondes* (1872), Th. Bentzon, had a long article on Whitman, starting from the ridicule offered by Alfred Austin and continuing much in the same vein. He called Whitman's religion, philosophy, and morals "bizarre," his verses a *galimatias* which "passed the limits of absurdity." He admitted, however, "a certain grandeur and much passion," and the latest collection of poems, *Drum-Taps,* he found "trembling with emotion, patriotism, and universal love," even approaching correctness of form. Though the critic maintained that the French who took account of good taste would still regard Longfellow as the foremost of American poets, he did not despair of Whitman. At least the silence about him was broken.

In the same year Rudolf Schmidt, the chief editor of the Danish magazine with the significant name "For Ideas and Reality" (*For Ide og Virkelighed*) of which the Norwegian poet Björnson was co-editor, brought out a laudatory article on Whitman and translated some of his poems. Later (1874) he translated the whole of *Democratic Vistas*. In Russia, Turgenieff was busy translating verses of Whitman's, but was unable to have them published.

The new generation of authors who grew up in the 1860's and 70's were powerfully impressed by the works of Whitman. John Addington Symonds has said that *Leaves of Grass* "influenced me more perhaps than any other book has done, except the Bible; more than Plato, more than Goethe," and that it "has deeply entered into the fibre and marrow of my being. . . . It revolutionized my previous conceptions, and made another man of me." Whitman, he said, "added conviction, courage, self-reliance to my sense of cosmic enthusiasm." In a similar vein Robert Louis Stevenson said of Whitman's work: "It tumbled the world upside down for me, blew into space a thousand cobwebs of genteel and ethical illusion, and, having thus shaken my tabernacle of life, set me back upon a strong foundation of all the original and manly virtues." Edward Carpenter's first work, *Towards Democracy* (1883), was admittedly inspired by Whitman.

The remarkable thing is that his influence was in the ascendant as the years passed. In the 1890's all young English poets stood under the sign of his star. Since 1895 new editions of *Leaves of Grass* have appeared almost annually. Since 1892 new books on him have multiplied; I have noted almost a full score in the succeeding half century.

In Germany, the battle for him began in 1883 when the Irishman T. W. Rolleston, a pupil of Dowden, gave a lecture on him before the Literary Society of Dresden and proclaimed his poetry as the necessary engine for the rehabilitation of the declining idealistic philosophy of the Germans. Afterwards Rolleston, together with the German-American Karl Knortz, translated Whitman and in the 1890's Whitman became the leading spirit in the literary and social rebellion of the time in Germany. Impressionistic and expressionistic poets followed in his tracks, monists accepted his philosophy, socialists his democratic program. In the German revolution of 1918 he was celebrated as the champion of the new age, and Thomas Mann developed his ideas on the moral forces of democracy. Unfortunately other forces seized power in Germany.

In Russia too the revolutionary parties adopted Whitman as one of their own. But magazines and books that would present him to the public were immediately banned. Nevertheless he was an inspiration to the young poets who entered the literary arena on the eve of the revolution of 1917, and after the revolution he became the favorite poet of youth.

At the same time the group of Danish poets who rose to literary leadership in their country were above all inspired by Whitman.

In France, the sway of his poetry was inaugurated by articles by Gabriel Sarrazin in *La Revue nouvelle* in the 1890's and finally by the brilliant translation of Léon Bazalgette. In 1913 it could be said that not since France discovered Poe had its literature been so deeply affected by anything American.

There was everywhere, however, a marked difference between the impact of Poe and that of Whitman. Poe's influence was essentially literary or artistic, it had a moral aspect only insofar as it braced the conscience of the authors toward their art and made them more intensely aware of the duties of craftsmanship. Whitman in a way dissolved what Poe had tightened under severe rules. He reinstated the liberty of the poet. In particular, he made the rhythm of verse something far more flexible and free than had previously been regarded as permissible. But such formal freedom only increased the necessity of the absolute conformity of individual truth and artistic expression. Every author became obliged to express himself unreservedly through his work. Whitman would not allow him to be simply an artist. Whitman had a message for the world. His poetry was action, was fight, inspiring as well as inspired. That was what made his influence so profound.

At the present moment, translations of his poems are to be found in most European languages. American idealism has had no more effective spokesman in Europe than Walt Whitman; he has been a force for mental and literary liberation everywhere.

The immediate battle against the money power in America only rarely had direct repercussions in Europe. The reason was twofold. On the one hand, the organization of the great economic corporations was so different on the two sides of the Atlantic as to make the American methods of regulating them to a large extent unsuitable for imitation. On the other hand, the social mentality of the New World, shaped as it was by the abundance of opportunities for private enterprise, did not adjust itself to the ideals of economic collectivism which more or less prevailed in the countries of the Old World. While European labor movements almost without exception adopted programs of an essentially socialistic character and everywhere formed independent political parties, American trade unions generally had no intention of fighting the capitalistic system as such and were content to keep their political activities within the framework of the old parties.

Nevertheless during the 1880's there came from the United States two works that stirred old Europe to both action and thought in the battlefield of social politics. One was Henry George's *Progress and Poverty*, which appeared in America in 1879 and was translated in quick succession into several European languages. It based itself on an old idea that had followed man almost through the whole history of civilization—that all men had an equal right to apply their labor to the resources of nature. But from what George saw happening in California, he came to a conclusion that struck him, and after him others, as the manifest and easy panacea against the violation of that human right. He noticed that in that young country the value of the soil was mounting irresistibly simply by virtue of the increasing population so that the owners of land were able to earn manifold profit without doing a day's work. He was incensed by this injustice to the real working men, and he proposed to take away from the landowners the profit of their robbery by a sweeping tax on the unearned increment of their fortune. With the economic progress that constantly went on in all countries, such a tax would virtually make all other taxes superfluous. This single tax would suffice for all public purposes.

Henry George proclaimed his idea with such fervent eloquence and such effective illustrations that it impressed the common man with convincing force and even became a tenet of many politicians. J. A. Hobson reports that *Progress and Poverty* was the "first book of serious economic import which ever reached the outer circle of the English reading public," and the same may be true of other countries. Nearly a hundred thousand copies were sold in England. In 1883 Henry George himself went there and lectured about his ideas; the Land Restoration League was founded, and he gave an impetus to the social thought of such men as Bernard Shaw and Keir Hardie.

In Norway his book was translated by a man who shortly was to become the leader of the largest political party of the country, Viggo Ullmann, the most brilliant stump speaker of the time, who carried the idea of Henry George to wide circles in the nation. One of the most prominent authors of Norway, Arne Garborg, made himself a consistent spokesman for the same program. In Denmark a group of radicals formed a single-tax party which worked to influence opinion through books and special magazines.

If the idea of the single tax was nowhere put into practice and thus proved utopian, the idea of severely taxing the unearned increment of land values could be adapted with success to existing systems of taxation. It was put into practice in German and English cities in the 1890's, and later in Copenhagen and Oslo. As for its application to agricultural lands, England with its great landlords was a far more fruitful field for agitation even than America. There Lloyd George appropriated the program. As Chancellor of the Exchequer he introduced his first budget in 1909 with the proposal of a tax of twenty percent on the increment of land values. That was the signal for battle. The House of Lords ventured to assert its right to vote on the budget and rejected the proposal. There followed the vehement campaign against the usurpation of the Lords, who in the end were compelled not only to swallow the radical budget but also to see their constitutional power seriously curtailed. Thus a whole revolution was brought about. Denmark immediately followed Britain's example, and Sweden began to discuss similar plans. The ideas of Henry George proved capable of stimulating far-reaching practical measures.

Such was not the effect of the other work to be mentioned here, Edward Bellamy's *Looking Backward,* which appeared in 1888. It was not a call to action but an appeal for the revision of traditional concepts. Written in the form of a utopia, it purported to give a picture of a socialistic society such as had developed in the year 2000. It had a far more practical character than all previous utopias. It took into consideration the general nature of men, their self-interest and their common sense, and quite methodically attempted to show, even to the details of daily life, how socialism would function and satisfy both intellectual and economic needs. Precisely by virtue of a certain factual dryness, the book made an impression of reality such as no earlier utopia had attained. It was really effective socialistic propaganda.

The book was immediately translated into all European languages, from Portuguese to Russian, and was a great hit everywhere. For thousands upon thousands of people it was the first introduction to socialistic ideas which they had hitherto known only by name. It helped powerfully in strengthening the new wave of socialism which rose in the 1880's in Europe and reached a temporary climax in the centenary of the French Revolution with the foundation of the Second International in Paris in 1889. Thus strangely enough, even European socialism received an impetus from America.

XII

WORLD CO-OPERATION IN TECHNOLOGY
AND SCIENCE

AFTER the transatlantic cable was laid in 1866 and after steamboats became regular carriers of the traffic between America and Europe, the two great continents of western civilization were drawn so closely together in all their activities as to make their progress increasingly interdependent. In all domains of civilization they came to constitute a firm unity that made it difficult to single out the contributions from the one or the other side. International coöperation became the prevailing characteristic of life and work in all countries within this unity.

With the immensely mounting population and wealth of America—once the territory of the United States was completely settled and the country had ceased to be a land of pioneers—the center of gravity of western civilization would inevitably tend to move in such a way as to attain a more even balance among the nations included. Then the question would naturally arise whether the leadership of civilization would pass into the hands of new nations. Was it possible that the leadership would be taken over by America?

In the 1880's, the French Socialist Victor Considérant expressed his conviction that the movement of civilization would lead westward and end in America. "When we observe the general march of humanity," he wrote in his pamphlet *The Great West* in 1854, "we easily perceive that progress, while advancing in Time, displaces itself in Space, and that the focus of social light and impulsion has always proceeded from the East to the West like the Sun." This appeared to Considérant a law of nature, and everything indicated, he said, that the last phase of social evolution would be attained on the new continent of America.

No law has ever been discovered governing the appearance

of the highest forms of genius. It is not an absolute certainty that large nations produce the largest number of men of genius. The great Belgian historian Pirenne once told me that during the First World War he had billeted in his house a German officer of considerable intelligence with whom he often discussed the problems of our times. This officer ventured the assertion that a great genius could only be born in great nations. When Pirenne asked him to name a great genius produced by Germany after the establishment of the German Empire, the officer unhesitatingly answered: Ibsen! It was easy for Pirenne to ridicule this proof of German greatness. Whether he succeeded in convincing the officer of his error, I don't know. At all events, other conditions being equal, human probability would seem to be in favor of the assumption that a nation of fifty or a hundred millions might give birth to more men of genius than one of five or ten millions. In a country like America, where so many European nations meet and compete—where there is so much social and mental friction to strike vigorous sparks of human intelligence—where the opportunities of individuals are great as nowhere else—in such a country we may well expect to see human genius rise to the highest peaks of effort and achievement in all domains of civilization.

What the future may bring, nobody knows. During recent times, however, America has achieved amazing feats of intellectual energy, and individuals of the highest genius have appeared. But the greatest results have been won by the coöperation of united forces within the nation and by coöperation with other nations. Is it possible to state whether America has been, is, or will be the strongest power in this universal coöperation?

In the last year of the nineteenth century, Brooks Adams, the American historian, thought himself entitled to say, as already quoted, in his book *America's Economic Supremacy*, that the seat of wealth and power, migrating westward, had at that time entered America. In the first year of the twentieth century, the brilliant English journalist William T. Stead published a book entitled *The Americanization of the World,* in which he tried to prove that the whole of Europe, and all the European colonies, were rapidly adjusting themselves to American patterns in economic, political, religious, and other matters. He saw American ideas and forms of life penetrating everywhere together with American products and American machines. The only resistance to American influence he discerned in Germany under the leadership of the Kaiser. But even the Kaiser appeared "driven to Americanize when he resisted Americanization." Stead affirmed that there were no more Americanized cities in Europe than Hamburg and Berlin: "They are American in the rapidity of their growth, American in their nervous energy, American in their quick and great appropriation of the facilities for rapid transport." He pointed to the quick adoption of the latest American machines by German manufacturers and engineers, and he believed it true to say that the Social Democratic Party in Germany received inspiration from German immigrants in America. In this he found an analogy to the relations between the Irish-Americans and the Irish in Ireland.

The fundamental fact in all this seems to be the unification of the world, particularly of western civilization. In this community of life and thought America is one element, certainly a very strong one and one of determining power.

* * * * *

Throughout the nineteenth century, communication and commerce between Europe and America was on the whole a mutual affair. But toward the close of the century a remarkable change set in. American historians have often fixed their attention on the fact that by about 1890 the whole territory of the United States was settled so that there was no longer an internal frontier of settlement. Another important fact is that at the same time American capital and enterprise started expanding beyond the boundaries of the country. Until that time, Great Britain had been the greatest investor nation of the world, and she had invested considerable capital in enterprises in the United States. Other foreign capital also sought a profit in America. Toward the close of the nineteenth century, United States businessmen began to invest capital abroad, at first in the neighboring American countries, Canada and Mexico. When the twentieth century opened, they began to invade Europe.

It was a significant occurrence when in 1901 a European government, that of Great Britain, for the first time sought and received an American loan. That was the beginning of a new epoch which transformed America from a debtor to a creditor nation. The First World War struck a serious blow to Great Britain's economic supremacy; after that war, English foreign investments were reduced by a quarter, and the main fact of this decline was the repatriation of American securities. During the following years, the United States began to replace Great Britain as an investor nation on a large scale. In that period American capital showed an annual net export averaging about 600 million dollars. In 1930 when the depression set in, American foreign investments amounted to fifteen billion dollars, more than a third of this sum being in European countries.

The expansion of American capital had another aspect which was almost more impressive. That was the invasion of Europe by the big American trusts. The oldest of them, the Standard Oil Company, organized in 1882, soon established branches in one European country after the other. Rival oil companies followed its example. So did American shoe companies. The United Shoe Manufacturing Company in 1899 set up at least one branch in England. The American Tobacco Company, which in 1901 had acquired the United Cigar Stores Company, combined in 1902 with the Imperial Tobacco Company in England for the organization of the jointly owned British-American Tobacco Company, which took over the foreign trade of both firms.

Together with American capital, American methods of manufacture and business entered victoriously into the whole field of European production and commerce. European business leaders were frightened when they saw American products invading their home markets and crowding out their own articles. At first they were inclined to complain of unfair competition and condemn the American methods as unethical. But soon they understood that efficient machinery and closely knit sales organizations were what made it possible to offer cheap goods. Discovering that business was a science demanding scientific study, they began to establish both technical schools and business schools after American patterns, and American merchandizing methods were adopted one after the other. Efficiency became the slogan of economic life in Europe as in America.

If anything could be called Americanization, it must be this infiltration of American capital and business spirit into European economic life. At any rate, it meant an increasing combination of the interests of both continents. This community of interests found a formal expression in the changes that occurred in the activities of the Chambers of Commerce. Such institutions had been formed in a very distant period—in the United States as far back as colonial times (1768) for the purpose of defending domestic interests, originally for no more than individual cities. The American example had been followed in Europe, where, a hundred years later, in one country after the other city chambers were united into national instruments. They became representative of all the commercial interests of their country and charged themselves with many new tasks. In the twentieth century a new phase of their activities was opened with the establishment of national Chambers of Commerce in foreign cities where they coöperated with the domestic Chambers. Finally in 1920 all of them combined in an International Chamber of Commerce. It is interesting to notice, in view of the fact that W. T. Stead in 1901 had pointed to Hamburg and Berlin as the most Americanized cities in Europe, that it was those two cities which led in the movement for this extension of the functions of the Chambers of Commerce. Their efforts for world commerce in turn reacted upon the American commercial world in advancing universal conceptions.

* * * * *

The close connection of American and European economic life is perhaps nowhere better illustrated than in the progress of the American steel industry, the basic element of modern industrial civilization by virtue of the vital part which steel plays in all domains of production and transportation. Since the last decade of the nineteenth century the United States has been the leading country in the production of steel, not only in absolute quantities but also in the output of steel per man and per blast furnace. That means that American methods are more efficient than those of any other nation, although the fundamental advances of technique in steel production were first made in Europe.

It was an Englishman, Henry Bessemer, who in his quest for a material with the quality of malleable iron to be used in the casting of cannon, discovered in 1856 the pneumatic method of making steel. At the same time an American, William Kelly, discovered the same principle. But Bessemer developed it more completely and more successfully, and it was his discovery that made an epoch in the steel industry. The whole world speaks of "Bessemer steel."

Alexander Holley brought the Bessemer method to America and combined it with the Kelly processes in his steel plant at Troy, N. Y., in 1865. He did not limit his work to his own plant; he helped make the new method general in America. He became the foremost steel-plant engineer and designer in the United States, and made many original improvements in design, so that he has been justly recognized as the father of modern steel manufacture.

A German immigrant in America, John A. Roebling, transferred the Bessemer method to a new article. In the 1840's he had made his specialty the manufacture of iron wire, which he utilized in the construction of suspension bridges. He made a sensation, when in 1851 he began the construction of the suspension bridge over the Niagara River. With the Bessemer method he could supplant wrought iron in the wire by mild steel; in 1868 he was able to undertake the building of the Brooklyn Bridge, the largest suspension bridge ever attempted at that date. When it was finally completed by his son in 1883, it was admired as one of the wonders of the world.

The Bessemer converter had a disadvantage in that it was only serviceable for iron poor in phosphorus. It was therefore an event of major importance when Sidney Gilchrist Thomas, again in England, in 1879 constructed a furnace that rendered phosphoric iron ores completely available for the manufacture of Bessemer steel. The introduction of this reformed converter spelled a great increase in American production.

Before the Bessemer method had been widely accepted, a German immigrant in England, William Siemens, had demonstrated that both a heightened temperature and an economy of fuel could be obtained by the use of gas to heat the furnace hearth. When his process by 1865 had been improved by the brothers Martin in France, the converter was gradually replaced by the open hearth, and the combination of the Bessemer method with the Siemens-Martin method—the combination thus of British, German, and French genius—gave a new stimulus to the steel industry. One new gain from these inventions was the possibility of using all kinds of scrap iron for the manufacturing of steel, with the result that the annual output of steel soon exceeded the annual production of pig iron.

On the foundation of all these discoveries and inventions American practical genius carried the production of steel to a constantly enhanced perfection. The billion-dollar trust called the United States Steel Corporation worked systematically on the improvement of technical methods for efficiency as well as for economy. Labor-saving devices were applied in all operations, electricity was introduced in all stages of manufacturing, and extensive standardization was made the rule for all products. An important saving of labor was attained by a process whereby the steel furnaces received hot metal directly and continuously from the blast furnaces. Another remarkable new process was continuous strip sheet rolling without reheating of the steel. All such inventions increased the productivity of the mills immensely. The Americans were not alone in making such progress; the German steel works, for instance, achieved many practical improvements. But America kept her position in the vanguard of production. None could beat her, although she owed much of her superiority to the adaptation of European ideas.

*　　*　　*　　*　　*

In another important domain of industry, discoveries and researches by an American opened a whole new epoch. This was in the chemical industries, and the man was a quiet professor of mathematics, apparently secluded from the bustle of life—Josiah Willard Gibbs. Although not completely heedless of the problems of technology, he achieved and published his far-reaching results in mathematical physics without ostentation and without any attempt to demonstrate their practical effects. His great work *On the Equilibrium of Heterogeneous Substances* (1876–78) laid the foundation of a new science—physical chemistry. But it took time for its importance to be understood, and even after other scientists had begun to emphasize and develop the new ideas contained in Gibbs's work, many conservative chemists continued to reject the new science. Today Gibbs is one of the most shining names in the history of science.

His victory came first in Europe. There his studies were carried on by brilliant men of research in many countries—by Bakhuis Roozeboom and other great Dutch physicists and chemists, by Wilhelm Ostwald and Fritz Haber in Germany, by Svante Arrhenius in Sweden, by Kristian Birkeland in Norway. There too his ideas were transformed into technics and created giant industries. The chemical industry was simply revolutionized. Chemistry entered virtually every industrial field, but more especially those branches of production called chemical-process industries. The simple enumeration of the major groups in the chemical industry fills twenty-four lines in the *Encyclopaedia of the Social Sciences* (1935), and more or less directly most of them owe their existence to the genius of Gibbs.

In America, the Aluminum and Standard Oil companies were among the first to exploit the new opportunities offered by the new formulas and methods. In 1888, George Eastman's construction of the Kodak camera made photography an art which could be practiced even by amateurs; it became an indispensable tool for newspapers all over the world, and introduced a new hobby to large numbers of people.

In America also the Atmospheric Products Company in 1902 was engaged in experiments to solve the problem of making ammonia by the synthesis of nitrogen and hydrogen drawn from the air by electricity. It was an urgent practical problem as well as a scientific one. In a presidential address to the British Association at Bristol in 1898, the famous physicist and chemist, Sir William Crookes, had drawn a gloomy picture of the future of mankind by predicting the imminent exhaustion of the nitrate deposits in Chile, whereby the world's agricultural production would be seriously diminished and general starvation would follow. Many people discussed the possibility of finding another fertilizer in the nitrogen of the air. The first man who succeeded in solving the problem was the Norwegian Physicist Kr. Birkeland in 1903. Together with the engineer Sam Eyde he started the Norwegian Company of Electro-Chemical Industry for exploiting the method. The immense quantity of electric power needed was easily available in Norway at a price that made the production profitable. The original company became the mother of a whole family of plants for various electro-chemical products, aluminum, carborundum, carbide, and explosives. A few years later, the German physicist Haber discovered a similar method of making nitrate from the air; he too associated himself with a practical engineer, Robert Bosch, and the Haber-Bosch method became the foundation of the powerful I. G. Farbenindustrie. It formed a cartel with the Norwegian company, and the two companies proceeded to divide the market of the world between them.

Both in Germany and in Norway the new chemical industries became the leading elements in the national industrial life. In England they were consolidated in the Imperial Chemical Industries, Ltd., in Italy in the Montecatini Societa per l'Industria Mineraria e Agricola. Everywhere the laws of physical chemistry were applied, and all kinds of synthetic products were manufactured in large quantities—dyestuffs like indigo, drugs like aspirin, rubber, etc. The production of synthetic resins as applied to the metal industry or in sound-reproducing devices (radio) has been called "one of the modern romances of chemistry." During the First World War, American scientists constructed new types of optical glasses through chemical processes. The intimate connection between science and industry was never so strikingly illustrated as in the rapid growth of the chemical industries; plants in this field regularly maintained laboratories for experimenting and research.

* * * * *

In 1840 Tocqueville had predicted that in America there would be a mounting interest in science, particularly in efforts to make discoveries useful to industry. The impetuous enterprise characteristic of all domains of industry and the enormous wealth created by it both contributed to carrying America forward to a leading part in the progress of science; the New World coöperated with the Old on equal terms and even surpassed it in the effective organization of research work. Apparently the great American industrialists grasped the importance of scientific research more fully than their European colleagues, as witnessed by the large endowments given by them to institutions for research and study.

In some cases such endowments were directly instrumental in furthering European studies also. That is one aspect of the constantly increasing coöperation within the whole of western civilization, evident perhaps in no field more than in the sciences. Another external sign of this unity has been the awarding since 1901 of the Swedish Nobel prizes for scientific research to eminent Americans as well as to Europeans. In our day, in fact, every advance in scientific knowledge immediately becomes the property of all workers in the same field, and every new gain in understanding or mastering the forces of nature is the stepping-stone to other new gains to be won by other students. Publications of academies and universities, scientific reviews of all kinds are links of mutual assistance. Still this universal coöperation is only partially organized, but there are already in existence international associations for research in general as well as special branches, which are bringing men of research ever more closely together.

* * * * *

A typical instance of world unity in scientific research may be seen in the studies that led to the discovery of vitamins. In the 1880's, the Japanese surgeon-general Takaki began experiments on beriberi, the disease that was incapacitating so many soldiers in his army. In the 1890's the Dutch investigator Christiaan Eijkman took up the same problem. He arrived at the conclusion (1897) that some quality of the food was the reason for the disease, and in particular he stated that in the polishing of rice something was taken away which would have prevented beriberi. Shortly thereafter, in the first years of the twentieth century, the Norwegian professor Axel Holst was officially commissioned to examine why in recent times, despite careful regulations, beriberi and scurvy had become common among seamen on long voyages and on polar expeditions. He was able to state that such diseases were caused by the want of certain substances in vegetables that were killed by modern processes of canning. Further researches into food substances were conducted in England by Charles Martin and Sir Frederick Hopkins, in the United States by McCollum, Mendel, and Osborne. At the meeting of the Far Eastern Association of Tropical Medicine at Hongkong in 1912, American, English, French, and Japanese investigators were nearly unanimous that beriberi was of dietetic and not of infectious origin. Meanwhile the Polish investigator Casimir Funk, who had studied in Berne, Paris, and London, had already drawn the same conclusion from his own and others' researches into beriberi and had proclaimed (1911) the existence of vitamins—this was the name he gave to the unknown substance needed for health. Now it is called Vitamin B-1, for a whole series of vitamins has since been discovered, and the study of them has been carried on in laboratories all over the world. Their problems have not yet been completely resolved, but all civilized nations share in the work on them.

✿   ✿   ✿   ✿   ✿

Similar is the history of the hormones—the name given to the internal secretions of glands in animal and human bodies by two English physiologists, W. M. Bayliss and E. H. Starling, who published the results of their researches into the highly important effects of these secretions in 1919. They were not the first to observe these effects. Before them French, German, Swiss, and other investigators had studied the glands and their secretions. A

French-American, Brown-Séquard, born at Mauritius of a French mother and an American father, later living and working as a doctor in America and in France, had in his experiments come very close to the conclusions of Bayliss and Starling as early as 1891. As with vitamins, the general idea embodied in the concept of hormones stimulated rivalry in research throughout the world. An Austrian doctor, Eugen Steinach, announced in 1920 a method of rejuvenating people by the implantation of new glands. An American doctor, Louis Berman, drew a vivid picture in 1921 of how the hormones determined and regulated personality. A more practical effect sprang from the isolation and production of one of the hormones by two Canadian doctors, Banting and Best, in the laboratory of Professor MacLeod at the University of Toronto in 1922. They called it insulin, and it proved an effective remedial agent in the treatment of diabetes. As such it was later improved by a Danish doctor, Hagedorn. Laboratories of universities and other scientific institutions in America worked eagerly on the study and use of insulin and other hormones, and indeed many European students came to America to observe the progress of the researches.

❊   ❊   ❊   ❊   ❊

The discovery of both vitamins and hormones, resulting from the study of diseases, had important consequences for practical medicine. In this latter field America gave the world something of her best. She had been the leader in dentistry at an early date and had discovered the first methods of anaesthesia. The next great advance in medicine—that represented by bacteriology— was due to the researches of French, German, and British investigators (Pasteur, Koch, Lister), but America carried them forward, both in practice and in research. The study of toxins was founded by two professors at the University of Pennsylvania, Mitchell and Reichart, who first demonstrated that the most powerful poisons known are proteins, the poisonous proteins later called toxins. Sewell of the University of Michigan in 1887 discovered methods of securing immunity from the action of toxins. The German Paul Ehrlich extended these methods by the production of serums. To a large extent chemical pathology was the result of his work, and he instigated the manufacture of synthetic drugs which became, as it were, a specialty of America. One of the most important toxins, the diphtheria antitoxin, was first isolated in pure form by Dr. John Northrup of the Rockefeller Institute of Medical Research. Dr. Bela Schick of New York was the discoverer of the method for determining immunity. The sulfa drugs, developed first in Germany and France after 1935, and the still more recent penicillin, first made in England in 1940, found their most extended use in America where they were made the objects of mass production. An eminent medicinal discovery of another kind was the feeding of liver for the cure of pernicious anemia; that was the work of two Boston doctors, Minot and Murphy, in 1926.

Such activities have made American doctors and American hospitals famous through the whole world. In recent years, people have learned to look to America for all the best features in matters of healing and health.

* * * * *

Paradoxically, the true unity of the world was most strikingly demonstrated by the Second World War, not only in drawing almost all nations into totalitarian warfare, but also in making all of them rivals in exploiting one of the greatest discoveries in the history of mankind—the method of releasing atomic energy for practical use. The definitive experiments in the long series of researches for the desired aim were undertaken in America, but they were made with the coöperation of scientists from Germany, Denmark, Italy, Great Britain, Canada, and other countries. Saboteurs in German-occupied Norway did their share of the work by preventing the enemies of mankind, the Nazis, from completing their similar experiments.

At the close of the war the tremendous destructive power of atomic energy was proved by the bombing of two Japanese cities, and it posed at once new and far-reaching problems for the whole of humanity, problems which cannot be solved without universal coöperation. If the world succeeds in such a solution, the new power won for the service of mankind will open a new epoch of progress and all nations will benefit from it.

XIII

ONE WORLD OF IDEAS

In the world of ideas America has not been so creative as in that of the sciences. Even in science it has to be admitted that the large synthetic concepts have generally originated with European men of research. And in philosophical thought Europe has largely shown the way. Kantian idealism was able to release intellectual forces in America strong enough to react again upon Europe through Emersonian transcendentalism. This movement demonstrated to the world the existence of a vigor in the American mind capable of translating European ideas into active life. But the philosophical system—so far as there was a system—that figured as the basis of such ideas was wholly borrowed from Europe. Even the Kantian idealism which proved such a force in America was not widely accepted among the educated classes. What really appealed to their mental needs and tastes and prevailed through most of the nineteenth century was the Scottish "common-sense philosophy" which distrusted abstract reason and made it its chief task to defend traditional morals and religion. At the end of the 1860's evolutionary ideas began to force their way into American thought, particularly with the works of Herbert Spencer, and Americans limited themselves to accepting and absorbing his economic liberalism with its emphasis on laissez-faire. Presently, however, evolution attained such an influence upon general thought as to amount to a revolution, and under its influence America created a philosophy distinguished by a character that made it felt in Europe as a new and valuable contribution to the common treasure of ideas.

The leader of this new America philosophy was William James. He had a firm footing in the European tradition, having been to a great extent educated in Europe; nevertheless his American character was unmistakable. He came to philosophy from psychology, and to psychology from physiology. That too

218

was in accordance with the new ways of proceeding in Europe. It made James above all an observer and investigator. In 1876 at Harvard he established the first American psychological laboratory; this was only a few years later than the first one in Europe. Toward the close of the 1870's he began to publish articles on psychology in European reviews which evoked immediate attention. James was fully imbued with the evolutionary conception of the human mind; he regarded the whole conscious field as a function of the nervous system. But he brought a new idea, or rather a new emphasis, into the study of consciousness. That was something truly American: he stressed the active and interested aspect of consciousness, asserting it as a causal force of thought and life, and insisting on the continuity of the stream of consciousness. To him this psychological flux was the true and fundamental existence. Mind became a function of living, never static, always dynamic, and life became an effect of progressive selection.

This was the view that give the impetus to the French philosopher Henri Bergson for the elaboration of his "vitalism," the idea of the *élan vital* as the essential force of life, as presented in his essay on the immediate ideas of the consciousness (1889). Likewise it was at the basis of the German Gestalt psychology. Therefore, when James in 1890 collected his studies in his *Principles of Psychology*, the book took its place as a monumental work in the development of this science. It even reached far beyond the circle of students in the field because it was so extremely well written, forgoing much of the professional terminology, illuminated by practical examples from daily life and—strange to say—even by wit.

As a good American James steadily appealed to common sense, using it, not to defend conventional ideas, but on the contrary to break through them. In the presence of authorities and theories he was always prompted to question, doubt, and disregard them. He based his work on what he called radical empiricism, and he was suspicious of generalizations. He accepted, however, as facts not only experiences that could be observed and charted, but also the thoughts and beliefs that might be formed in the minds of individuals. That was the reason why he was interested in religious conceptions, not as doctrines but as important emotional and imaginative phases of the life of mind. There was in him a double current, one stemming from the rational Enlightenment of the eighteenth century, another closely related to the inveterate Christian traditions of his nation. The truth of religion could not be to him a purely intellectual question; it would prove itself by experience and by life, and faith was by itself a power of reality. When in 1902 he published *The Varieties of Religious Experience*, it conveyed a new understanding of mental forces, and gave a great impetus to more systematic research in the psychology of religion.

Obviously much of this psychological research contained a philosophy of life. As a natural consequence came his two philosophical works, *Pragmatism* (1907) and *A Pluralistic Universe* (1908). They were as undogmatic as his psychological treatises. Professors of metaphysics found his philosophy incoherent and contradictory, but that did not disturb James. So he found life itself. He consciously rejected all absolutes. Half jestingly he could exclaim: "What a curse philosophy would be if we couldn't forget all about it!" According to him, the meaning of an idea consisted in the particular consequences it led to, and he looked to life for the final test. Like Walt Whitman, he himself had faith. He believed in human free will, in individualism and all the ventures of freedom, in the promises of the future. He regarded life as an unfinished experiment with unpredictable changes. In its valuing of all ideas according to their practical bearing upon human interests, his pragmatism struck Europeans as an eminently American philosophy, but one adaptable to the European mind. It was felt as a liberation from coercive systems and it influenced ways of thinking in large circles, even when it was not consciously accepted.

A younger American philosopher, John Dewey, stood forth beside William James and became after him the leader of the pragmatic movement. He was even more active in practical life than James, and his practical influence in Europe was greater. He defined thoughts as plans of action or as imaginative projections of possible lines of action. Philosophy, he said, "is at once an explicit formulation of the various interests of life and a propounding of points of view and methods through which a better balance of interests may be effected." He studied the origin and process of ideas and valuations in order to determine their use for the shaping of the future. He conceived life as the steady adjustment of individuals to their environments, and he praised democracy as the experimental method of testing ideas on the stage of social issues. He concluded that such a democracy "must have a type of education which gives individuals a personal interest in social relationship and control, and the habits of mind which secure social changes without introducing disorder." He called it the "socialization of mind." Thus pure individualism was not enough for him, nor was the limitation implied by the national unit. He looked forward to the universal community of man. In this spirit he started and led the movement for "progressive education." At first, in the 1890's, at the University of Chicago, afterwards at Columbia University, he established experimental schools for the practice of his ideas. These schools became famous over the world. From all the countries of Europe teachers and scholars came to see them, and they stimulated both research and new practices in education in all democratic countries. The old stiff and sterile scholasticism was definitely conquered. Dewey's little book *Democracy and Education* (1916) became the program of a world movement.

The prominence of pragmatic philosophers like William James and John Dewey does not imply that America did not at the same time produce thinkers of a more purely metaphysical type. But they were few, and they attained almost no attention or influence outside their own country. Best known in Europe was Josiah Royce. Books about him and his philosophy appeared in France (1927) and in Norway (1934). He was an exponent of post-Kantian idealism. "As an American," it has been said of him, "he was predisposed to individualism, and sought earnestly to reconcile this motive with the absolutistic trend of his philosophy." But he did not reach a large audience in Europe.

In psychological studies, on the other hand, America worked

her way to the forefront. The new psychological school of behaviorism had its birthplace there. It was founded by a zoölogist, Herbert Spencer Jennings, a student of animal psychology (*Behavior of Lower Organisms*, 1906). His methods were transferred to the study of human psychology, particularly by John B. Watson (*Behavior*, 1914). As a general theory behaviorism always remained in dispute. But as a method of investigation it exerted universal influence. It made no use of introspection and it omitted all consideration of consciousness, but it was useful because of its insistence on the observation of the slightest movements of psychical reactions.

The highly original economic theories of Thorstein Veblen attracted some attention outside of America, and Richard T. Ely's more conservative textbook on political economy (1889) was in use in many European universities. Among the social sciences, it was only in the field of historical sociology, however, that America made a contribution which was recognized by European scholars as eminently important and which left a profound mark upon European research. That contribution was the work of Lewis Henry Morgan. Starting from inquiries into the family organization of the Iroquois (1859), he finally arrived at general conclusions as to the original organization of the human family (1871 and 1877). Into the romantic conception of an ancient matriarchy he brought a realistic view of the laws of consanguinity and descent. Even today his researches still have an important place in the study and discussion of these problems. His conclusions have found both adherents and opponents, but everyone acknowledges that he greatly furthered the comprehension of ancient society.

In other respects it was a long time before Europe took an active interest in American history. There was a general opinion that, apart from Indian studies, America was too young a country to offer anything truly instructive to the historian. The German Balt H. E. von Holst, who had lived in America for five years between 1867 and 1872, and who, twenty years later, returned to become an American citizen, made a real break with his solid and sympathetic work *Verfassung und Demokratie der Vereinigten*

Staaten, of which the first volume appeared in 1873. In Great Britain, quite naturally, the study of national history could not but touch on American history. In particular, the American Revolution demanded treatment. This event was finally explained not only from the British but from the American point of view as well in the fourth and following volumes of W. E. H. Lecky's *History of England in the Eighteenth Century* (1882). Six years later came James Bryce's great work *The American Commonwealth* which marked an epoch in British understanding of modern America. It attested to an intimate, critical, but thoroughly sympathetic knowledge of the country, and was written in a spirited way that made it attractive reading. Through the next fifty years the book appeared in numerous new editions, steadily revised and kept up to date by the author. There were even abridged editions for use as a textbook at colleges and universities. It was translated into several European languages, including even Croatian.

Nevertheless, on the European continent American studies were still not much in fashion. I remember the amazing experience I had when, as a student at the University of Leipzig in the winter of 1897–98, I went to hear the lectures on American history by the fine scholar Professor Erich Marcks. Only three students took his course, and only one of them was a German; the other, beside myself, was an American (I presume it was the later Professor and Ambassador William E. Dodd). Ten years later, German, Italian, Norwegian and other historians began going to America to study its civilization on the spot. Old professors shook their heads at the idea of studying history in America, but the younger generation went anyway. In Germany, textbooks were written in American history for the universities, at least one of them (by Paul Darmstädter, 1909) being very good. In Norway, at the University of Oslo, a course in American history was made obligatory for students majoring in history. The first World War brought America still more forcibly before European minds, and American history began to take its place as an obvious object of study.

On the other hand, America actively entered all fields of European studies. In that respect, the foundation in 1876 of the

Johns Hopkins University, organized exclusively for postgraduate studies, marked an epoch. The American nation felt mature in intellectual matters; no longer would it be content to remain in the attitude of a pupil. Its will to assert its equality in research work was demonstrated by the establishment of the Archaeological Institute of America in 1879 from which was born in 1882 the American School of Classical Studies at Athens. American universities and other scientific institutions sent out scholars for excavations in the Orient as well as in Greece. Oriental and classical studies were cultivated at leading universities and museums. The brilliant Russian archeologist and historian, Michael Rostovtzeff, became an American professor and published his works in English. Soon there was no branch of history or philology in which America did not participate by research, by books, by lectures, by reviews. In the twentieth century, American scholars really took their place side by side with Europeans, and in certain fields (for example, Chinese studies) they came to the forefront. Much of this work was organized on an international basis. It was the director of the American Council of Learned Societies, Waldo G. Leland, who took the initiative in creating in 1926 the International Committee of Historical Sciences.

Unfortunately, however, the humanistic studies have not attained to such a degree of international coöperation as have the sciences, and American contributions have not been so generally noticed or appreciated in Europe as they may have deserved, although they formed natural links in the progress of research. Frederick Jackson Turner's thesis concerning the influence of the frontier on American development was similar in nature to the interpretation of Russian history advanced by the Russian historian Vasili Kluchevski, but it was a long time before either author found recognition for his ingenious and stimulating idea outside his own country. Brooks Adams' provocative theories concerning the growth and decay of civilizations and their connection with the movement of the centers of exchange attracted little attention in Europe, although Oswald Spengler's *Decline of the West* (1919) may well have been a belated echo of Adams' pessimistic hypothesis. Until recently the creative works of Henry Adams remained almost unknown in Europe.

An economic interpretation of American history more conformable to the Marxian conceptions that exerted such a strong influence on historical thought in Europe was initiated by Charles A. Beard's challenging book *An Economic Interpretation of the Constitution of the United States* in 1913, and continued in later works by him and others. European historians, however, even those of the Marxian creed, witnessed these beginnings in America with relative indifference. Their importance lay in the fact that they attested to the correspondence of ideas in American and European intellectual life.

*   *   *   *   *

Such correspondence was evident in literature and art as well.

What Europeans had perceived as something distinctly American when they first became aware of American literature was its humor, particularly in the sketches of Washington Irving. Not that humor was foreign to European literature. English humor indeed became world-famous through the works of Charles Dickens, and North-German humor was represented by Fritz Reuter. But Americans were reputed to possess humor as their peculiar gift. They won this reputation particularly through the lectures given in London in 1858 by the great showman Barnum on "the science of money making and the philosophy of humbug." Since he was regarded as typically American, as in certain respects he was, his philosophy was received as specifically American. Europeans, first of all the English, formed their idea of American humor upon Barnum's specimen, and they clung to it with singular stubbornness. When G. K. Chesterton wrote on American humor in 1902, he defined it as "purely exaggerative." He called it "wild, sky-breaking." And to all Europeans the "tall tale" was its true characteristic, the natural overflow of the exuberance of youth and of national expansion. It made you laugh heartily, but it did not bring the tear to the eye that would come from a sympathetic heart. Therefore, when

Chesterton met the humor in Bret Harte's California stories, he could recognize that the author was "a genuine American and a genuine humorist," but he denied that he was "an American humorist," because he found knit closely into the texture of Bret Harte's humor the two (in his opinion) un-American qualities of reverence and sympathy. The world at large, perhaps, did not make such a subtle distinction. When, at the end of the 1860's, Bret Harte's stories began to be known in Europe, they were at once accepted as truly American. His characters were pictured against the background of a rough society and were often grotesque, but one felt the good in their hearts and loved them in spite of their absurdities. Why shouldn't that too be American? Isn't there sentimentality enough in America?

When Chesterton delimited American humor as he did, he mentally contrasted Bret Harte with Mark Twain. With Mark Twain Europe became acquainted with a humor which was rightly conceived as genuinely American and by most people as the only American form of humor. He made a hit with his lectures in England in 1873, and from that time on he represented in Europe for half a century the great American humorist, a kind of successor of Barnum. Mark Twain was not sentimental, and he had a good deal of "exaggerative" humor, though he could use understatement as well. A true child of the frontier, with its aggressive individualism and its democratic insolence, he respected no one's dignity. Besides, as his friend W. D. Howells said, he was "the most unliterary man in his make and manner" —"he wrote as he thought, and as all men think, without sequence, without an eye to what went before or should come after." It is, of course, a great art to write in a natural way, and Mark Twain was a master of that art. He had what has been called the Western "swaggering extravagance of speech," and he could tell a tall tale as no one else could. He made all of Europe laugh. But if Chesterton found him deficient in reverence, it was because Mark Twain had reverence for other idols than those of Chesterton. He did not revere monarchy or past greatness or conventional morals, nor had he any veneration for the Church of England or for any other church. His humor was truly iconoclastic, as was that of Cervantes, and Kipling was right when he said that Mark Twain was a relation of Cervantes. His most fundamental quality was a profound respect for healthy, uncorrupted human nature.

What Europe finally retained out of his production, after it had laughed over his droll stories, was mainly his two boys' books, *The Adventures of Tom Sawyer* (1876) and *The Adventures of Huckleberry Finn* (1884). They are excellent boys' books, but I suspect that only adults can enjoy the full humor of them. Previously, in his *Sketches,* he had written a "Story of the bad little boy" and a "Story of the good little boy," and it was evident from them that he "hated moral boys." In the full-length boys' books he demonstrated his hatred and contempt of tyrannical educators and pretentious moralists, of affected phraseology and misplaced sentimentality, of all kinds of humbug and fraud. Tom and Huck were rebels against the conventions of their surroundings, and they represented the rebellion of the human heart against social coercion, because they were boys following the natural impulses of boys. The two books about them were translated into all European languages, including Finnish, Croatian, and almost any language one can think of, and new translations have appeared right down to yesterday. Surely they have helped to liberate education in all countries from many old chains of strictness and severity. Not only have they amused millions of boys, but they have also created for them better conditions for a freer development.

Mark Twain's works are wholly American, but they are at the same time immensely human. W. D. Howells was a little puzzled at the universal acceptance of his humor. But Howells himself offered the explanation: "I suppose that Mark Twain transcends all other American humorists in the universal qualities. . . . There is a poetic lift in his work, even when he permits you to recognize it only as something satirized. There is always the touch of nature, the presence of a sincere and frank manliness in what he says, the companionship of a spirit which is at once delightfully open and deliciously shrewd." In brief, he not only made people laugh, he made them think and feel too. That is why his best works endure even in far-off countries.

* * * * *

On the whole, popular literary taste was not very different in Europe and America. European girls were quite as enthusiastic as American girls about Louisa M. Alcott's *Little Women* (1868) and her later girls' books, and they were equally moved by Frances Hodgson Burnett's *Little Lord Fauntleroy* (1886) which, in contrast to the adventures of Tom Sawyer and Huckleberry Finn, was the sentimental story of "the good boy," and perhaps therefore more favored by girls than by boys. Among adults, Lew Wallace's *Ben-Hur, a Tale of the Christ* (1880) was a tremendous success and a great best seller in Europe as well as in America; in both hemispheres it struck the same chords of religion and romanticism. Highly popular for at least two decades at the end of the century were the superficial novels of Marion Crawford, which offered glamorous pictures from foreign worlds; they satisfied innate longings for exotic adventures, and briefly entertained a large public, but were quickly forgotten.

Generally speaking, the currents of more serious creative literature were the same on both sides of the Atlantic. This was eminently true of the predominance of the realistic novel which began in Europe in the 1850's with authors like Flaubert, George Eliot, Gottfried Keller, and Björnson, continued in the 1860's with the great Russians Turgenieff, Tolstoi, and Dostoievski, with Zola, and others, and reached its zenith in the 1870's and 80's, its last powerful representative being Strindberg. America had its active share in the beginning of this movement in the works of Hawthorne, and it came to the forefront in the 1870's and 80's with two remarkable authors, William Dean Howells and Henry James. From the European point of view, Howells was rather a respectable fellow fighter than a leader; only one of his novels, *The Rise of Silas Lapham* (1884), the typical story of an American businessman, won a worldwide

reputation and was translated and read all over Europe. Henry
James won for himself a much broader place and was recognized
as one of the leading men in European literature. He was perhaps the greatest artist of all the novelists of the realistic school.
If America had not produced such authors of artistic perfection
as Poe and Hawthorne, one would have been tempted to say
that James appeared un-American in being seemingly so absorbed by the artistic criteria of his work rather than by any
social aim.

There is, of course, room for dispute as to whether he can be
regarded as an American author. Like his brother, the philosopher William James, he had had much of his education in
Europe, he had received determining influences from French,
English, and Russian authors, and during his whole life as an
author (more than forty years) he lived constantly in Europe.
By his mastery of two hemispheres he became more cosmopolitan in his outlook than any of his European colleagues. In large
measure he treated cosmopolitan subjects; one of his chief studies
was the American in Europe. For that purpose he had to picture
and investigate the impact of two different backgrounds, what
he called "the international situation," and his contemporaries
often called him the Balzac of English and American society.
Although, as a true realist, he was always careful to place his
characters firmly in their milieu, his keenest interest was in the
psychology of the individual character of the various persons
who populated his novels. In this field he gradually developed
a subtlety that made him the master of his age.

In the middle of the 1890's, the French *Grande Encyclopédie*
called him "*le chef de l'école analytique dans la littérature
anglaise contemporaine.*" He maintained this position through
the early years of the twentieth century, when the *Encyclopaedia
Britannica* called him "a modern of the moderns . . . a very sen-
sitive impressionist, with a technique that can fix the most elu-
sive phase of character and render the most baffling surface. The
skill is unending with which he places his characters in such relations and under such lights that they flash out in due succession
their continuously varying facets." This judgment is particularly

valid with respect to the last period of his authorship, and the same article of the *Encyclopaedia* concludes: "For speculative readers, for readers who care for art in life as well as for life in art, and for readers above all who want to encounter and comprehend a great variety of very modern and finely modulated characters, Mr. James holds a place of his own, unrivalled as an interpreter of the world of today." A similar judgment can be found in the German *Meyers Groszes Konversations-Lexikon.*

Henry James was a power in world literature. He was overwhelmingly productive, and almost every one of his books offered something new and interesting. They were translated and read everywhere, they set the standard of art and taste for wide circles, and profoundly influenced the younger generations of novelists, particularly English writers, such as John Galsworthy.

The younger American novelists had much more of a fighting spirit in them than Henry James had manifested. To that extent they followed, perhaps unconsciously, rather in the footsteps of some of the great European realists. They joined the battle of Walt Whitman and Thorstein Veblen against the oppressive power of modern capitalism. To indicate which books of this character have attracted widespread attention in Europe is not to point out the best of them in the literary sense. During the twentieth century, American literature has generally been closely watched in Europe and forms part of the general reading on a par with European literature. But what makes a book appeal to a broad public is not always its finest qualities. I think it is true to say that the first great sensation came with *The Jungle* by Upton Sinclair (1906). It was such a colorful picture and such a harsh indictment of the atrocities of the Chicago stockyards as to evoke the fiercest indignation of Europe, the more so since the Chicago packers had recently been charged with exporting poisoned meat to the European markets.

Then followed the works of Jack London, not only *The Call of the Wild* which was a little older, but almost all of the books that made him the novelist of the proletariat. He became more generally popular than any other twentieth-century American author, and he certainly influenced the great European novelists of the proletariat, the Russian Maxim Gorki, the Dane Andersen-Nexö, the Norwegian Kristofer Uppdal.

Upton Sinclair's book also drew attention to the works of Frank Norris, in particular *The Octopus* (1901) the indictment of the big railroad companies.

Later (1922) came Sinclair Lewis' *Babbitt,* which was a roaring success over all of Europe and even won for the author the Nobel prize for literature. Through Babbitt the American businessman revealed himself to Europe with all his prejudices and became the symbol of his class. Others of Lewis' books were also read in Europe, but none of them took a similar hold of the public until *It Can't Happen Here* appeared in 1935. That was a striking success, an alert ringing out over the world, warning everybody of the dangers of Nazism.

There were other American literary successes in Europe, books by Booth Tarkington, Dorothy Canfield, Willa Cather, Pearl S. Buck, and others. But their significance was not so incisive. The American author who really came to wield a more penetrating influence in Europe was Ernest Hemingway. The intensity of his feeling and the impressionism of his style made a great impact on both readers and fellow authors. After the First World War there was in all European countries much talk about the new "post-war literature" that might be expected. In *A Farewell to Arms* (1929) Hemingway really gave expression to what the war had done to the new generation, the new values it had impressed on the young, and he came to stand for both the literary and the moral ideals of post-war youth.

In a peculiar way a work by an immigrant in a foreign idiom expressed something of the same mentality as the result of another kind of war—the war to conquer the land of America. That was *Giants in the Earth* by Ole E. Rölvaag (1927). It had been written and first published in Norwegian, but it was, as Vernon Parrington has said, "deeply and vitally American." It presented the tragedy of the frontier, the fight, the failure, and the victory, with the severe earnestness of life itself. It was the epic of how America was born and it portended the future of the nation.

In sum, the American literature of the twentieth century conveyed to Europe a sort of disillusioned virility, something hardened and yet burning beneath the crust. There was fight in it, that kind of spirit that will fight on even against apparent superiority because self-respect forbids surrender. These authors might have abandoned all ancient beliefs, but they acted on the old American certitude: "The soul is marching on." That meant strength to Europe too.

*   *   *   *   *

A new vitality came to the European press, as a result of influences from America. Of course, the mere technical development, the introduction of the rapid rotary press, of machine typing and other accelerating devices, counted for much in speeding up the trade of journalism. The telegraph too had an electrifying effect. But then, the very spirit of the American newspapers was contagious. Around 1850, Richard Cobden exhorted British journalists to take an example from their American colleagues. The conservative London *Times* answered by quoting items from American papers regarding people's private life that could not but strike English readers as odious. In transcribing a report from a fashionable American watering-place on the relative prettiness of girls assembled there, the *Times* asked indignantly: "What would our Mammas say to such a sketch from Cowes or Brighton?" The ruthlessness and sensationalism represented by James Gordon Bennett and his followers could not invite imitation either. In the 1880's, however, the press of all European countries began eagerly to adopt American features. That was particularly due to the innovations of Joseph Pulitzer.

Like Bennett, Pulitzer was an immigrant. Coming from Hungary, he made his debut in the United States as an editor of German-language papers. When, in 1883, he took over the New York *World*, he became the pioneer of new forms of journalism, and all the different features which he introduced were almost immediately imitated in Europe. Most conspicuous externally were the large headlines which seemed to call aloud to the

readers and excite their interest. Then there were all the pictures and cartoons that accompanied the text; the use of them
was facilitated by the development of the photograph. But even
in the text of the papers a transformation went on. Variety and
vivacity became the watchword. All kinds of "features" and
"stunts" were introduced. Swift condensation alternated with
broad detailing. Even the language changed. Terseness became
the first commandment of style, and the American journalists
created a picturesque vocabulary of striking power. I would not
pretend that this last development left any deep marks on European journalism. But in other respects, European papers generally began to resemble the American. Only one feature has not,
as yet, become usual in Europe—the "comics,"—although in recent years their invasion is apparent.

Sensationalism, such as prevailed in the "yellow" press, has
also found imitators in Europe, but has not generally infected
European newspapers. This aspect of the American press is frequently represented by Europeans as its salient characteristic,
and from that point of view the "Americanization" of the press is
often deplored. The vitalization of the press, however, seems to
me the fundamental fact, and it has helped powerfully to increase the influence of the press on the public mind.

❋   ❋   ❋   ❋   ❋

Closely connected with the development of the press was
the growth of the art of advertising. In fact, it was America that
made advertising an art. Barnum had impressed on the world
the advantages of publicity, and agencies of advertisement had
existed in America since 1840. The boom of economic enterprise
that set in after the Civil War found a natural expression in a
hectic publicity. In particular, the enormous development of
the patent medicine industry demanded an increasing perfection
of the technique of advertising. Illustrations were required, and
the psychology of the public had to be studied. In the 1880's and
90's, experts took the lead in the adaptation of advertisements to
changing conditions: the first color advertisement appeared, artists were called in to assist, novelty became an important factor,

illustrated catalogues became usual, streetcars and other vehicles of transportation were utilized for business publicity, posters and billboards were erected along railroad lines and highways. Nothing was neglected that would strike the eye and draw the attention of prospective customers wherever they might be. Advertising became exciting.

All these features, one after another, were gradually imitated in Europe. There too advertising was made a vital element in business, a proof of progressive enterprise. Now Europe too came to see full-page advertisements in certain newspapers, American business catalogues were studied as models, the peculiar mentality of customers in different countries was investigated, even public authorities learned how to advertise. In fact, advertisements became the basis of existence for many newspapers and to some extent for magazines. At the same time they stimulated the development of artistic methods and media—woodcut and lithography, and different methods of color printing. They became an integral part of modern life.

*   *   *   *   *

In the pictorial and sculptural arts modern America has produced many fine works, mostly, however, following the line of European development. Only one American artist really exerted an independent influence on European art. He was James McNeill Whistler, who learned his art in Europe. He was a pupil of the French painter Gustave Courbet, one of the precursors of the school of impressionists that took the leadership in art for decades from the beginning of the 1860's. Together with Edouard Manet, Whistler was the sensation of the *Salon des Refusés* in Paris in 1863 with his picture of "The White Girl." That achievement in itself would have made him one of the pioneers of the impressionist movement. But Whistler could not remain within the limits of a given school, however broad its scope. He went his own way, and his creative mind brought something truly new into the art of painting.

The titles he gave his works indicate plainly his intentions. Whether they were portraits or landscapes, he loved to call them "symphonies" or "harmonies" or "arrangements" in one or more colors, in white, in yellow and blue, in gray and gold, etc. That was what he called the poetry of sight: the colors alone should speak to the onlooker. Unlike many of his fellow impressionists he was completely un-literary in his art; he never had a "story" to tell, but simply wanted to communicate a mood, "divesting [to quote his own words] the picture from any outside sort of interest which might have been otherwise attached to it." Together with the other impressionists he resuscitated the cult of color which had been the greatness of the masters of the Baroque. Whistler himself felt most akin to Velasquez.

In Paris he associated mostly with the bohemian poets who rallied under the banner of Edgar Allan Poe. Whistler too fought for the idea of art for art's sake, or perhaps it would be more to the point to say, for the dignity of art independent of all conventional rules. That was what motivated his sensational libel suit against Ruskin who in 1877 defined his art, exemplified by a "Nocturne in black and gold," as "flinging a pot of paint in the public's face." He lost the case, and at the moment the public was ranged against him. But hardly more than a decade later the victory was his. The portrait of his mother or, as he renamed it, "arrangement in grey and black," became in 1891 a world success and appeared in thousands of reproductions in all countries. From that time on, his position as a painter might be compared with that of Henry James in literature, except for the significant fact that Whistler kept aloof from all groups. He did not form a school, but preferred to cultivate "the gentle art of making enemies."

His combative individualism might have been defined as his most truly American quality, if it had been found also in other American painters of that time. At any rate, he conceived of himself as the American rebel in the Ruskin case, and in Europe he certainly was a rebel. His work, genuinely personal as it was, was a challenge to the younger generation that accepted his artistic program. His influence was particularly strong in the art of etching and lithography, which he virtually renewed. His prints were fully as apt as his paintings to express moods with a singular power, to convey the poetry of the unsaid and suggest what was to be found between the strokes. He left a deep impress on all prominent later etchers and lithographers; his marks can be discerned, I think, even in the works of that great Norwegian artist Edvard Munch.

In the eyes of the general public another American painter, John Singer Sargent, was much more in vogue than Whistler, though I hardly know in what sense, except the merely legal one, he may be classed as an American artist. He was born and educated in Europe and spent almost all his life there. His works had nothing specifically American in them. He was one of the great virtuosos of modern times, possessing a facile and fluent technique, and he was for several decades one of the most fashionable portrait painters of the world, rivaling such a master as the great Swede Anders Zorn. His best pictures were a feast of colors to the eyes and recalled the English masters of the eighteenth century. But one does not sense the presence of a strong or original nature behind his work. Although I feel bound to cite the view of a judicious English expert, Frank Rutter, that Sargent "has been perhaps the greatest influence in portrait painting in our time," and that in the field of watercolor he "created a new and distinct style which had a great effect on his contemporaries," I nevertheless feel that the influence of Sargent was merely transitory.

A still more fleeting popularity was the lot of the amiable creator of the "Gibson Girl," Charles Dana Gibson, whose portraits of the sentimental American glamour girl flowed through all the magazines and newspapers of the world. If this girl was truly American, she was so in the most philistine way imaginable.

* * * * *

In one art, namely architecture, America gave to the world something totally new. Throughout the nineteenth century, America, like Europe, had lived essentially on imitations. America was so dominated by the classical style in all kinds of public buildings—state houses, banks, libraries—that it had almost become the American style, although romanticism had brought in the Gothic too. But new techniques and new materials called for new forms. Towards the close of the century, the skyscraper entered the field, made possible by the electric elevator and steel construction. As the first automobiles were formed on the pattern of horse-drawn wagons, so the first skyscrapers tried to imitate brick houses. But soon they made themselves independent. This was first achieved by the Chicago architect Louis H. Sullivan, who formulated the slogan of the new style: "Form follows function." According to that rule he made his skyscrapers form themselves around the skeleton of steel and concrete and won a new beauty for them by throwing away all false adornments.

The skyscraper never conquered the old cities of Europe. But what Sullivan had done for the skyscraper, a pupil of his, Frank Lloyd Wright, did for general house construction. In fact, he drew consequences from the rule of function which virtually revolutionized architecture. It is worthy of notice that he was an enthusiastic adorer of Walt Whitman, the poet of the young, realistic democracy, and he presented his program in a paper on "The Art and Craft of the Machine," read in 1894 before an audience in Jane Addams's Hull House, one of the characteristic institutions of the same democracy. Wright proclaimed the ideal of the architecture of the machine age. "Get rid of everything useless and false," he said. He considered walls, roof, windows, all the single parts of the building, as parts of one organic whole. His principle of design was an organic simplicity: the outside of the house should be the natural result of the inside. On that principle he built, and thus he created functionalism.

It became a world movement. Designs of his buildings were published in Germany in 1910, and students from foreign countries came to Chicago to learn from Wright. After the revolution in Russia in 1917, the new regime adopted the new architecture. Social workers, intent on housing reforms for the benefit of the poorer classes, saw the advantages of the new ideas, and after the First World War functionalism conquered one country after the other. New books on Wright and his principles appeared in German, in Dutch, in French, in Czech. Houses in his style were built in Frankfurt, in Oslo, in Moscow, and out in the country as well as in the cities. In his autobiography (1932) he could justly state that "new values came into the architecture of the world." The new houses were more fit for human habitation than many of the older ones, they appeared more natural on their sites, and the quiet streamlined effects gave a new sense of repose to the eyes. Sometimes unoriginal architects adopted features natural to the conditions of the land of origin as essential elements even in a different milieu and, in that way, made functionalism a hard and fast "style" instead of a principle to be adjusted to the actual conditions. This was a deviation from the fundamental idea. But it showed the strength of the movement that had come from America.

Frank Lloyd Wright drew other conclusions too from modern conditions. He maintained that the new easy mode of travel made possible by the automobile should lead to the disappearance of cities as places of habitation, and, as a matter of fact, the housing reforms of the twentieth century resulted in the construction of suburban garden cities outside of many of the great urban centers—Liverpool and London, Brussels, Oslo, Copenhagen, and many others. That was the way in which democracy built.

*   *   *   *   *

Thus in all possible ways America proved an active coöperator in Western civilization. In small and great matters its contributions made themselves felt in the life of Europe. Perhaps the small things were most conspicuous in the so-called "Americanization" of the world. Characteristic American movements easily spread to Europe. In the 1870's, America started correspondence schools which, in the 1890's, entered upon international activities and soon were imitated in Europe. From America in the twentieth century came the Rotary Clubs with their special form of effort to shape an international mind. Several times Europe was visited by that peculiarly American phenomenon called "Pussyfoot" Johnson, the violent crusader for a dry world, who was mobbed in London in 1919.

Even in the taste for all kinds of pleasures America exerted

distinct influences, not only with natural products such as tobacco but also with new creations such as those produced by
the botanical wizard Luther Burbank. From America came the
cocktail, said to have been invented by a woman innkeeper in
New York at the beginning of the nineteenth century. Football
in Europe largely got its impetus from America. Then there was
jazz and Negro dances in the twentieth century. Popular American tunes like "Daisy Bell" were whistled in the streets all over
Europe. Card-playing received repeated impulses from America.
Edgar Allan Poe, in one of his mystery stories, exalted whist as
a game which greatly tasked the faculty of analysis. A special
American form of whist was the game called Boston. Finally, the
most modern form, bridge, was systematized by Ely Culbertson,
and when European players sat down at the card table their
first question would be: "Do you play Culbertson?"

After the close of the 1860's, American tourists flocked to
Europe in increasing numbers. They went to Italy, Switzerland,
Norway, wherever beauties of nature and art were to be seen,
and everywhere they brought their demands for comfort and
cleanliness, the daily change of towels, the daily bath, etc.

On the other hand, America drew freely on Europe for its
entertainment. Barnum started the calling of European celebri-
ties to America when, in 1850, he made himself the impresario
of the Swedish nightingale Jenny Lind. Since then a steady
stream of artists has been brought over to America—singers,
pianists, violinists, actors—some to tour the country, some to
stay. Some have gone the other way, from America to Europe.
An article in *The Cosmopolitan* in 1902 told about an "American
invasion of the London stage," enumerating a score of American
actors who played prominent parts in the theaters of London. It
must be admitted that they were not so vital to the European
theater as, for instance, European singers were to the Metropolitan Opera of New York. European immigrants to a large extent
shaped the musical life of America; Germans organized the
brilliant orchestras of the big cities, Scandinavians made choral
singing popular.

When famous European artists settled down in America, attracted by higher salaries, that was obviously a loss to Europe. So was it when eminent scholars went the same way. The loss was self-inflicted when tyrannical governments, like the Nazis in Germany, expelled great talents because of their race or political opinions. More material was the loss which resulted when wealthy Americans brought monuments and objects of art, ancient and medieval as well as modern, over from Europe and established large museums in many cities. In such action the Americans were only following the example of Europe, where many fine treasures had been taken away from their homeland for the glory of foreign countries. Much of this moving must be deplored because things are torn away from their true environment. It is disconcerting to find one half of a unique work of ancient art in Rome and the other half in Boston. But one benefit is indisputable: the wandering of things and persons across the Atlantic has confirmed and strengthened the spiritual unity of Europe and America.

A question of another order arises from the activities of immigrants in America: Can it be said that what they achieved in their new country was a truly American contribution to the world's civilization? On several occasions in this book I have had to mention achievements of universal importance due to immigrants. In many cases it may be argued that the special American conditions determined the performances of these immigrants. But their personal talents and their European education were essential elements of their activities, and it is not easy to distinguish between what such men brought and what they received.

There is, for instance, the English immigrant John W. Draper whose *History of the Intellectual Development of Europe* (1863) was translated into nearly every one of the known languages and had a profound influence on nineteenth-century thought. It was a parallel work to that of H. T. Buckle which had appeared some few years before and helped popularize still more the idea of evolution and of the impact of nature in human history. His later work, *History of the Conflict between Religion and Science* (1874), continued the same line of thought; this work too, which has been called a "rationalistic classic," was translated into many languages. Both works came to Europe from America. But did they truly constitute an American influence on Europe? I think not.

Engineers like the steamship-constructor John Ericsson, a Swede, the inventor of the telephone Alexander Graham Bell, a Scotchman, and the bridge-builder John A. Roebling, a German, all of them mentioned before, at least pursued an American line of action. The same holds true as to many other engineers who came over from Europe and made themselves co-workers in American technology; I mention at random the Icelander Chester H. Thordarson, who perfected the electric transformer, or the Swede E. F. W. Alexanderson, who made the radio broadcast possible by his alternator, or the Serbian Michael Pupin, who invented the self-induction coil for long-distance telephoning. The most eminent of all, Nicola Tesla, born in Croatia, educated in Austria, continued the work of Edison with his brilliant electrical researches and inventions. But was not he, and most of the others, more a gift of Europe to America, than the reverse?

That must truly be said of such medical men as the Danish master surgeon Christian Fenger or the Norwegian physician Ludvig Hektoen. It was Europe that came to America when the Englishman J. Sylvester, one of the foreigners who were called to the Johns Hopkins University in 1876, established the first *American Journal of Mathematics*. But all of them helped make America more able to return new gains to Europe.

The only American composer who, in the nineteenth century, won world fame, was John Philip Sousa. His stately marches were played by the orchestras of all countries. But he was a Portuguese immigrant.

George Santayana was a professor at Harvard and wrote his philosophical works in America. But can he justly be called an American philosopher? Was not his Spanish character the strongest element in him? Perhaps the American surroundings stirred him to opposition, but even his opposition, his pessimistic philosophy was essentially un-American.

The whole problem of the immigrants as representatives of America illustrates in a peculiar way the interplay of Europe and America in the progress of Western civilization.

*　*　*　*　*

In contemporary intellectual life nothing seems so distinctly American as the "movies." They are much more than a glorious technical invention; as such they are mentioned in a previous chapter. Their appearance on the world stage may best be compared with the invention of the art of printing in the fifteenth century. They have become, in the twentieth century, admirable instruments of entertainment, art, and education. Vulgar and immoral films may, like bad literature, have a detrimental effect on unfortified minds. But that cannot detract from our appreciation of the tremendous power of civilization inherent in the moving and talking pictures. America created them and has stamped them with its spirit. Experts assert that so far as artistic perfection is concerned, French films have attained the highest level. But most of the films circulating over the world come from America. Their pattern stems from Hollywood. The "stars" of the movies belong to many different nations; in so far Hollywood is an international world. They are, however, instructed by American managers and have adjusted themselves to American demands. In all matters relating to movies, America decidedly has the lead. Its influence on the world through this art is immense.

It is unquestionable that a rather considerable proportion of the films that present pictures of American life give a lopsided representation of what America is, and consequently are apt to create false conceptions in the minds of European playgoers to the disadvantage of the American nation. That is an aspect of the movie industry which it will be for the Americans themselves to correct. Indubitably it impedes mutual understanding.

As long as the movies were silent, they spoke to the world, as it were, in an international language, like that of music. After they had become "talkies" the English language which they used tended to become still more international than it previously had been.

English naturally had a dominant position as the language of such a truly international empire as the British Commonwealth of Nations. When America rose as a new and powerful center of civilization, the superiority of English as an international language became ever more manifest. The American movies carry this development still further. At this moment, English seems predestined by the natural course of progress to be the world language that many people have dreamed of creating in an artificial way. Thus in the intellectual field America has worked its way forward to the status of a truly international power and has made decisive contributions towards the unity of the world.

XIV

AMERICA AS A WORLD POWER

SUMMING up the American contributions to civilization in 1896, Charles W. Eliot spoke first of what America had achieved for the abandonment of war as the means of settling disputes between nations. In particular, he felt proud to point to a series of questions which had been settled by arbitration. The Mexican War of 1846 he presented as an isolated exception. Little did he dream that within two years the American government would enter into war under the pressure of an excited public opinion, and that conquests and imperialism would become factors, however disputed, in American politics.

Two opposite tendencies were at that time making themselves felt in American relations with foreign nations—on the one hand a natural consciousness of the strength of the nation and of its right to assert its interests, a certain impatience with obstacles thrown in its way and an inclination towards high-handed treatment of opponents, and on the other hand an equally natural respect for the freedom of others, a desire to extend the principles of liberty and law everywhere, and a certain high-mindedness towards the weaker and the oppressed. Both ideas manifested themselves simultaneously in the year that may be regarded as the turning-point in American foreign politics—the year 1890.

In that year Congress adopted a joint resolution in favor of international treaties of arbitration. This undoubtedly originated in the discussions of the first Pan-American Congress which met in Washington in the fall of 1889. Senator John Sherman, the father of the Anti-Trust Act of 1890, took the initiative in a general extension of the arbitration idea; his resolution was voted by the Senate on February 14 and by the House of Representatives on April 3, 1890. For the time being, it had no practical consequences. By a remarkable coincidence, a resolution in the same sense was adopted exactly at the same time, on March 5, 1890, by the parliament (the Storthing) of Norway on the initiative of Paul Koht. There too it led to no immediate practical result because the Swedish government was opposed to it, and foreign affairs, at that time, were handled in common by the two countries.

No other parliament of the time adopted resolutions of the same order. But the next few years saw a universal movement for arbitration, one of whose first results was a general treaty of arbitration between the United States and Great Britain in 1897. Its conclusion was hailed with enthusiasm by friends of peace all over the world. It was the first time that any great power had made such a treaty. The Senate, however, refused to give consent, chiefly because it wanted to preserve its authority to pass on every single case of dispute that might arise. The disappointment of the world was as profound as the expectations had been high.

This insistence by the Senate on its power in foreign matters became for half a century the great obstacle to American action for international peace. For that reason America resisted the adoption of compulsory arbitration at the Hague Conference of 1899. On the other hand, when Germany threatened to overthrow the whole idea of establishing a court of international arbitration, it was largely American pressure that brought Germany back into the general accord. The Senate ratified the treaty of voluntary arbitration which was concluded on that occasion, and it deserves to be recalled that President Roosevelt in 1902 first brought the new Hague Court into action by referring to it a controversy with Mexico.

The same Congress that adopted the resolution in favor of treaties of arbitration voted in June 1890 a naval act that started America on a program of naval expansion of a character previously unknown. It inaugurated an era of imperialism. It was the response of the Congress to the report of the recently appointed Secretary of the Navy, Benjamin F. Tracy, laid before it in December 1889. This report was a forceful appeal for a strong navy; it proposed to build up two powerful fleets of a completely new type, composed of armored battleships and fast cruisers, one for the Atlantic and another for the Pacific. A still more extravagant program, but based on the same principles, was put forward in January 1890 by the Navy's Policy Board. This latter report pointed out that America was entering a period of sharp commercial competition which would make a strong navy necessary. And the Board bluntly stated that in a naval war offense was the best defense. Its proposals raised a storm of protest. Public opinion in America was still unprepared for such a change of policy. The nation had not yet felt the full impact of its own growth. It thought in terms of peace, not of war. Therefore even those people in Congress who in their hearts agreed with the new naval ideas did not dare to support the whole program of the naval authorities. But they could and did succeed in beginning the construction of a fleet of battleships of the new type in the hope, soon realized, that the near future would bring a continuation.

Europe, of course, could not but be aware that something new was brewing in America—that a new power was in the making. Europe itself at that moment was stirring with unrest, searching for new combinations. Then came from America not only the warning of a new power arising, but the impulse for a general program of wide ramifications. That was the book of Captain Alfred T. Mahan, *The Influence of Sea Power upon History*, which was published in May 1890.

Beyond a doubt Secretary Tracy, and probably the Navy's Policy Board, were acquainted with the ideas of Mahan before his book appeared. It was finished before the end of 1889. His philosophy of history was simple enough and it was propounded with great energy and consistency. It was virtually mercantilism renewed. Foreign commerce, he said, was essential to national prosperity and power; a strong nation must have also a strong merchant marine; and for the protection of this marine it must have the mastery of trade routes and of safe ports at the ends of them; in other words, colonies and a superior navy. Mahan stated with regret that the United States had allowed its merchant marine to decay, and observed that "the dwindling of

the armed fleet and general lack of interest in it are strictly logi-
cal consequences." This lack of interest could have been counteracted by strong aggressive impulses, but unfortunately he did
not discern such impulses in the American nation. He had a
hope that the opening of the projected canal through the Central American Isthmus might awaken the nation to aggressive
purposes, but he doubted it "because a peaceful, gain-loving
nation is not far-sighted, and far-sightedness is needed for ade-
quate military preparation, especially in these days."

Naturally Captain Mahan addressed himself primarily to his
own nation; he wanted to stir it to an interest in the navy, and
his book had a great effect. It stimulated thinking even farther
afield. It was translated immediately into French, some years
later into German, and was eagerly discussed everywhere in
Europe.

It became the Bible of the young Kaiser Wilhelm II who, in
the spring of 1890, had just dismissed his old chancellor Bismarck
and had begun to steer his own course. He went in for colonial
politics and for the development of a great navy, and though his
chief aim was to outrival Great Britain on the seas, he succeeded
in persuading the British government to cede Heligoland to
him. He summed up Mahan's program when, in a speech in
1898, he proclaimed: *"Unsere Zukunft liegt auf dem Wasser"*
(Our future rests on the seas). In that year a German Navy
League was founded.

In England, Mahan's book played directly into a growing
current of imperialistic thought. It certainly gave a firmer shape
to the empire ideas of Joseph Chamberlain and at the same time
bound him more closely to America. He had been there in 1887
to negotiate an agreement regarding the long-standing dispute
over the Canadian fisheries, and though the treaty he signed was
not ratified, he at least won a wife in America. He soon became
the outspoken champion of an Anglo-American alliance, and
his imperialism was a prominent element in British politics while
he was Secretary of State for the Colonies during the years
1895–1903. Imperialism meant a battle against all types of
"Little Englanders," the union of the forces of all British domin-

ions, and a struggle to maintain the mastery of the seas. Mahan had made the connection and necessity of these ideas visible to everybody. His influence can be plainly seen in the founding of the British Navy League in 1894, and quite as plainly in the poetical propaganda of Rudyard Kipling. When Kipling in 1892 published his *Barrack Room Ballads,* with their subjects from army life, he pointed to a new interest in his mind by dedicating the collection to his American brother-in-law. Just that year he had married an American, and he began to take motifs for his poetry from the life of the seas. One of the songs he included in the collection *The Seven Seas* (1896) was a kind of poetical transcription of Mahan's ideas. That was the song "The Liner She's a Lady," with this significant stanza:

> The Liner she's a lady, and if a war should come,
> The Man-o'-War's 'er 'usband, and 'e'd bid 'er stay at home;
> But, oh, the little cargo-boats that fill with every tide!
> 'E'd 'ave to up an' fight for them, for they are England's pride.

Navy leagues, like the British and the German, working to rouse public opinion for the building of strong navies, were formed in many countries—in France, Italy, Spain. Everywhere the ideas of Mahan were working.

❉　　❉　　❉　　❉　　❉

The United States had been well-nigh forced into colonial politics by the establishment of a tripartite condominium—German-British-American—in the Samoan Islands in 1889. In the following years, American mercantile interests were active in Hawaii and even instigated revolts in order to effect an annexation. Mahan directly urged it. Simultaneously in 1890, an American corporation was working on an inter-ocean canal through Nicaragua. In 1894 a revision of the treaties with Japan began which opened the country more completely to foreign commerce. Thus several facts demonstrated a widening of American interests in the Pacific. Yet Congress obviously did not favor political expansion and Europe was not disturbed.

Then in 1895 came an event which suddenly made all of Europe sit up. It originated from a long-drawn-out dispute between Venezuela and Great Britain over the frontiers of British Guiana. The United States government had tried to mediate and proposed arbitration, but Great Britain refused both good offices and arbitration. Then President Cleveland had his Secretary of State Olney send a note that brought the dispute to a head. The question, Olney wrote, on July 20, 1895, was one which concerned the Monroe Doctrine, the principles of which he maintained had become a "doctrine of American public law," and, addressing himself more to the European than the Latin-American public, he continued: "To-day the United States is practically sovereign on this continent, and its fiat is law upon the subjects to which it confines its interposition." That was fairly strong language, and in the following December it was published, together with a message from the President to the Congress which was just as belligerent. The President demanded authorization from Congress to appoint a commission to investigate the question of boundaries, and he said that after such investigation he would regard the frontier defined by the commission as final. Then, he declared, it would be "the duty of the United States to resist by every means in its power, as a willful aggression upon its rights and interests," any attempt by Great Britain to appropriate territory beyond the said frontier. He added: "In making these recommendations I am fully alive to the responsibility incurred and keenly realize all the consequences that may follow." And he went on to say that "there is no calamity which a great nation can invite which equals that which follows a supine submission to wrong and injustice and the consequent loss of national self-respect and honor beneath which are shielded and defended a people's safety and greatness."

That was a new note in American foreign politics. The emphasis on honor and national greatness was the more surprising coming from a President who was known as an anti-imperialist. It made a great stir in the world. For the first time people in Europe began to realize that across the Atlantic a power had grown up which must be taken into account in political considerations. Most of all the English were amazed. A virtual ulti-

matum was laid before them, a completely unexpected one. They
were just then beginning to feel a little restless in their "splendid
isolation," which was no longer so splendid as conflicts loomed
on all sides. They had started looking around for friends, and
it now dawned upon them that perhaps America might be the
friend they needed. For a century the relationship between
Great Britain and the United States had been one of steady
rivalry and more or less open hostility. The crisis of 1895 opened
the eyes of both sides to the natural community of the two nations. It was at this moment that Joseph Chamberlain stood forward as the advocate of their alliance. On January 25, 1896,
he said in a speech at Birmingham:

> War between the two nations would be an absurdity as well as a crime.
> . . . The two nations are allied and more closely allied in sentiment and
> in interest than any other nations on the face of the earth. While I should
> look with horror upon anything in the nature of a fratricidal strife, I should
> look forward with pleasure to the possibility of the Stars and Stripes and
> the Union Jack floating together in defense of a common cause sanctioned
> by humanity and justice.

Even before that speech, Chamberlain had urged Lord
Salisbury "to make a serious effort to come to terms with America." A year later, Great Britain and Venezuela signed in Washington a treaty of arbitration on the boundary question, and the
conflict was thus resolved in peace and good understanding.

❖ ❖ ❖ ❖ ❖

American imperialism broke upon the world with intervention in Cuba and war with Spain in 1898. In Europe popular
opinion was not very favorable to Spain; the Cuban revolutionists who fought Spanish tyranny were generally followed
with sympathy, at least by the liberal newspapers. When the
American Congress in 1896 declared itself in favor of Cuban
independence, the act was received with approval by all liberals.
When Congress in 1898 finally empowered the President to use
the military forces of the country against Spain, it was ostensibly done for the independence of Cuba, and liberals again
approved. The governments of the Great Powers felt differently,

for they never loved insurrections, and they feared the consequences of a war. They presented a joint note to the President cautioning against war for humanity's sake, and they prepared a further note (never delivered), which was intended, according to the expression of Arthur Balfour, temporarily in charge of the British foreign office, "to give the United States a lecture on international morality." After war had begun, Queen Victoria wrote in her diary: "It is monstrous of America."

When the war was over and peace concluded, opinions changed. President McKinley had stated in his annual message of December 1897 in regard to Cuba that there could be no question of annexation—"that, by our code of morality, would be criminal aggression." But Mahan, Theodore Roosevelt, and others wanted annexation, and the President, guided by prayers to God, saw no alternative left to him but to take what the war had given. The result was a protectorate over Cuba and the annexation of Puerto Rico, Guam, and the Philippines. At the same time the Hawaiian Islands were annexed by a treaty with the revolutionary government there, and Wake Island, between Hawaii and Guam, was occupied. Of a sudden, the United States appeared not only as a Pacific power but even as an Asiatic power. It was imperialism, no longer in the British sense of uniting the Empire, but in the sense of creating an empire by conquest.

There was violent opposition within the United States to this departure from traditional policies. People who still kept to the old "code of morality" recently proclaimed by McKinley could not easily reconcile themselves to the new methods. Such a man as William James said that he felt like a man who has lost his country. But these misgivings were swept away by a current of triumphal elation at the easy victory that carried the large majority of the people along.

In view of later events, some American historians have judged the conquests of 1898 as an aberration and a blunder, even as "the greatest blunder of American diplomacy." That is a point of view that does not concern a foreign historian. He has only to state that the policy chosen at that moment was just one step in an advance that had begun at an earlier date and was continued in the years to come. It was the natural result of a commercial expansion which, under the prevailing economic system, must lead to political rivalry and struggle for power. The liberal friends of America in Europe were highly disappointed to see that America was no better than the other sinners, the European Great Powers. It was a disappointment of the same kind as that which gripped many socialists when they saw the Soviet Union waging power politics similar to those of capitalistic powers. Liberals could not but think that America would govern its new colonies in a more enlightened way than Spain had done, though some experts doubted the administrative ability of the Americans. Nevertheless it was a surprise, and not a pleasant one, that America should become a colonial power.

At one stroke America was taken out of the political isolation in which it had hitherto lived. In many respects that might mean a considerable advantage to the rest of the world. One, at least, of the old Great Powers hailed the appearance of America on the stage of world politics with satisfaction. That was Great Britain. British statesmen quickly realized that here was arising a desirable counterweight to some of their own country's rivals. They foresaw that America would build a navy that would place it among the principal powers of the world, and they began to speak of having it admitted to the concert of the Great Powers.

*   *   *   *   *

This consequence was not slow in coming. It was the result of the course of events in East Asia. There Japan suddenly appeared as an aggressive power with its victorious war upon China in 1894–95. The Japanese advance stirred up all the European powers which had interests in China, and there was a general scramble for part of the loot. A partition of China into a number of spheres of influence seemed imminent. Great Britain did not like this development. The United States acted against it. Secretary of State John Hay in 1899 addressed to all the powers concerned a note demanding their adherence to the principle of the Open Door in China. Most of the powers assented; only Russia held back. It was, at any rate, a preliminary victory. America had begun to assert its influence.

In China, however, a nationalist movement, organized as "the Righteous Harmony Fist," (called "Boxers" by Europeans) arose to combat foreign exploitation, and in the summer of 1900 the situation became critical. Violence and murder increased. At first the United States took a conciliatory attitude and refused to join in military measures. Secretary Hay was suspicious of the true motives of the other powers. But when it became clear that the Chinese government supported the Boxer movement and was laying siege to the foreign legations in Peking, Hay and his colleagues, the Secretaries of the Navy (Long) and of War (Root), acted with speed and energy. It was, in fact, the American impetus that overcame the dilatoriness of the allied commanders in Tientsin and hastened the relief expedition to Peking. A German newspaper admitted it frankly: "If the movement upon Peking has now really begun, America undoubtedly deserves great credit." In a couple of weeks Peking was occupied and the foreigners there rescued.

The impression of the American action may be rendered in the words of John Hay's friend Henry Adams, who at that time was in Europe:

Nothing so meteoric had ever been done in American diplomacy. . . . For a moment, indeed, the world had been struck dumb at seeing Hay put Europe aside and set the Washington Government at the head of civilization so quietly that civilization submitted, by mere instinct of docility, to receive and obey his orders; but, after the first shock of silence, society felt the force of the stroke through its fineness, and burst into almost tumultuous applause.

Later times will perhaps not speak so glibly of "civilization" in this connection as Henry Adams did. It must be said, however, that America behaved in a more civilized way than some of the European governments. The firm but considerate note of John Hay's despatches shone out finely in comparison with the notorious speech with which the Kaiser sent his soldiers off for China: "Spare nobody! Make no prisoners! Use your weapons so that for a thousand years hence no Chinaman will dare look askance at any German! Open the way for civilization once for all!" The civilization that the German soldiers brought along was the plundering of Peking, and when, after the liquidation of the affair, China requested the return of the treasures taken away, the German government coolly answered: "Come and take them!" Only by the treaty of peace after the First World War was Germany compelled to deliver up its plunder. The United States, on the other hand, repaid to China the largest part of the reparations which the Chinese government had to pay for the murders of its nationals.

America was honestly interested in maintaining the integrity of China. During the Boxer disturbances, Secretary Hay stated this principle in circular notes to the other powers. Together with the Open Door, it became the steady objective of American policy in East Asia.

* * * * *

The conquests in the Pacific made the question of the Isthmian canal more burning than ever. John Hay tried to exploit the new friendship with Great Britain to make the United States the sole master of the projected canal, and in 1901 he succeeded in concluding a treaty that would allow the American government to fortify the future canal which, in that way, would be a powerful link in the military system of the United States. Great Britain acquiesced in the predominance of the United States in the Caribbean, withdrew its principal naval forces, and reduced its permanent garrisons in the West Indies.

Dramatically the American government asserted its predominance in this part of the world in the Venezuelan conflict of 1902. The question had to do with the foreign debts of Venezuela, and Germany proposed to use armed force to compel their payment. In order not to let Germany act alone, Great Britain joined in the action and together they blockaded the coast of Venezuela, bombarding two forts and seizing some gunboats. The Argentine Foreign Minister Luis M. Drago submitted to the United States a memorandum containing the principle that a public debt due to private individuals does not entitle their governments to armed intervention. And President Roosevelt, who now had succeeded McKinley, warned earnestly against any action in violation of the Monroe Doctrine. The American press raised a great cry against the interference of the European powers in the Western hemisphere, and the American fleet was mobilized. Great Britain willingly acknowledged the validity of the Monroe Doctrine, and finally even Germany gave in and accepted arbitration.

European opinion was, to begin with, divided. There was some doubt as to the assertion that a refractory debtor state should not be forced to pay; that might seem to set a premium on default. But the aversion to the use of arms in international affairs, in particular for private claims, was stronger, and some years later the Drago doctrine was embodied in an international convention. It was an American victory. Roosevelt had planned to build on this principle a kind of receivership of the United States for other governments of the American hemisphere, and he really established a financial protectorate over the Dominican Republic. In his hands the Monroe Doctrine tended to be an instrument of power, and people in Europe began to think of him as a leader of American imperialism.

That America now had really gone in for full-fledged imperialistic policies appeared confirmed beyond any doubt when in 1903 Roosevelt, according to his own boast some years later, "took Panama." To be sure, he had tried to get the concession for the Panamanian canal by treaty. When he did not succeed in this effort, he threw aside all consideration of the rights of little Colombia and acted on behalf of what he conceived to be a vital need of his own country as a great power. It is true that he tried to cover his act by a presumably spontaneous rising of the people of Panama. But the veil of legality was too thin to conceal the reality of violence. The American fleet was on the spot before the rising, and American forces prevented the Colombian government from fighting the insurrection. The new republic of Panama was too obviously a puppet state created for the benefit of the United States. European opinion was not deceived on this point, and all liberals regretted that the American government had made itself a party to these worst methods of power policies.

Many years later, in 1921, the United States agreed to pay Colombia an indemnity, a kind of conscience money, for the use of the Colombian territory; but that could not wipe out the impression of the act itself. It must be noted, however, that the Great Powers themselves did not object to the American procedure; they were rather more inclined than ever to accept America as a fellow power.

*   *   *   *   *

Apart from particular cases, there was one element in this development that made the entrance of America into world politics inevitable. That was the natural growth of American power by reason of its increasing population and wealth. It was impossible for the previously existing Great Powers to neglect the weight that America naturally would throw into any balance of power. And America could not be indifferent to the shaping of this balance; it could not but influence American interests in different parts of the world. Without a neatly adjusted balance of power America might easily risk suffering material losses.

Theodore Roosevelt was well aware of this fact, and it determined his policies both in Asia and in Europe. In Asia the rivalry of forces led to war between Russia and Japan in 1904–5. Before that war Russia had seemed to be the most disturbing element in the situation. That was the major reason why Great Britain in 1902 made a formal alliance with Japan, although her action was not uninfluenced by the idea of keeping a close watch on the movements of the latter country. More secretly President Roosevelt encouraged Japan to resist Russia's pushing forward. The victory of Japan changed the situation materially. Both Great Britain and the United States wanted a peace that would not give too dominant a position to Japan. Therefore Roosevelt proffered his good offices for negotiating a peace between the belligerent parties, and on the basis of his suggestions the treaty of peace was concluded in Portsmouth, New Hampshire. He

appeared as the great pacificator, and the Norwegian Nobel
Committee awarded him Nobel's peace prize.

The whole affair was actually one of power politics. Roosevelt and the British government thought it advantageous to the
balance in East Asia to leave Japan a free hand in Korea and
make Russian and Japanese interests balance each other in Man-
churia. On the other hand, Japan disavowed any aggressive designs whatever on the Philippines and pledged itself to respect
the Open Door in China. The main result was that Japan definitely established its position as a world power. That event was
so closely bound up with the parallel admission of the United
States into the concert of Great Powers that the interdepend-
ence of the two powers became a permanent element of their
policies. Consideration of Japanese moves would always play a
prominent part in American decisions.

That would not mean that the United States could remain
indifferent to the balance of power in Europe. On the contrary,
in 1905 and 1906, President Roosevelt took an active part in
the negotiations over Morocco, which threatened to bring about
a European war. By alternately supporting Germany and
France, Roosevelt helped to carry the dispute to a compromise
that preserved the precarious peace in Europe for some further
years. It is interesting to note that in his correspondence with
Roosevelt the Kaiser emphasized that if Great Britain and
France should succeed in destroying the German navy, they
would be strong enough to partition China and make an end
of the Open Door in East Asia. Thus European and Asiatic questions were bound together and both of them placed within the
sphere of American interests.

The efforts of Roosevelt to maintain the balance of the European powers were mostly made in deep secret, so that only much
later could Europe become aware of them. What Europe saw,
however, was the significant fact of America's participation in
the Conference of Algeciras where the Moroccan questions were,
at least preliminarily, settled. That was the official admission of
the United States into the circle of the Great Powers. It was,
indeed, a far cry from the time back in the 1820's when America

was not counted worthy of a seat in consultations about questions regarding its own southern neighbors to the day when it was called, in 1906, to join in the discussions and decisions concerning Old World affairs. It had been sitting in already at the Congo Conference in Berlin in 1885, but merely for deliberative purposes, not for decisions; and the United States never ratified the Berlin Act. As early as 1880 it had signed an international convention regarding Moroccan affairs, but that was nothing more than a definition of extraterritorial protection with no political involvement. The Algeciras convention was an act of much larger consequence: it brought America actively into European politics. It did not matter much that the Senate, in ratifying this new treaty, stated that there was no "purpose to depart from the traditional American foreign policy which forbids participation by the United States in the settlement of political questions which are entirely European in their scope." In the definition of the true purposes of the treaty, the Senate had to include "aiding by its friendly offices and efforts in friction and controversy" between European powers. Obviously that spelled stepping out of isolation.

In order to demonstrate the power and new self-reliance of America, President Roosevelt sent its battleship fleet out on a world cruise which, in the course of 1907–8, carried it across both the Pacific and the Atlantic to both Asiatic and European ports. It impressed even the popular mind with the conspicuous strength of the new Great Power.

❊　❊　❊　❊　❊

The active and partly aggressive imperialism of America during the decade 1898–1908 was softened down after the retirement of Theodore Roosevelt from the presidency. But the consequences of the new situation of the country as a world power could not be undone. Politically, as well as economically and intellectually, the world had become one, and America was an integral part of it.

Clearly, America was interested in universal peace. Secretary of State Elihu Root concluded in 1908 a series of arbitration treaties with twenty-five different nations, weakened, however, by the proviso that in each case of dispute a special agreement would have to be adopted by the Senate. In 1913, Secretary of

State William J. Bryan concluded another series of "Treaties for the Advancement of Peace," providing a term of one year for the investigation of every case of dispute, thus creating a "cooling-off" period.

But even the institution of general arbitration by the Hague Conferences of 1899 and 1907 could not prevent the mounting tension between the opposed groups of Powers in Europe, and the First World War broke out in 1914. President Woodrow Wilson repeatedly offered his good offices for the reëstablishment of peace, but in vain. He tried to keep his country out of the war as long as possible. But the war tended steadily to become totalitarian, without much regard for the rights of neutrals. The Germans even plotted within the territory of the United States, and their increasingly ruthless submarine warfare against neutral shipping finally drove America into the war in 1917. American sympathies had all along been mainly with the Entente, the Western Powers; thus it was only natural to associate with them for the defeat of German militarism.

How far the outcome of the war was changed by America's entry nobody, of course, can state with absolute certainty. The fact is that in the course of 1917 Russia was put out of the war, and Germany was able to concentrate its forces on the Western front. It seems a well-founded conclusion that the best the Entente powers might have hoped for without American assistance was a stalemate and no decisive victory. With the reinforcements from America their lines were materially strengthened, and the victory was won.

What America—or more particularly President Wilson—unquestionably did was to make the war a struggle for high ideals. In his war message to Congress he said:

The right is more precious than peace, and we shall fight for the things which we have always carried nearest our hearts,—for democracy, for the right of those who submit to authority to have a voice in their own government, for the rights and liberties of small nations, for a universal dominion of right by such a concert of peoples as shall bring peace and safety to all nations and make the world itself at last free.

Wilson was not the first to look forward to such a peace. Both in Europe and in America there was on foot a movement to make this war the last by establishing an order of universal justice. In Europe it called itself the Central Organization for a Durable Peace, in America the League to Enforce Peace. In both continents it was a continuation of the movement for peace which had been gaining strength along with liberalism and democracy since the last decades of the nineteenth century. When President Wilson stood forth as the spokesman of this idea, all the hopes of a better world were united in him.

On January 8, 1918, he laid before Congress and proclaimed to the world his program of peace, containing the famous Fourteen Points. I quote here only the fourteenth of them: "A general association of nations must be formed under specific covenants for the purpose of affording mutual guarantees of political independence and territorial integrity to great and small States alike." This program was hailed with enthusiasm both abroad and at home. It even was cheered by people of the enemy nations. Wilson supplemented it in later addresses in which he emphasized the principles of impartial justice and of the free self-determination of peoples. He disavowed entirely what he called "the great game, now forever discredited, of the balance of power." When Germany acknowledged defeat and asked for peace, it did so explicitly on the basis of the Fourteen Points and Wilson's subsequent pronouncements, although nothing of this found a place in the articles of armistice.

When President Wilson went to Europe for the Peace Conference, he met a reception such as no man had received before. Wherever he appeared, in France, England, Italy, innumerable crowds gathered to see him and cheer him. They saw in him "the people's man," a man who did not talk of national advantages but of permanent peace. He spoke for the people, not for the governments or the powers, and he was acclaimed with frenzy. Again and again newspapers had to state that such throngs of people were unexampled in their countries and that enthusiasm was roused to a pitch exceeding anything that the oldest observer could remember. An American historian (J. Franklin Jameson) wrote to Lord Bryce in England: "Rightly or wrongly, I formed the notion that the prodigious welcome accorded to President Wilson when he first came to Europe was simply an ebullition of popular feeling in favor of a more internationalized world-order, evoked by a symbol of disinterested idealism, and rather surprising to statesmen and politicians, who, in Europe as in America, have had it as their main business to look out for *national* interests!" That was true. It was not the man Wilson who was acclaimed. It was the ideas he stood for. But as a champion of them he became the idol of the peoples of Europe.

This is not the place to retell the sad story of the disappointments and the defeats which he suffered at the Paris Conference and the compromises he was forced to accept. It must be emphasized that they were not all due to the hard-headed national egotism of European statesmen, but that some of them stemmed from opposition by narrow-minded American politicians. As to Europe, it is worth while to say that, in spite of all efforts for international peace, it was not mentally well prepared to accept and practise the idea of an effective League of Nations as proposed by Wilson. The resistance was partly related to these earlier efforts in the sense that in general opinion they had proved their futility in not being able to prevent the outbreak of war. The inability to avert this World War seemed to be the doom of all the hopes of the pacifists and to confirm the skepticism of the "realists" who were accustomed to declare that war was an inherent element of human life. The activities of the Central Organization for a Durable Peace and similar organizations had been mainly limited to the neutral countries which were not invited to share in the establishment of peace, and at the conference table at Versailles President Wilson met the "practical" politicians who did not believe in the efficiency of a League for the security of their countries. They accepted it only half-heartedly. The general delight at the achievement found a formal expression in the award of Nobel's peace prize to the two men who had done most to make the League a reality—Woodrow Wilson and the Frenchman Léon Bourgeois.

The League of Nations was made a part of the Versailles Treaty of Peace. This was later made an objection to it by the Germans who found it attached to a treaty humiliating to them.

It must, however, be remembered that Wilson wanted it included in the treaty of peace in order to secure adherence to it by the Great Powers of Europe. Then he met with the greatest misfortune of his life in the rejection of the League by his own country. All his noble efforts did not avail to rouse such a popular opinion as to compel a sufficient majority of the Senate to adopt it.

The disappointment in Europe at this event can only be measured by the immense enthusiasm that had greeted Wilson and his struggle for the League of Nations. After its adoption at Versailles, Dr. Fridtjof Nansen in Norway took the initiative in forming a society for the advancement of the idea of the League, and such societies were formed in other countries too. I remember speaking at a large meeting in Oslo where the establishment of the League was applauded as inaugurating a new epoch in history and America was cheered as the champion of the future of humanity. Suddenly all this enthusiasm fell flat to the earth. Not a few people in the neutral nations thought that since America had failed to join the League which was created by American efforts, it might just as well be abandoned to the care of the victors. They did not attach great hopes to it.

How far the slight success of the League of Nations during its less than twenty years of existence was determined by the absence of the United States, it is impossible to say. Certainly it would have stood a better chance had America joined it. The United States was the only Great Power that had the trust of the small nations as acting for universal principles of justice without secret motives of power or other interests, and that was essentially a fruit of Wilson's work. The United States might have been able to prevent the prevalence of power politics within the League. As it was, the Great Powers of Europe never came to conceive of the League as the main forum of international politics; they managed their most important affairs outside it. Consequently, as a political instrument the League withered into comparative insignificance.

*   *   *   *   *

Although America remained outside the League of Nations, the American government sought other means to help establish world peace. In 1921, after the close of the Wilson administration, a conference was called in Washington to discuss limitation of armaments. Secretary of State Charles E. Hughes opened the negotiations by proposing an agreement that "preparations for offensive war stop now," and according to the plan which he offered, a naval treaty was concluded fixing the limits of capital-ship construction for the leading naval powers. Inasmuch as it meant more scrapping of battleships for the United States than for any of the other powers, it demonstrated clearly the peaceful intentions behind American policies.

Further efforts towards the limitation of armaments did not prove successful. But America constantly continued to urge upon the world the abandonment of offensive war. Out of negotiations with France regarding the renewal of a treaty of arbitration came the idea of a general international treaty for what was sometimes called "outlawing war." The proposal was formally put forward by Secretary of State Frank B. Kellogg, and the Pact of Paris that was signed in 1928 is often called the "Kellogg Pact." By this treaty all the signatory parties solemnly declared that they condemned recourse to war for the solution of international con-troversies and renounced it as an instrument of national policy in their relations with one another. In consequence they agreed that they would never seek to settle any disputes or conflicts among them except by pacific means.

It was a high-sounding declaration, and almost all nations in the world, among them all the Great Powers, signed it. The Great Powers, however, and among them the United States itself, made so many reservations to the announced principle as to make it rather illusory. No authority was established to enforce the treaty, and it never served to protect any country against aggres-sion. Norway again came forward with Nobel's peace prize. But if the Kellogg Pact exerted any practical influence, it was rather to create an imaginary feeling of security.

The United States not only scrapped battleships, it also began to scrap imperialism, at any rate, in the sense of dominating other nations. Under the Wilson administration, before America entered the World War, intervention in unruly Latin-American States still took place; thus American troops were sent to Nicaragua and a protectorate established over Haiti. But after 1930, the policies of the "big stick" were definitely superseded by "good neighborliness." Beginning under President Hoover, it was firmly developed and maintained under President Franklin D. Roosevelt. By a Pan-American treaty of 1933, intervention in the internal or external affairs of another state was formally disclaimed. The next year saw the end of the American protectorate in Cuba and Haiti; in Panama it was ended in 1939, in the Dominican Republic in 1941. Still more significant, from the point of view of political principles, was the act of 1934 for the independence of the Philippines, intended to come into force in 1946; the events of the Second World War led Congress to resolve in 1944 that the Philippine Republic should be organized as soon as the Japanese invaders had been driven out, and this became a fact the next year.

None of these changes in American politics immediately concerned Europe. But they made a profound impression on European minds. The suspicions and fears evoked by the aggressive policies of 1898 were gradually allayed and at last almost completely wiped out. The hopes that had been so sadly frustrated by America's failure to join the League of Nations began to rise again. The United States regained its position as the power the nations could trust as the champion of freedom.

A feature of the new Rooseveltian policies that had a direct implication for Europe was the reciprocal trade program sponsored by Secretary of State Cordell Hull. In 1934 he secured from Congress full powers to make arrangements with other states for a mutual lowering of customs by 50 per cent, with the understanding that every such lowering agreed upon with one state should become valid for all other states. That was the first break with the high-tariff policies that had prevailed in America since the Civil War, and all Europe felt happy about the slackening of the strings that hitherto had narrowed commerce with America. Only Germany under the Nazi administration would have none of the new reciprocity. It must be said that the change on the American side was not followed by a corresponding change of commercial principles by the European nations; there the idea of equal exchanges won increasing ground. Only the so-called Oslo States (the Nordic and Low Countries governments) struggled for lower customs. Generally, however, the new American policies were felt as a friendly act that brought the Old and the New World closer to one another. Europeans were grateful for it.

*   *   *   *   *

Then came the Second World War. And again it proved impossible for the United States to stay outside. Anti-Nazi Europe watched and admired the way in which President Franklin Roosevelt prepared his nation for the inevitable outcome.

During the interval between the two wars a mounting wave of isolationism had flowed over America, submerging many old ideals. The first political measure by which the isolationist spirit gave evidence of itself was the Johnson Act of 1934, forbidding loans to any foreign government which had defaulted on its war debts to the United States. Then followed the Neutrality Acts of 1935 and 1937, intended to prevent America from being dragged into European wars by violations of its neutral rights, as had been the case in 1917. These acts implied the voluntary renunciation by America of all those rights it had been fighting for since the Napoleonic wars. It was made a crime to exercise them. By these acts it was forbidden to grant loans to any belligerent government—to ship arms, munitions, and other implements of war to such government, to travel on merchant ships of belligerents, to send American ships into waters proclaimed as combat zones, to arm American merchant ships. It was an astounding act of self-abnegation, made by the nation hitherto regarded as the most self-assertive in the world. Aggressor nations exulted; all others were depressed.

President Roosevelt approved and signed these acts. But soon he understood how dangerous they really were because they encouraged aggression and violation of rights far more valuable than neutrality. In his heart he agreed with Woodrow Wilson's declaration that "the right is more precious than peace." He realized that in a crisis America could not stay out of the battle for democracy and freedom. He had the foresight to recommend in the first year of his administration (1933) the resumption of naval construction. At least as early as 1937 he foresaw a new war coming. It was the Japanese attack on China that year that occasioned his famous "quarantine" speech of October 5, 1937, in which he declared that aggressor nations ought to be put into quarantine. But he spoke at the same time about the "international anarchy and instability" created by violations of treaties everywhere. He said that "mere isolation or neutrality" was no means to prevent such acts. In referring explicity to the Covenant of the League of Nations and to the Kellogg Pact he made it clear that he wanted all "peace-loving nations" to unite their efforts for averting war. It was the first official warning of the imminent world war, and the speech made a sensation all over the world.

When, during the next few years, one crisis followed the other, Roosevelt indefatigably appealed to the dictators as well as to the democratic governments to make all possible efforts to reach peaceful settlements. Hitler for one laughed at him. He would not believe that Roosevelt could stir America out of isolationism, and besides, he imagined that the Americans were a degenerate soft people that could not wage a war.

In April 1939, after Hitler had seized Czecho-Slovakia and Mussolini Albania, Roosevelt asked them to conclude non-aggression treaties with all the small nations hitherto not attacked. Hitler actually offered such treaties to all the Nordic and Baltic States, and some of them accepted the offer. Some of them refused because they did not see any safety in treaties of that kind with Germany, and, as a matter of fact, the nations that concluded the non-aggression treaties were wantonly attacked by Germany some few months later.

In the summer of 1939, Roosevelt proposed to Congress a change in the Neutrality Acts, and after the war in Europe had broken out, the embargo on shipments of implements of war was relaxed, at least with respect to non-American ships, in the so-called "Cash-and-Carry" act. In 1940 and 1941 other measures were taken to make America what Roosevelt called the "arsenal of democracy." Most important and significant was the "Lend-Lease" agreement of March 11, 1941, by which virtually all the material forces of America were made available for defense against the aggressors. Finally, by Japan's insidious attack on Pearl Harbor, December 7, 1941, America was brought directly into the war. Immediately Germany too declared war and took its place as the major enemy.

This is not the place to attempt even an approximate evaluation of the American military contribution to the Second World War. At America's entry into the war the situation was almost the reverse of what it was when it came into the First World War. On the earlier occasion Russia had been on the eve of complete collapse and Germany was no longer under the necessity of fighting on the eastern front. In 1941, Russia had only recently been attacked by Germany and the chief fighting was on the eastern front, while France was crushed and no western front existed. It was the task of America, together with Great Britain, to establish a second front and thus place Germany between two fires. In addition, American *matériel* had to be brought into play on all imaginable battlefields. Both tasks were fulfilled in the most brilliant manner. An expeditionary force of more than four million men was brought overseas—an achievement of unprecedented magnitude. And in the spring of 1945 the war in Europe was carried to a victorious end.

Could the war have been won without the help of America? Probably—or I think it is proper to say—certainly not. But then two other questions ought also to be put: Could the war have been won without the heroic efforts of Russia? And could it have been won without those of Great Britain? These questions too must be answered with a No. Furthermore, many smaller nations —Poland, Norway, the Netherlands, Greece, Yugoslavia, and all the British dominions outside Europe—took a very important part in the European war and helped materially in winning it. The fact is that the whole war was a common task for all the nations united for defense against Nazi tyranny. They fought together and they won together. All of them gave their utmost for the victory, and all of it was needed.

The principle of the indivisible community of the united nations in this war was the declared basis of the Lend-Lease agreement which effected the pooling of all their forces. And when President Roosevelt, on January 6, 1941, laid the proposal of this unprecedented arrangement before Congress, he said that the idea behind it was to prepare for a world founded upon four essential human freedoms. He went on to define these freedoms:

The first is freedom of speech and expression—everywhere in the world.

The second is freedom of every person to worship God in his own way —everywhere in the world.

The third is freedom from want—which, translated into world terms, means economic understandings which will secure to every nation a healthy peacetime life for its inhabitants—everywhere in the world.

The fourth is freedom from fear—which, translated into world terms, means a world-wide reduction of armaments to such a point and in such a thorough fashion that no nation will be in a position to commit an act of physical aggression against any neighbor—anywhere in the world.

This was a new program for the war, born of a vision, not of a distant millennium but of a future to be attained by practical measures after the defeat of the aggressor dictators. And it was grasped by all the people of the United Nations. The "four freedoms"—though somewhat contradictory because two of them were true liberties while the other two implied what men should be freed from—became a slogan all over the world and raised a common standard over the common war.

It was an act of large consequence that Roosevelt should have put forward such a program. And it was highly significant that it came from an American statesman. If in several respects America came to take the leadership of the United Nations in the military field, it certainly took it with respect to political aims even before entering the war. It was America that most clearly and explicitly made the war a fight for universal ideals.

From the very beginning, of course, it had been a war against Nazi aggression and Nazi dominion. But this idea was obscured by the appeasement policies previously conducted by the European powers, which made it look more like the traditional struggle for a balance of power. Germany brought out the fundamental issue more conspicuously by its invasion of one after another of the small nations. But it was President Roosevelt who fixed the ideas of the struggle in a clear, common, and inspiring program.

While Winston Churchill, the dauntless leader of the British fighting force, used to say that the only matter to be discussed was the winning of the war, Roosevelt never ceased to point to the shaping of the future peace, and he persuaded Churchill in their first meeting to issue with him a declaration of war aims, the so-called Atlantic Charter of August 14, 1941. This declaration stated the principles of self-determination and self-government of all nations; it held out the prospect of equality and collaboration in all economic matters; it promised a stable peace that would afford the assurance that all men in all lands might live out their lives in freedom from fear and want.

It was a simple declaration by two political leaders, but it had a world echo, and it immediately consolidated the public opinion of all the anti-Nazi nations. After America had become one of the belligerents, the declaration was embodied in a document, signed in Washington on January 1, 1942, by representatives of all the United Nations. In subscribing to the program formulated by Roosevelt and Churchill, all these nations pledged themselves to employ all their resources "to defend life, liberty, independence and religious freedom, and to preserve human rights and justice in their own lands as well as in other lands."

The ideas contained in all these declarations attained a more positive form when the secretaries for foreign affairs of the "Big Three"—the United States, the Soviet Union, and Great Britain— met in Moscow in the fall of 1942 to discuss their common political problems. Without contradiction it has been stated that the American Secretary of State Cordell Hull was the initiator of the central article of the declaration of war aims issued from this meeting on November 1 and signed also by the ambassador of China, namely "that they recognize the necessity of establishing at the earliest practicable date a general international organization, based on the principle of the sovereign equality of all peace-loving States, and open to membership by all such States, large and small, for the maintenance of international peace and security."

On the basis of this declaration the State Department in Washington set to work on a complete plan for such an international organization. In the fall of 1944, representatives of the "Big Three," later joined by representatives of China, met at Dumbarton Oaks, Washington, D. C., and sat for several weeks discussing all the details of the plan which was subsequently published on October 9. This plan was placed before a conference of all the United Nations in San Francisco on April 25, 1945, and there, with several amendments, definitely adopted.

This whole series of discussions gave evidence of the mounting realization of the unity of the world, and America was the leader in the effort to make it come true.

✻   ✻   ✻   ✻   ✻

President Roosevelt lived to see neither the final surrender of Germany (May 7, 1945) nor the San Francisco conference. With an energy and a vitality that seemed inexhaustible he had carried the heavy burden of twelve years' administration in times of the greatest difficulties, internal and external, coupled for more than three years with the duties of the commander-in-chief of the American armed forces. In spite of his crippled body he went abroad repeatedly to confer with national leaders of foreign countries, to Canada and Mexico, to Europe, Africa, and Asia. Everywhere his presence had a tonic effect on the minds and efforts of men, and at the same time he was a uniting element by virtue of his good humor and his ability to reconcile different views. The last such trip took him to the Crimea and Egypt, and after a strenuous trip of six weeks he came back to Washington on February 28, 1945, a worn-out man. He died on April 12.

The tragic news of this event was received in Europe with a consternation and a sorrow that recalled the impression created by the death of Abraham Lincoln, eighty years before, except that Roosevelt was still better known and more widely loved. Of course, the enemies who were still left fighting rejoiced because he seemed to them their most dangerous adversary, and they imagined that after his death the United Nations might split. At the German headquarters there were such high spirits as almost never before during the whole war. When the news burst upon Hitler, hiding in the bomb shelter of his chancellery in Berlin, he threw his arms into the air in obvious glee; he laughed and laughed, and cried: "I knew it! I knew it!" He told his generals that he had always felt that something would happen to Roosevelt, and he kept repeating that phrase, intermingled with exclamations of *"Donnerwetter"* and chuckling all the time. It was a devil's laughter—certainly the last of his life. Within the month he himself was dead.

World history during the past twelve years had in a way been a duel between Hitler and Roosevelt. Simultaneously, in the beginning of 1933, each of them had attained the leading position of his nation. But they had used their power in entirely opposite ways. One of them had ruled by oppression, concentration camps and blood purges, by drilling the minds of his subjects into unthinking discipline, and by extirpating all traces of human mercy and good morals. The other had felt his highest satisfaction in winning the voluntary following of a free people and calling forth to action their sense of social responsibility and their human sympathy. One had exerted himself to sow hatred and contempt for foreign nations and races; the other had striven to build up a universal coöperation of peace-loving nations. The accession of Hitler to the German chancellorship had thrown horror into the souls of mankind; the election of Roosevelt to the presidency of the United States had raised the hopes of all suffering people.

The war gave him a unique position. As the British nation, in the direst calamities of the war, turned to Winston Churchill as its leader and savior and took indomitable courage from his unflinching will to fight to the bitter end, as Russian patriotism rose to unconditional sacrifice and heroic strength under the leadership of the "man of steel," Josef Stalin, so the whole world looked to Franklin Roosevelt as the inspiring symbol of unity and victory, of justice and freedom. No wonder his death seemed a disaster for all, and that for the second time the decease of an American president was mourned by all people in the world more than that of any other man. The most significant feature was not the official mourning, even though that was on a larger scale than anything of the kind dedicated to foreigners or foreign sovereigns in any European country. The most remarkable fact was the genuine grief of the man in the street.

Roosevelt's sudden death had not the same horrid implications as that of Lincoln, but it was felt throughout the world as a more direct blow to common hopes and ideals. He had possessed the magnificent gift of making people feel his heart speaking to them. Everywhere was heard the sentence: "We have lost a friend." People said: "He was the friend of the common man." As one commentator wrote: "Poles, Greeks, Italians, Serbs, Belgians, Syrians, Zionists, the hungry, the dispossessed and the oppressed of Europe looked to him for support." In a commemorative speech in the House of Commons, Churchill summed up the sentiments of all Europe in saying that in Roosevelt died "the greatest champion of freedom who has ever brought help and comfort from the New World to the Old."

* * * * *

His death did not split the United Nations, it rather drove them together into vigorous action for common ideals. In Europe the victory was won within a moment. His absence might render some negotiations and agreements more difficult. But people in general felt that they could honor his memory in no better way than by uniting for the goals which he had set before them.

America remained the hope of the nations of Western Europe. Naïvely it was expressed in a letter from an American boy, one of a flying crew who came to Oslo soon after the German surrender. Writing to his family in Brooklyn, he described at length the more than enthusiastic welcome he and his comrades received there. "We'd walk through the streets," he wrote, "and in a flash, two hundred people would have us surrounded and we could hear the whisper around, 'Amerikanere! Amerikanere!' They really believe America is the wonderland and thereby, the Americans the wonder people."

Maybe Americans would not meet quite the same exuberance of gratitude everywhere. But in the hearts of the common people there was and is living a vivid consciousness of what America did during the war and what it might be able to do in times of peace. People in Europe were waiting for food and other material assistance from America. But still more they expected that America would help create that better world that everybody is longing for—indeed, that America should be the strongest power for establishing that brave new world.

XV

OUTLOOK

THERE is a distinct rhythm in American history as related to the outside world. In the beginning, the settlements on the western shores of the Atlantic were nothing but an offshoot of Europe and were for a long time dependent on Europe for all the elements of their civilization. Gradually they developed a character of their own and then suddenly jumped to independence. The period that followed was one of establishing the American nation as a separate political and intellectual body, able to live by its own resources and to develop a civilization of its own. Inevitably there were many connections between the New and the Old World, many currents running to and fro, but on the whole the two continents lived their own life and constituted different individualities. The very growth of America, however, led it into a powerful expansion and threw it out into a whirlpool of international life where all its forces were matched with those of all other civilized nations. It even became one of the vital centers of the universal movement of civilization.

That is the way America has gone: from colony to independence, from national consolidation to leadership of Western civilization. A magnificent task and immense responsibilities lie before the young nation. Who can predict what the future will bring?

In all human life, in the fate of the nations, there are so many unknown elements and so many conflicting tendencies as to make all prophecies futile. Future historians will be able to point out the determining forces and explain the reasons why events took the course they did. The strength of the different forces cannot be measured in advance with any kind of certainty. We may discern some wishes and efforts that seem to unite large bodies of people behind them, and we may presume that such combinations of human wills may succeed in shaping at least part of the future. We may imagine that we have discovered some general tendencies or even laws of social change, the influences of known economic or psychological forces. But even when we discuss the past, students often disagree about the fundamental causes of events or developments.

It is easy to see that America represents a tremendous power in the present and, presumably, in the future world. But it is not so easy to know how that power may be used, still less what form the interplay between America and the other forces of human civilization may take.

Despite two world wars—partly by reason of them—the twentieth century has brought all the nations encompassed within what we call Western Civilization, the nations of Europe and those of European stock, together into an effective, indissoluble, and prospectively ever widening unity. In the mutual relations of all these nations we may observe a striking parallel to the development of those of individuals.

Manifestly through the course of long centuries every individual has acquired an increasing mental independence and a marked difference of character. At the same time, however, the social ties between individuals have multiplied; the conformity of education, the community of religion and morals, of ideas and interests, make all of them associates in a large brotherhood with mutual responsibilities in all domains of life.

In the same way, nations have developed their peculiar character and their national consciousness to a previously unknown degree, though the basic similarity of their civilization is evident and more strongly felt than ever. The overwhelming number of international organizations for all imaginable purposes is perhaps the most outstanding positive fact of this world unity. World trade, world-embracing transportation and communication, the immense literature of translations, are other such facts. The continual interchange of all elements of civilization, intellectual as well as material, makes for a world-wide mutual influencing of all nations.

In this great seething pot of international life two nations today are strongest, both in actual and potential power—the United States of America and the Union of Socialist Soviet Republics. Tocqueville foresaw more than a hundred years ago that Russia and America would grow to determine the fate of the world. Today we can discern more clearly the nature of their impact. They are the strongest not merely by virtue of their numerous population and the abundance of natural wealth contained within their boundaries, but still more by reason of the expansive energy that animates their activities.

The difference between them is obvious and could under certain conditions be dangerous. They are the most extreme exponents of the two most significant tendencies of modern life. In the Soviet Union the spirit of collectivism, in the United States that of individual enterprise, have attained the peak of development and the most remarkable results, each in the same field— the industrialization of society. Both in collectivism and in individualism a fierce spirit of conquest prevails. Both of them address themselves to the rest of the world wth a mighty urge for imitation that comes very near to coercion and cannot but exert a powerful influence. One calls for freedom, the other calls for solidarity. Is conflict inevitable? And which of the two will win?

I wonder if it would be too audacious to predict that in the final issue both of the two ideas will come together and help to shape the future of the world. It is not necessary to take a footing on Hegelian dialectics to suggest the probability that collectivism and individualism may in the future unite into a social organization that preserves comprehensive coöperation as well as individual liberty. The whole history of mankind seems to point in that direction. Nowhere, in fact, will one find individual liberty or collectivist society ruling in absolute purity. For the high development of both ideas, I venture to instance my own country, Norway. There we meet an outspoken, almost violent spirit of individualism, such as that embodied in the work of its most famous author, Henrik Ibsen, combined with a national solidarity that has expressed itself in economic and social measures of a distinctly collectivist character. The same orientation can be observed in the other Scandinavian nations, and the like tendency asserts itself in Great Britain and other countries of Western Europe. The way of progress seems clear.

No uniformity is to be expected, nor would it be desirable. The complexity of the world will remain and become even more multi-colored than before. But above this complexity and in spite of all controversies it is possible to perceive a mutual *rapprochement* of different ideals and aspirations that will make the world still more firmly one.

A fundamental condition of such a fortunate and beneficial development is lasting international peace. That is the preliminary task of America and of all other civilized nations, and the test of their civilization.

SELECTED BIBLIOGRAPHY

Bernard Faÿ, *L'esprit révolutionnaire en France et aux Etats-Unis à la fin du XVIIIc siècle*, Paris, 1925.

Georg Jellinek, *Die Erklärung der Menschen- und Bürgerrechte*, Leipzig, 1895.

G. H. Guttridge, *English Whiggism and the American Revolution*, Berkeley, Cal., 1942. (University of California Publications in History, Vol. XXVIII.)

Samuel F. Bemis, *A Diplomatic History of the United States*, Revised Edition, New York, 1942.

———, *The Latin American Policy of the United States*, New York, 1943.

Dexter Perkins, *The Monroe Doctrine, 1823–1826*, Cambridge, Mass., 1927; *1826–1867*, Baltimore, 1933; *1867–1907*, Baltimore, 1937.

———, *Hands Off, A History of the Monroe Doctrine*, Boston, 1941.

William A. Dunning, *The British Empire and the United States*, New York, 1914.

Franklin D. Scott, "American Influences in Norway and Sweden," *Journal of Modern History*, Vol. XVIII, 1946.

E. H. Thörnberg, *Sverige i Amerika, Amerika i Sverige*, Stockholm, 1938.

Harald Elovson, *Amerika i svensk litteratur 1750–1820, Lund, 1930*.

Jane Louise Mesick, *The English Traveller in America, 1785–1835*, New York, 1922.

Max Berger, *The British Traveller in America, 1836–1860*, New York, 1943.

George Ives, *A History of Penal Methods*, London, 1914.

Merle Curti, *The American Peace Crusade, 1815–1860*, Durham, N. C., 1929.

A. C. F. Beales, *The History of Peace*, New York, 1931.

Edson L. Whitney, *The American Peace Society*, Washington, 1928.

History of Woman Suffrage, ed. by Elizabeth Cady Stanton, Susan B. Anthony, and Matilda Joslyn Gage, Vol. 1, New York, 1881.

John Allen Krout, *The Origins of Prohibition*, New York, 1925.

Charles Nordhoff, *The Communistic Societies of the United States*, New York, 1875.

Edith Abbott, *Historical Aspects of the Immigration Problem*, Select Documents, Chicago, 1926.

George M. Stephenson, *A History of American Immigration, 1820–1924*, Boston, 1926.

Marcus L. Hansen, *The Atlantic Migration, 1607–1860*, Cambridge, Mass., 1940.

B. J. Hovde, "Notes on the Effects of Emigration upon Scandinavia," *Journal of Modern History*, Vol. VI, 1934.

Halvdan Koht, "When America Called for Immigrants," *Norwegian-American Studies and Records*, Vol. XIV, Northfield, Minn., 1944.

Holland Thompson, *The Age of Invention* (Chronicles of America, Vol. 37), New Haven, 1921.

Roger Burlingame, *March of the Iron Men: A Social History of Union Through Invention*, New York, 1938.

———, *Engines of Democracy: Inventions and Society in Mature America*, New York, 1940.

J. G. Crowther, *Famous American Men of Science*, New York, 1937.

Bernard Jaffe, *Men of Science in America*, New York, 1944.

Charles T. Rodgers, *American Superiority at the World's Fair*, Philadelphia, 1852.

Louis P. Betz, *Studien zur vergleichenden Litteraturgeschichte der neueren Zeit*, Frankfurt a.M., 1902.

C. P. Cambiaire, *The Influence of Edgar Allan Poe in France*, New York, 1927.

William B. Cairns, *British Criticisms of American Writings, 1783–1815*, Madison, 1918; *1815–1833*, Madison, 1922. (University of Wisconsin Studies in Language and Literature, No. 1 and No. 14.)

Clarence Gohdes, *American Literature in Nineteenth-Century England*, New York, 1944.

Robert Magidoff, "American Literature in Russia," *Saturday Review of Literature*, Nov. 2, 1946.

Donaldson Jordan and Edwin J. Pratt, *Europe and the American Civil War*, Boston and New York, 1931.

Ephraim D. Adams, *Great Britain and the American Civil War*, 2 vols., London, 1925.

J. M. Ludlow, "The Growth of American Influence over England," *Atlantic Monthly*, Vol. 74, Boston, 1894.

Edward Rodhe, *Den religiösa liberalismen*, Stockholm, 1935.

Karl Federn, *Essays zur Amerikanischen Litteratur*, Halle, 1899.

Julius Simon, *R. W. Emerson in Deutschland, 1851–1932*, Berlin, 1937.

William Sloane Kennedy, *The Fight of a Book for the World: A Companion Volume to Leaves of Grass*, West Yarmouth, Mass., 1926.

Harold Blodgett, *Walt Whitman in England*, Ithaca, N. Y., 1934.

Harry Law-Robertson, *Walt Whitman in Deutschland*, Giessen, 1935. (Giessener Beiträge zur deutschen Philologie, XLII.)

Richard H. Heindel, *The American Impact on Great Britain, 1898–1914: A Study of the United States in World History*, Philadelphia, 1940.

INDEX

Adams, Brooks, quoted, 163; influence of, 224
Adams, Charles Francis, quoted, 144, 148–50
Adams, Henry, quoted, 138, 253; influence of, 225
Adams, John Quincy, 30
Advertising, influence of American, 233–34
Agricultural machines, influence of American, 97
Agriculture, influence of American, 160–61
Airplane, influence of, 177–78
Alabama claims, 150–51
Alcott, Louisa May, influence of, 228
Alexander I, Czar, 28
Alexander II, Czar, 133
Alexanderson, E. F. W., 178, 241
Alfieri, Vittorio, 21
Algeciras Conference, 257–58
Allen, Hervey, 118–19
Amana community, 61
American Anti-Slavery Society, 47
American history, European interest in, 112, 222–23
American Peace Society, 40–41, 42
American Revolution as a European revolution, 7–25
American School of Classical Studies, 224
American Society of Dental Surgeons, 89–90
Amerikanische Bibliothek, 120–21
Ampère, André Marie, 85–86

Anaesthesia, influence of discovery of, 90–91
Andersen, Tryggve, 119
Andersen-Nexö, Martin, 231
Arbitration, 150–51, 244–45, 258–59
Architecture, influence of American, 236–38
Arnold, Matthew, 179, 181–82, 190
Arrhenius, Svante, 212
Atomic energy, influence of release of, 217
Austin, Alfred, 198
Austria, influence of electrical telegraph in, 87
Automobile, influence of, 176–77

Bache, Alexander D., 85–86
Bacteriology, influence of discoveries in, 216–17
Baird, Robert, 57
Balfour, Arthur, 251
Baltimore College of Dental Surgery, 89
Bancroft, George, influence of, 112, 124; quoted, 125
Banting, Frederick G., 216
Baptists, 67; Seventh-Day, 60
Barbey d'Aurevilly, Jules Amédée, 118
Barlien, Hans, 74.
Barlow, Joel, 20, 101
Barnum, Phineas T., 91–92, 93, 225, 233, 239
Bastiat, Claude Frédéric, 43
Baudelaire, Charles, 118, 120
Bayliss, W. M., 215

281

Bazalgette, Léon, 201
Beard, Charles A., influence of, 225
Beecher, Henry Ward, influence of, 188
Belgium, influence of American Revolution on, 23–25; influence of electrical telegraph in, 87
Bell, Alexander Graham, 172
Bell, Henry, 81
Bellamy, Edward, 204
Bennett, Emerson, 121
Bennett, James Gordon, 86–87, 232
Bentzon, Th., 199
Bergson, Henri, 219
Berman, Louis, 216
Bernays, Charles L., 139
Bessemer, Henry, 210
Best, Charles H., 216
Birkeland, Kristian, 212, 213
Björnson, Björnstjerne, 163, 172, 185–86
Blackwell, Elizabeth, 52, 54
Bloomer, Amelia, 53
Bond, William Cranch, 93
Borden, Gail, 93, 95
Bosch, Robert, 213
Bourget, Paul, 118
Boxer rebellion, 253
Brandes, Georg, 55
Bremer, Fredrika, 35, 52–53, 80, 88, 104, 191–92
Bright, John, 137, 138, 145, 148, 181
Brissot de Warville, Jacques Pierre, 17–18, 19
British and Foreign Anti-Slavery Society, 48
Brooks, Phillips, influence of, 188
Brooks, Van Wyck, 119
Brown, Antoinette Louisa, 52
Brown, Charles Brockden, 102
Brown-Séquard, Charles E., 216
Bryan, William Jennings, 259
Bryant, William Cullen, influence of, 113–14

Bryce, James, 223
Buchanan, James, 126, 152–53
Buchanan, Robert, 198, 199
Bull, Ole, 75–76
Burbank, Luther, 239
Burke, Edmund, 6, 7, 9, 10, 14
Burnett, Frances Hodgson, 228
Burritt, Elihu, 41–45, 156

Cabet, Etienne, 61–62
Cairnes, John Eliot, 137
Cameron, Simon, 133
Canning, George, 29–30, 31, 33
Carlyle, Thomas, 182, 197
Carnegie, Andrew, 180
Carpenter, Edward, 200
Castlereagh, Viscount, 27–28
Central Organization for a Durable Peace, 260
Chamberlain, Joseph, 247, 250
Chambers of Commerce, 209
Channing, William Ellery, influence of, 188
Chateaubriand, François René de, 32
Chemical industries, influence of American, 211–14
Chesterton, Gilbert Keith, 225
Churchill, Winston, 269, 271
Civil War, influence of American, 130–51
Clay, Cassius M., 132
Clay, Henry, 28
Clemens, Samuel L. See Twain, Mark
Cleveland, Grover, 249
Collett, Camilla, 53
Colt, Samuel, 93, 164–66
Commerce, freedom of, 11–13, 128–30; influence of American, 159–60
Commercialism, American, 179–86
Condorcet, Marquis de, 17
Conrad, Joseph, 107

Considérant, Victor, 62, 205
Cooper, James Fenimore, influence of, 106–11
Copley, John Singleton, 3
Crawford, F. Marion, 228
Crawford, William, 37
Crimean War, 128, 165
Crookes, Sir William, 213
Crystal Palace, 92

Danish Sound dues, 127–28
Declaration of Independence, 14, 16, 17, 187
Democracy, influence of American, 2, 34–35, 148–50, 187
Denmark, restrictions on trade with, removed, 13; influence of steamboat in, 83; influence of electrical telegraph in, 87; influence of American literature in, 199–200, 201; influence of Henry George in, 203
Denmark-Norway, i n f l u e n c e of American Revolution on, 21–23
Dentistry, influence of American, 89–90
Dewey, John, influence of, 220–21
Dick, D., 93
Dickens, Charles, 35, 38, 120
Disraeli, Benjamin, 126
Dostoievski, Feodor, 120
Dowden, Edward, 198
Doyle, Sir Arthur Conan, 120
Drachmann, Holger, 100
Drago Doctrine, 254–55
Draper, John W., 240

Eastman, George, 212
Economic power, influence of American, 152–62, 207–9
Economic theories, influence of American, 222
Edison, Thomas A., 170, 174, 175
Ehrlich, Paul, 216

Eijkman, Christiaan, 215
Electric lamp, influence of, 169–70
Electricity, influence of, 169–74
Elevator, influence of invention of, 167–68
Eliot, Charles W., 79, 184, 244
Ellsworth, Henry W., 153
Ely, Richard T., influence of, 222
Emancipation Proclamation, reaction to, 141–42
Emerson, Ralph Waldo, influence of, 190–95; mentioned, 197
Emigration to America, influence of, 63–78, 156–58
England. See Great Britain
Ericsson, John, 150
Exhibition of the Industry of All Nations (1851), 92–98, 164
Exports, influence of American, 159–60
Eyde, Sam, 213

Falsen, C. M., 22
Faraday, Michael, 86
Favre, Jules, 146
Federn, Karl, 195
Feminism, influence of American, 45–55
Fenger, Christian, 241
Field, Cyrus W., 88
Finney, Charles G., 190
Ford, Henry, 177
Forgues, E. D., 117
Foster, Stephen, 77, 100–101
Four freedoms, 268
Fox, Charles James, 9
France, influence of American Revolution on, 15–21, 23; influence of steamboat in, 83; influence of electrical telegraph in, 87; influence of American literature in, 117–18, 120, 199, 201
Franklin, Benjamin, 5–6, 14, 16, 17, 19, 22, 80

Frederick II, King of Prussia, 15
Freiligrath, Ferdinand, 199
French Revolution, influence of American Revolution on, 16–21
"Friendly Addresses," 42, 44
Friends, Society of. *See* Quakers
Fröding, Gustaf, 187
Fulton, Robert, 81, 101
Funk, Casimir, 215

Galsworthy, John, 230
Garborg, Arne, 203
Gautier, Théophile, 118
Geijer, E. G., 38
George, Henry, influence of, 202–3
George, Lloyd, 203
Germany, influence of electrical telegraph in, 87; influence of American literature in, 110, 194, 199, 200–201; influence of Mahan's navalism in, 247
Gibbs, Josiah Willard, 212
Gibson, Charles Dana, influence of, 236
Gladstone, William E., 135
Glidden, Carlos, 173
Good Templars, Independent Order of, 58
Goodyear, Charles, 91, 93
Gorki, Maxim, 231
Gortchakoff, Prince, 133
Gosse, Edmund, 119
Gourmont, Remy de, 118
Great Britain, influence of American Revolution on, 8–10; economic relations of United States with, 12–13, 155, 208; relations of United States with, 27-31, 129, 139, 140, 248–50, 252, 254; influence of American feminism in, 50–52, 54–55; influence of American temperance movement in, 57; influence of emigration on, 66; influence of

Great Britain, steamboat in, 83; influence of electrical telegraph in, 87; influence of American literature in, 104, 115–16, 119, 120, 194, 198, 199, 200; attitudes toward Civil War in, 135, 136–38; influence of American democracy in, 148–49; influence of American religious leaders in, 188, 189; influence of Henry George in, 203; influence of Mahan's navalism in, 247–48.
Great Exhibition (1851), 92–98, 164
Greeley, Horace, 96, 97
Green, Anna Katharine, 120
Grieg, Nordahl, 175
Grimm, Hermann, 192, 193, 194

Haber, Fritz, 212
Haerne, Désiré de, 23–25
Hall, Basil, 34, 37, 46
Hall, Thomas, 173
Hamilton, Thomas, 34
Hamsun, Knut, 182–83, 184, 195–97
Hardie, Keir, 203
Harmonists, 60–61
Harte, Bret, influence of, 226
Hawthorne, Nathaniel, influence of, 121–22
Hay, John, 252, 253, 254
Hektoen, Ludvig, 241
Hemingway, Ernest, influence of, 231
Henry, Joseph, 85–86
Hitler, Adolf, 266, 271
Hjelm-Hansen, P., 75
Hobson, J. A., 203
Holley, Alexander, 210
Holst, Axel, 215
Holst, H. E. von, 222–23
Holy Alliance, 26, 30–31, 33
Homestead Act, 156
Hopkins, Sir Frederick, 215

Hormones, influence of discovery of, 215–16

Howells, William Dean, quoted, 226, 227–28; influence of, 228–29

Hughes, Charles E., 263

Hugo, Victor, 43, 118, 120

Hull, Cordell, 264, 269

Ibsen, Henrik, 76, 146–47, 183, 185

Idealism, influence of American, 188–204

Imperialism, influence of American, 245–56

Incandescent lamp, influence of, 169–70

International Committee of Historical Sciences, 224

International Council of Women, 55

International Exposition of Electricity, 168, 170

International law, American contribution to, 125

International Woman Suffrage Alliance, 55

Inventions, influence of American, 79–98, 163–78

Ireland, influence of American temperance movement in, 58

Irving, Washington, influence of, 103–6; quoted, 113

Isaachsen, Peter, 21–22

Italy, influence of American Revolution on, 21

James, Henry, influence of, 229–30

James, William, influence of, 218–20

Janson, Kristofer, 185, 189, 197

Jefferson, Thomas, 4, 17, 19

Jennings, Herbert Spencer, 222

Johnson, "Pussyfoot," 238

Jones, John Paul, 16, 21, 107

Joseph II, German Emperor, 15

Journalism, influence of American, 232–33

Judd, Norman B., 142

Kellogg, Frank B., 263

Kelly, William, 210

Kerosene lamp, influence of, 169

Key, Ellen, 189, 194

Kipling, Rudyard, 248

Kluchevski, Vasili, 224

Knortz, Karl, 200

Knudsen, Gunnar, 172

Koecker, Leonard, 89

Koht, Paul, 245

Kosciusko, Thaddeus, 14, 15

Ladd, William, 40

Lafayette, Marquis de, 14, 15, 17–19, 25, 33

Lamartine, Alphonse Marie Louis de, 43

Lamennais, Félicité Robert de, 24

Lamp, kerosene, influence of, 169; incandescent, influence of, 169–70

Latin America, American attitude toward, 27–33, 126, 248–51, 254–56, 263–64

League of Nations, 261–62, 266

League of Universal Brotherhood, 42, 44

League to Enforce Peace, 260

Leland, Henry M., 176

Lemaître, Jules, 118

Lend-Lease agreements, 266–68

Lessing, Gotthold Ephraim, 14

Lewis, Sinclair, influence of, 231

Library schools influence of American, 174

Lie, Jonas, 107

Lieber, Francis, 74

Lienhard, Friedrich, 194

Lincoln, Abraham, assassination of, 144–47

Literature, influence of American, 99–123, 190–201, 225–32

Livingston, Edward, 38–39

London, Jack, influence of, 230–31

Long, Crawford W., 90
Longfellow, Henry Wadsworth, influence of 114–16; quoted, 134–35
Louisiana, criminal code of, 38–39
Lowell, James Russell, influence of, 186

McCollum, Elmer V., 215
McCormick, Cyrus H., 93, 95–96
McKinley, William, 251
Madison, James, 22
Maeterlinck, Maurice, 194
Mahan, Alfred T., influence of, 246–48; mentioned, 251
Mallarmé, Stéphane, 118
Mann, Thomas, 200–201
Manufacturing, influence of American, 158–59, 166–67
Marcy, William, 126–28, 129–30
Marryat, Frederick, 34, 107, 110
Martin, Charles, 215
Martineau, Harriet, 35, 54, 137
Marx, Karl, 138 n, 146
Materialism, American, 179–86
Mathew, Father Theobald, 58
Mauclair, Camille, 119
Maury, Matthew, 84–85
Medicine, influence of discoveries in, 214–17
Meidell, Ditmar, 76
Mendel, Lafayette B., 215
Mercantilism, 12, 153
Merchant marine, growth of American, 8
Methodists, 47, 67, 182
Metternich, Prince, 32
Mexican War, 42, 125, 164, 244
Mill, John Stuart, 54–55, 137, 148
Mill, Mrs. John Stuart, 50–51
Minot, George R., 217
Mirabeau, Comte de, 14, 15, 17, 19
Monroe, James, 27, 28–29, 30

Monroe Doctrine, influence of, 30–33, 249, 255
Moody, Dwight L., 189–90
Morelly, 2
Morgan, Lewis H., 222
Morley, John, 192–93
Mormons, 68
Morse, Samuel F. B., 86
Morton, William T. G., 90
Motion pictures, influence of American, 175–76, 242–43
Motley, John Lothrop, influence of, 112; quoted, 134, 135, 136, 141, 142
Mott, Lucretia, 47–50
Munch, Edvard, 236
Murphy, William P., 217
Murray, Lindley, 4

Nansen, Fridtjof, 262
Napoleon III, Emperor, 139–40, 141
Navalism, influence of American, 246–48
Netherlands, influence of electrical telegraph in, 87
Neutrality Acts, 265, 266
Nightingale, Florence, 54
Norris, Frank, 231
Northrup, John, 217
Norway, restrictions on trade with, removed, 13; influence of American Revolution on, 21–23; influence of American feminism in, 53; influence of American temperance movement in, 57, 58, 59; influence of emigration on, 72, 74–77; influence of steamboat in, 83; influence of electrical telegraph in, 87; influence of electric power in, 172; influence of Henry George in, 203

Olds, Ransom, 176
Olney, Richard, 249

Open Door policy, influence of, 252–54, 257
Ørsted, H. C., 80, 85, 88
Osborne, Thomas B., 215
Oscar I, King of Sweden, 38
Ostwald, Wilhelm, 212
Otis, Elisha G., 167–68
Owen, Robert, 61
Owen, Samuel, 82

Pact of Paris, 263, 266
Paine, Thomas, 4, 9, 19–20
Painting, influence of American, 234–36
Palmerston, Lord, 126, 140
Panama Canal, 254–56
Paris, Pact of, 263, 266
Parker, Theodore, influence of, 188–89
Payne, John Howard, 99, 103
Peace movement, influence of American, 39–45
Penal laws, influence of American, 36–39
Phillips, Wendell, 48, 49, 50
Phonograph, influence of, 174–75
Pike, James S., quoted, 135–36, 140, 142–43, 147
Pirenne, Henri, 206
Pitt, William (Lord Chatham), 9
Pitt, William the Younger, 9, 10
Poe, Edgar Allan, influence of, 116–20, 201
Pragmatism, influence of, 220–21
Prescott, William Hickling, 111–12
Prussia, restrictions on trade with, removed, 12; influence of electrical telegraph in, 87
Psychology, influence of American studies in, 218–19, 221–22
Pulaski, Casimir, 14
Pulitzer, Joseph, 232–33
Pupin, Michael, 172, 241
Pushkin, Alexander, 104

Quakers, 40, 47, 49, 67
Queen, Ellery, 120

Radio, influence of, 178
Reciprocal trade agreements, 264
Reform movements, influence of American, 36–59
Reid, Mayne, 121
Richard, Rev. Henry, 43
Richepin, Jean, 118
Roebling, John A., 210
Rogers, Moses, 82
Rogers, Samuel, 113–14
Roland de La Platière, Jean Marie, 19
Rolleston, T. W., 200
Rölvaag, Ole E., 231
Roosevelt, Franklin D., 264, 265, 266, 268, 269, 270–72
Roosevelt, Theodore, 251, 255, 256–57, 258
Root, Elihu, 258
Roozeboom, Bakhuis, 212
Rossetti, W. M., 198
Rostovtzeff, Michael, 224
Rotary Clubs, 238
Royce, Josiah, influence of, 221
Rush, Benjamin, 56
Rush, Richard, 31
Ruskin, John, 115, 182, 183, 235
Russell, Lord John, 126
Russia, influence of American literature in, 104, 108, 120, 122, 200–201, 204; attitude toward Civil War in, 140; streetcars in, 168; functional architecture in, 237

Salvation Army, 190
Sanford, H. S., quoted, 143
Sankey, Ira D., 189–90
Santayana, George, 241
Sargent, John Singer, influence of, 236

Sarrazin, Gabriel, 201
Schick, Bela, 217
Schmidt, Rudolf, 199
Schurz, Carl, 74
Science, influence of American, 85–88, 214–17
Scott, Sir Walter, 102, 103, 106, 107, 110
Separatists of Zoar, Society of, 61
Seventh-Day Baptists, 60
Seward, William H., 130, 131, 139, 145, 154
Sewing machine, influence of, 97–98
Shakers, 60
Shaw, George Bernard, 203
Sherman, John, 244
Shipping, influence of American, 8, 155
Sholes, Charles, 173
Siemens, William, 211
Simms, William Gilmore, 121
Sinclair, Upton, influence of, 230
Singer, Isaac M., 98
Skyscraper, influence of, 237
Smith, Goldwin, 137
Sousa, John Philip, 241
Southey, Robert, 102
Southworth, Mrs. E. D. E. N., 121
Spain, influence of electrical telegraph in, 87; attitudes toward Civil War, 136
Spanish-American War, 250–52
Spengler, Oswald, 224
Spielhagen, Friedrich, 194
Stalin, Josef, 271
Standardization, influence of American, 163–67
Stanton, Elizabeth Cady, 50
Starling, E. H., 215
Stead, William T., 189, 206–7, 209
Steamboat, influence of, 81–85
Steel industry, influence of American, 211
Steinach, Eugen, 216

Stephanists, 67
Stephens, Mrs. Ann S., 121
Steuben, Baron, 14
Stevenson, Robert Louis, 120, 200
Stowe, Harriet Beecher, influence of, 122, 123
Streetcar, influence of, 168
Strindberg, August, 151, 189
Strodtmann, Adolf, 199
Stuart, Gilbert, 3
Sullivan, Louis H., 237
Sweden, restrictions on commerce with, removed, 12, 13; influence of American Revolution on, 21; influence of American penal laws in, 38; influence of American feminism in, 52–53; influence of American temperance movement in, 57, 58, 59; influence of electrical telegraph in, 87; influence of American democracy in, 148; influence of American economic policy on, 153; influence of American religious leaders in, 188–89
Swinburne, Algernon C., 198
Switzerland, influence of the steamboat in, 83; influence of electrical telegraph in, 87
Sylvester, J., 241
Symonds, John Addington, 200

Talleyrand, Charles Maurice de, 23
Tariff policy, influence of American, 152–55, 264–65
Technology, influence of American, 79–98, 209–14
Telegraph, electrical, influence of, 86–88
Telephone, influence of, 172–73
Temperance movement, influence of American, 55–59
Tesla, Nicola, 241

Thayer, William R., 191
Thomas, Sidney G., 210
Thompson, Benjamin, 4
Thompson, Holland, 170
Thordarson, Chester H., 241
Thrane, Marc. M., 74–75
Ticknor, George, 105
Tocqueville, Alexis de, 35, 36, 37, 38, 39, 43, 45, 46, 80, 85, 149, 214, 276
Toller, Ernst, 175
Transcendentalism, influence of, 186, 187, 190–95
Trollope, Anthony, 184–85
Trollope, Mrs. Frances, 34
Turgenieff, Ivan, 200
Turgot, Anne Robert Jacques, 11–12, 16
Turner, Frederick J., influence of, 224
Twain, Mark, influence of, 186, 226–28
Tyndall, John, 193

Ullmann, Viggo, 203
Unitarianism, influence of American, 188, 189
United Nations, 269–70, 272
Uppdal, Kristofer, 231

Veblen, Thorstein, influence of, 222
Venezuela, relations of United States with, 249–50, 254
Verlaine, Paul, 118
Versailles, Treaty of, 261–62
Victoria, Queen, 251

Villiers de l'Isle-Adam, Comte de, 118
Vinje, A. O., 183
Virginia Declaration of Rights, 16
Vitamins, influence of discovery of, 214–15
Voltaire, 14

Wallace, Lew, 228
Warner, Charles Dudley, 186
Warner, Susan, 121
Washington, George, 21, 106
Watt, James, 81
Webber, Charles W., 121
Webster, Noah, 4
Wergeland, Henrik, 38, 74
West, Benjamin, 3
Wheaton, Henry, 125
Whistler, James M., 234–36
Whitman, Walt, quoted, 180; influence of, 195–201
Whitney, Eli, 80, 164
Wilhelm II, Kaiser, 247, 253–54
Wilkes, John, 9
Willard, Emma, 46–47, 52
Willis, Nathaniel P., 120, 121
Wilson, Woodrow, 259–66
Women's rights. See Feminism
World War I, influence of American participation in, 259–60
World War II, influence of American participation in, 265–67
Wright brothers, 177
Wright, Frank Lloyd, influence of, 237–38

Zola, Emile, 118, 119